DESEGREGATION STATE

DESEGREGATION STATE

College Writing Programs after the Civil Rights Movement

ANNIE S. MENDENHALL

UTAH STATE UNIVERSITY PRESS
Logan

© 2022 by University Press of Colorado

Published by Utah State University Press
An imprint of University Press of Colorado
245 Century Circle, Suite 202
Louisville, Colorado 80027

 The University Press of Colorado is a proud member of the Association of University Presses.

The University Press of Colorado is a cooperative publishing enterprise supported, in part, by Adams State University, Colorado State University, Fort Lewis College, Metropolitan State University of Denver, Regis University, University of Alaska Fairbanks, University of Colorado, University of Denver, University of Northern Colorado, University of Wyoming, Utah State University, and Western Colorado University.

∞ This paper meets the requirements of the ANSI/NISO Z39.48–1992 (Permanence of Paper)

ISBN: 978-1-64642-202-9 (paperback)
ISBN: 978-1-64642-203-6 (ebook)
https://doi.org/10.7330/9781646422036

Library of Congress Cataloging-in-Publication Data

Names: Mendenhall, Annie S., author.
Title: Desegregation state: college writing programs after the civil rights movement/ Annie S. Mendenhall.
Description: Logan: Utah State University Press, [2022] I Includes bibliographical references and index.
Identifiers: LCCN 2021045123 (print) I LCCN 2021045124 (ebook) I ISBN 9781646422029 (paperback) I ISBN 9781646422036 (ebook)
Subjects: LCSH: College integration—Georgia—History—20th century. I Writing centers—Georgia. I English language—Rhetoric—Ability testing—Georgia. I Reading—Ability testing—Georgia. I African American college students—Georgia. I African Americans—Education (Higher)—Georgia.
Classification: LCC LC214.22.G46 .M46 2022 (print) I LCC LC214.22.G46 (ebook) I DDC 378.1/9829960730758—dc23/eng/20211021
LC record available at https://lccn.loc.gov/2021045123
LC ebook record available at https://lccn.loc.gov/2021045124

Cover photographs: courtesy, John Lavoie/SavannahNow.com (*top*); courtesy, Georgia Southern University Special Collections, Savannah (*bottom*)

CONTENTS

ABBREVIATIONS

ASTA	*Alabama State Teachers Association v. Alabama Public School and College Authority*
BSE	Basic Skills Examination
CCC	*College Composition and Communication*
CCCC	Conference on College Composition and Communication
CGP	Comparative Guidance and Placement Program
CLA	College Language Association
DOE	Department of Education
EOP	Equal Opportunity Program
ETS	Educational Testing Service
HBCUs	Historically Black Colleges and Universities
HEW	Department of Health, Education, and Welfare
HWCUs	Historically White Colleges and Universities
LCR	Literacy, Composition, and Rhetoric
LDF	NAACP Legal Defense Fund
MSIs	Minority Serving Institutions
NAACP	National Association for the Advancement of Colored People
NAEP	National Assessment of Educational Progress
NAFEO	National Association for Equal Opportunity in Higher Education
NCTE	National Council of Teachers of English
NTE	National Teacher Examination
OCR	Office for Civil Rights
SRTOL	Students' Right to Their Own Language
TSWE	Test of Standard Written English
USG	University System of Georgia
WAC	Writing Across the Curriculum
WCJ	*Writing Center Journal*
WLN	*Writing Lab Newsletter*
WPA	Writing Program Administrator/Writing Program Administration

ACKNOWLEDGMENTS

During most of the time I spent working on this project, I was doubtful I could finish it. Writing a book requires an immense system of support and encouragement that I do not think is adequately broadcast to graduate students and junior academics. The fact that I finished this book is thanks in large part to the people I mention here.

I first want to thank Evelyn Baker Dandy and Caroline Warnock for sharing their stories with me—I am honored that both of these outstanding educators took the time to contribute to this project. I also want to thank the archivists at Savannah State University and Georgia Southern University's Armstrong Campus for helping me by explaining finding aids, pulling boxes and documents, sharing the nuances of each university's history, and assisting with interview requests. Thanks to Ann Ogden at Savannah State for your guidance and stories about what Savannah State means to the community. Thanks to Caroline Hopkinson for enabling trip after trip to access the copious records in Lane Library and for checking so many small details I was piecing together while writing this project. I would be remiss if I did not mention Armstrong historian Janet Stone for her incredible work developing finding aids for the desegregation collection. My research assistant, Sierra Diemer, should be commended for sorting through endless student survey comments, perusing finding aids for the Georgia Archives, and completing other tasks—labor-intensive and sometimes unpleasant work. Credit goes to Kris Cook's excellent archival work in my Research Methods class for uncovering more about the Black American Movement on Armstrong's campus.

Thanks to the reviewers of this project for their generous, detailed feedback, which was invaluable in getting me on the right track, filling in gaps, catching my biases, and encouraging me to turn inward and understand my role—with all its complexity—in this project. If there is anything good about this project, it is due to the hard work of its reviewers. Any flaws are my own. Utah State University Press editor Rachael Levay provided guidance and much-needed encouragement throughout the process. Courtney Adams Wooten read every chapter at least three times, sometimes in a state of disarray, never ceasing to be critical and yet generous.

This research was completed with the aid of three generous research grants from the Department of Languages, Literature, and Philosophy at Armstrong State University, and additional funding from Georgia Southern's College of Arts and Humanities. I am grateful to David Wheeler, Beth Howells, and the members of the old LLP department for their assistance in securing the time and funds I needed to conduct archival research. Thanks to my Armstrong/Georgia Southern colleagues who encouraged my work on this project, including Kelly Benhase, Chris Cartright, Bill Dawers, Lisa Dusenberry, Cicelyn English, Amanda Konkle, Nicole Rivas, and Rob Terry. Thanks to ongoing support from colleagues who read various drafts or shared materials from their projects as guides during this process, including Jacob Babb, Paige VanOsdol Banaji, T. J. Geiger, Lauren Obermark, Erika Strandjord, Julia Voss, and Remi Yergeau. Thanks to Amy Potter for always supporting me.

Although this project did not come from my dissertation, I could not have completed the work without the years of guidance, support, and feedback I received from my mentors, Kay Halasek and Beverly Moss. Kay made historical work seem exciting and modeled the best ways of giving holistic writing feedback to a writer as a person. Beverly was there at the start—my introduction to composition—giving me countless lessons and opportunities over the years that led to this book.

Thanks, finally, to Shaun for making my work possible and to my children for reminding me every day to never give up fighting for a better world.

DESEGREGATION STATE

INTRODUCTION

On the first of September in 1977, the Board of Regents of the University System of Georgia (USG) submitted its *Plan for the Further Desegregation of the University System of Georgia* to the Office for Civil Rights (OCR) in what was then called the Department of Health, Education, and Welfare (HEW). The OCR was, throughout the 1970s, collecting desegregation plans from formerly segregated states whose university systems remained largely segregated more than two decades after *Brown v. Board of Education of Topeka* (1954) legally ended segregation. In this plan, the USG wrote, "the question of special compensatory activities speak directly to the heart of the problem of increasing minority student enrollment. Many minority students come from cultural and educational backgrounds which were not conducive to strong academic development. It is essential that appropriate programs be provided for such students if they are to have reasonable expectations of success in college level work" (Oxford et al. 1977, II:48).[1] The heart of the USG's desegregation plan was to remediate Black[2] students, not to remedy segregation.

When I began working for the USG in 2013 as an assistant professor at Armstrong State University, one of the USG's historically white colleges and universities (HWCUs)[3] in Savannah, I heard talk about efforts to desegregate Armstrong and nearby Savannah State University, one of the USG's Historically Black Colleges and Universities (HBCUs). As one colleague told me on a tour of campus, "Armstrong can't offer a business degree because of desegregation. We got teacher education instead." Having no idea what this comment meant, I did what most archival researchers would do: I went to the archives. It was there that I came across the USG's desegregation plan I quote above and realized that what happened during the 1970s desegregation period did more to transform the curriculum at Armstrong and Savannah State and in the USG than most people realized and had far-reaching repercussions nationally.

Up to this point in my career, I was like most white faculty in that I believed racism was important to address in my teaching, but I lacked

https://doi.org/10.7330/9781646422036.c000

direction for anti-racist action at my university (García de Müeller and Ruiz 2017; Perryman-Clark 2016). As I began perusing desegregation records, I was developing a methodology for reframing my perspective on racism as a central, not peripheral, force in higher education in the United States. I realized that white resistance to postsecondary desegregation informed the policies for remediation, retention, and assessment that exist today, particularly in my fields of literacy, composition, and rhetoric (LCR).[4] I read the writing of Black activists in desegregation who traced white supremacy in the institutional language of race neutrality and meritocracy. But, I realized, their most transformational demands—for a redesigned admissions process, for Black-centered courses, for a new core curriculum, for Black leadership, for grading and assessment—went unrealized. Nothing would stop universities or myself from reproducing racism if these institutional transformations were never to take place. Nothing will happen if we keep failing to remedy the past.

My concerns crystallized one fall when I went to teach my first class of English Learning Support, the USG's newest iteration of remedial writing for students, and I walked into a class of twelve students, nearly all of whom were students of color and a majority of whom were Black. This English Learning Support course was part of a USG initiative in partnership with Complete College Georgia (CCG). CCG (2019) asserts that redesigning learning support contributes to "removing common barriers for minority . . . students" by allowing students who placed into remediation to bypass the older non-credit-bearing three-credit-hour remedial writing courses required by the USG since desegregation. Learning Support was redesigned as a "co-requisite" course, meaning students must take it at the same time as a regular first-year composition class, allowing them to earn first-year composition credit immediately during their first term of college. I helped design the co-requisite English Learning Support class at Armstrong my first year as an assistant professor. At that time, I was swayed by arguments in basic writing scholarship that co-requisite support was more equitable, particularly if it eliminated conventional grades and provided a space for students to question writing conventions (Grego and Thompson 2007; Adams et al. 2009). I also helped administrators set an English Placement Index, a calculation used by the state for placement into learning support, which considered SAT or ACT scores, high school GPA, and Accuplacer writing test scores. Based on our enrollment data and admissions requirements, we agreed to set the score slightly higher than the minimum so we would be able to run a full section of the learning support course to better facilitate student interaction. It was a pragmatic, race-neutral decision. I felt I had helped create a course that our university system data showed eliminated a curricular obstacle for students and improved pass rates, particularly for Black students (Denley 2017). In reality, I had conflated improvement with justice and allowed myself to be satisfied with pedagogical changes rather than the harder work of institutional transformation.

Walking into a predominantly Black classroom on an HWCU campus as a visibly white, middle-class, able-bodied, straight woman, ostensibly there to remediate students' literacy "deficiencies," profoundly underscored for me the ways I was reproducing a racist educational history through literacy norms. After all, I am a third-generation college student who largely benefited from my parents' and grandparents' access to flagship state HWCUs and whose career trajectory was shaped by a line of white women writing instructors who told me I was a "good writer" and encouraged me to study English and go to graduate school. This classroom reproduced literacy norms defined during segregation, which manifest in racial disparities in writing placement, or "disparate impact," where conventional placement criteria disproportionately place students of color in remediation (Poe and Cogan 2016; Poe et al. 2014). I had viewed myself as transforming an older system, but co-requisite learning support merely lowered the credit hours and changed the timing of remediation without addressing the history of using literacy remediation to avoid more comprehensive anti-racist curricular reform. The state's guidelines still cast literacy in terms of deficit, stating that co-requisite courses must "strengthen both reading and writing competencies in which [students] have deficiencies" (University System of Georgia 2019, 30–31). If students performed better with less basic writing, were their writing deficiencies really the problem? Shouldn't we be questioning the entire structure of our required core writing courses? Shouldn't we be talking about how the same literacy standards that produce faculty like me reproduce the racist dynamics of (de)segregated educational spaces?

Furthermore, I realized that what involved only a dozen students at my university might involve a larger number of students at an access institution. Disparate impact reinforces institutional racism by placing the burden for remedial credit hours on the state's least selective institutions, where Black and Latinx students are disproportionately enrolled (Carnevale et al. 2018). Complete College America (2017) recommends that states assign funding based on institutions' retention rates for underrepresented and minoritized student groups. While one could argue that this directive allows states to direct funds to institutions with low retention rates, in reality, it typically penalizes attrition by removing resources, worsening the tendency for less selective institutions to have fewer resources to support student retention and contributing to higher attrition rates for Black and Latinx students (Jones 2017; Bombardieri 2019; Carnevale et al. 2018). This funding practice does not empower programs to hire secure faculty, reduce course caps and teaching loads, or develop more valid (but labor-intensive) placement or assessment practices—practices that contribute to retention but are typically sidelined in administrative decisions. These programs fail students by attributing racial disparities to students' deficiencies and placing students in a system largely taught by non-tenure-line faculty, who tend to be the most diverse and least secure faculty (Finkelstein et al. 2016). This system was designed to work against Black students. During desegregation, states, and in some cases the courts, relocated remedial writing primarily to less selective and open-access institutions, arguing that they provided a pathway to Black students attending more selective institutions even as southerners proclaimed "Segregation now, segregation forever" (Harbour 2020; Greene 2008; Sellers Diamond 2008).

I am not arguing against student support services or literacy instruction in college; I am arguing for changes to curriculum, policies, and assumptions about students and literacy formed in opposition to desegregation. Policy change requires negotiation with multiple stakeholders, particularly in a centralized university system like mine that mandates writing curricula across its institutions. And many stakeholders lack the historical knowledge to identify racist policies—something I know from personal experience. Using this knowledge myself has only resulted in limited success. For example, I worked with the center in charge of our university's Learning Support program to discontinue using SAT scores in placement. But I have had less success convincing them to implement directed self-placement, as recommended in scholarship and, I will show, by desegregation activists, or to share data supposedly showing that students with low Accuplacer scores would fail first-year composition without learning support. My efforts to explain how first-year composition hiring policies create instability and higher turnover for faculty of color have been met mostly with inaction or justifications of race-evasive policies.[5] And in 2019, much of my work had to be restarted from scratch, negotiated with new parties in chaos, when Armstrong was merged with Georgia Southern University—a "white flight" college for many white Armstrong students in the 1970s. This book is my attempt to detail a usable history of the racism in everyday institutional practices. It's a deeply personal project since I, my parents, and my grandfather all earned college degrees from HWCUs in the USG. My family history is intertwined with its history of segregation and desegregation in this university system. As Sara Ahmed (2012, 182, original emphasis) writes, "We need feminist and antiracist critique because we need to understand how it is that the world takes shape by restricting the forms in which we gather. The time for this is now. We need this critique now if we are to learn *how not to reproduce what we inherit.*" It is imperative for white faculty like myself to investigate how *we have reproduced* a racist system, to hold ourselves accountable for our failures, and to leverage our resources to advocate for change.

LITERACY AND HIGHER EDUCATION DESEGREGATION

Desegregation State argues that literacy requirements for admission, placement, retention, and graduation developed in opposition to the monitoring and enforcement of postsecondary desegregation in HWCUs and white-controlled university systems. This book contributes to existing studies of postsecondary desegregation by illuminating a period typically overlooked. Scholars have detailed desegregation from the 1930s through the 1960s, accomplished through the legal activism of the National Association for the Advancement of Colored People's (NAACP) Legal Defense Fund (LDF), the protests of Black students on college campuses, and the eventual defeat of the last, often violent holdouts for segregation in the South (Williamson-Lott 2018; Wallenstein 2008). Beginning in the 1930s, desegregation litigation attempted to upset the presumption of white superiority in white social spaces, resulting in the legal end to segregation in *Brown.* By the second half of the 1960s, even the most resistant state-funded HWCUs admitted Black students, threatened with the loss of federal funding after the passage of the 1964 Civil Rights Act and the 1965 Higher Education Act (Williamson-Lott 2018). But histories skip over the period between the tremendous progress of civil rights activists in the 1960s and the rollback of civil rights in the 1980s. What happened in the 1970s when the federal government began enforcing postsecondary desegregation was critical, as explicitly segregationist arguments against admitting Black students to HWCUs transformed into race-evasive justifications of ongoing segregation.

Federal desegregation enforcement gave states control over desegregation plans. Much to the LDF's frustration, states consistently attributed ongoing patterns of segregation to Black students' supposed lack of preparation for college and inability to acclimate to the academic "standards" of HWCUs. Remediation became a central focus of desegregation, based on the theory that Black students would be unsuccessful in HWCUs without it. Social scientific theories of cultural and linguistic deprivation in the 1960s and neoconservative policies in the 1970s and 1980s explained illiteracy, poverty, and protests among African Americans as a product of a deprived culture rather than racism (Raz 2013; Omi and Winant 2015; Smitherman 1977). Academic and political discourse claimed that the cultural norms of whites, particularly with respect to literacy conventions, were superior academic "standards." Writing programs, including writing centers and writing across the curriculum (WAC), were formed to remediate literacy skills, particularly dialect but also logic, organization, clarity, and punctuation—all racialized features of language. These programs expanded to support the labor-intensive work of testing and remediating students to determine whether they could enter or exit college, adding extensive and unrewarded work for writing programs at HBCUs that has affected their visibility in LCR scholarship (Jackson and Jackson 2016; Daniel 2016; Ford 2016; Fulford 2019; Lockett and RudeWalker 2016; Coupet 2017; Jackson et al. 2019).

The USG centralized its writing program policies in its desegregation plan. One of ten states cited in 1969 for ongoing postsecondary segregation, Georgia has a single university system for public colleges and universities that has operated since 1931 ("Overseeing" 2021). The USG is governed by a Board of Regents, which oversees the state's public colleges and universities and whose members are appointed by the state's governor to a seven-year term (2021). As a national example of the challenges of desegregating nearby Black and white colleges, Savannah State and Armstrong showcase the ways desegregation policies contributed to systemic disparities between HBCUs and HWCUs—particularly in the case of literacy policies—with disparate impact on the placement, retention, and graduation of Black students. In chapter 1, I describe how the social scientific theory of cultural deprivation redefined desegregation as remediation, prompting pilots of remedial writing programs and literacy tests in Georgia during the late 1960s and early 1970s. In chapter 2, I explain how Georgia's 1974 desegregation plan described remediation as a retention strategy, echoing national discourses. The plan expanded remediation at Savannah's two colleges, disparately impacting the growth of Armstrong and Savannah State. In the third chapter, I examine how Armstrong and Savannah State constituents negotiated a desegregation plan, with Armstrong asserting literacy standards to argue for preserving its white identity. In chapter 4, I show how the USG's mandated literacy competency test, the Regents' Test, harmed Savannah State, resulting in additional citations against the state by the OCR. With support from the Reagan administration, the USG responded to these citations by requiring its Black colleges to offer additional writing remediation, under surveillance by the state. In the coda, I discuss postsecondary desegregation after the 1990s, arguing that postsecondary desegregation literacy policies are a vestige of segregation that warrants anti-racist program and policy development.

LITERACY, RACE, AND RACIALIZED INSTITUTIONAL SPACES

Literacy policies are sites of power contest because in the United States, literacy is viewed as a possession that contributes to socioeconomic advancement (Pritchard 2017; Brandt 2001; Graff 1991). While typically defined as "discrete linguistic and scribal skills," literacy is an interpretive practice inextricable from social context and identity, including race (Brandt 2001, 3). I define race as a sociohistorical construct that shapes people's self- and perceived identification, which has influenced law, policy, and the systems for distributing resources and assigning worth in the United States and globally through a history of racist belief (Bonilla-Silva 2006; Omi and Winant 2015; Mills 1997). Given literacy's perceived social power, whites have historically controlled literacy norms and education since slavery by defining literacy as "white property," a resource legislated and evaluated by whites (Prendergast 2003). However, African Americans have used literacy for social change and empowerment and to resist requirements employed to block access to literacy learning, voting booths, schools, and other resources (Royster 2000; Moss 2003; Richardson 2003, 2004; Banks 2006; Lathan 2015; Pritchard 2017; Epps-Robertson 2018). Black literacy practices, Elaine Richardson (2003, 16) explains, developed a tradition of "vernacular resistance arts and cultural productions that are created to carve out free spaces in oppressive locations." Seeking to suppress Black social advancement, whites have historically asserted the superiority of white "literacy standards" to diminish, exclude, or penalize Black literacy traditions.

Literacy norms work in tandem with what April Baker-Bell (2020) calls White Mainstream English, the linguistic and rhetorical practices culturally associated with whites, often called Standard English. White Mainstream English is taught in schools as the path to socioeconomic mobility, presuming that whites will occupy positions of social power and that Black students who assimilate to white literacy norms will have equal opportunities. This anti-Black linguistic racism, as Baker-Bell (2020) calls it, labels Black ways of speaking and writing as unfit for professional advancement, yet it masquerades as a race-neutral "standard" equally applied to everyone despite well-established links among culture, race, and language. This is not to say that white or Black language practices are fixed or homogeneous. Differences within racial groups exist across regions, ethnicities, and different class, gender, and sexual identities. However, linguistic racism means that divergences from linguistic and rhetorical norms are racially marked by listeners and readers and differently understood and disparately evaluated because of that racialized identity (Pritchard 2017; Johnson and VanBrackle 2012; Lindsey and Crusan 2011; Davila 2016, 2017). For example, whites rarely use Standard English consistently, but their language practices are typically considered normal and standard, with deviations or "errors" more likely to be overlooked or rated as less severe (Johnson and VanBrackle 2012; Ball 1997).

Scholars today argue that race-evasive literacy instruction perpetuates anti-Black linguistic racism (Pimentel et al. 2017; Comfort et al. 2003; Richardson 2003; Ball and Lardner 2005; Lockett 2019; Baker-Bell 2020). As sociologist Edward Bonilla-Silva (2006) explains, race-neutral practices leave racist ideologies and institutional structures in place, perpetuating racism through race-evasiveness in the absence of explicit racist intent. Race-evasive views of literacy may take note of race, as the National Assessment of Educational Progress does when it reports that Black students perform lower than other racial groups on writing assessments, but they present racial disparities as a result of deficient literacy skills rather than anti-Black linguistic racism (National Center for Education Statistics 2011). Rather than dismantling anti-Black linguistic racism for its role in racism in housing access, hiring, criminal justice, and policing (Victorelli 2019; Baker-Bell 2020), proponents of "literacy standards" suggest that "better" education or remediation will result in parity. Writing assessments penalize Black students for dialect, stylistic conventions, or organizational strategies, depending on the assessment construct; and features of Black English are treated more harshly than writing features associated with other racial groups (White and Thomas 1981; Kynard 2008; Inoue 2015; Poe et al. 2014; Balester 2012; Fowler and Ochsner 2012; Johnson and VanBrackle 2012; Ball 1997). In contrast, studies demonstrate that teaching about Black literacy practices and anti-Black linguistic racism can improve students' rhetorical and language awareness—the foundational concepts in learning to write for diverse purposes and situations (Ball 1993; Smitherman 1993; Richardson 2003; Redd 1992, 1993; Redd and Webb 2005; Ampadu 2007; Stone and Stewart 2016; Perryman-Clark and Craig 2019a; Lockett et al. 2019).

Examining the intersection of race, literacy, and educational policy contributes to emerging scholarship on the racialization of higher education. In 1997, Charles W. Mills argued that racism is perpetuated by tacit agreement to a "white racial contract" that has justified colonization, slavery, segregation, and economic exploitation by defining white spaces, worldviews, and people as superior—biologically, cognitively, or culturally. The racial contract governs who is seen as belonging where and whether they are granted full personhood by the policies and laws governing that space. This theory explains how institutional spaces, such as colleges and universities, are racialized based on their student demographics and segregated histories, marking HWCUs as normal and Minority Serving Institutions (MSIs) as raced. Gina Ann Garcia (2019) argues that the racialization of institutions devalues and under-resources MSIs. Diane Lynn Gusa (2010) argues that HWCUs privilege white worldviews on academic achievement, resulting in a "white institutional presence" that contributes to the attrition of students and faculty of color. Others demonstrate that the racialization of colleges informs institutional rankings, funding policies, program evaluations, the distribution of resources for faculty and students, and media and community representations of institutions (Wooten 2015; Coupet 2017; Hill 2012; Fulford 2019; Daniel 2016; Spencer-Maor and Randolph 2016; Kirklighter et al. 2007; Newman 2007; Millward et al. 2007). The racialization of higher education also impedes efforts to create inclusive HWCUs. Sylvia Hurtado and colleagues (1998, 285) found that HWCUs' diversity initiatives are undermined by failing to acknowledge exclusionary histories and ignoring "embedded benefits" for white students on campus, focusing instead on interpersonal harmony among students.

Given the ideological role of literacy in higher education, diversity and inclusion projects often intersect with the work of writing programs and writing program administrators (WPAs) like myself. Whether directing first-year composition, basic writing, WAC, or writing centers, WPAs participate in admission, retention, and graduation initiatives. Writing is considered a high-impact practice, promoting retention, and a "gateway" skill often believed to predict success in later courses. (Though, since students are required to pass first-year composition before taking many other courses, this prediction itself may be a tautology.) Without historical knowledge of racism and literacy, such initiatives can exclude students, forward ineffective models for literacy learning, and exacerbate racial and institutional inequalities. While HWCUs certainly have a history of racism to examine, this work may also be useful for HBCUs in explaining the effects of constraints imposed by white trustees and accreditation systems or desegregation policies that mandated they recruit more white faculty and students. To develop racially just programs and policies, we need to understand the harm done by desegregation policies premised on anti-Black linguistic racism.

SEGREGATION AND DESEGREGATION IN THE HISTORY OF HIGHER EDUCATION

Thus far, I have used the terms *segregation* and *desegregation* as if they are self-explanatory, but that is far from the case. Defining *desegregation* in higher education is challenging, given student choice; institutional selectivity; and distinctions between private, for-profit, and state-funded (or public) institutions. Legal and education scholarship debates whether desegregation has been achieved or whether it can be achieved through law and the courts (Wilson 1994; Maples 2014; Wooten 2015). As M. Christopher Brown (1999, xviii) has observed, "Higher education is still without a prevailing legal standard that clearly articulates what it means for postsecondary education to be desegregated or to have dismantled dual educational structures." The history of resistance to desegregation is critical to understanding higher education today.

Defining the Terms of Desegregation

Histories of postsecondary desegregation focus on the first Black students who enrolled in all-white southern universities in the 1950s and 1960s, after the decision in *Brown* (1954) made segregation illegal. These first admissions were largely the result of court order after Black applicants were rejected, and in many cases, they were met with violence or protest through the 1960s (Wallenstein 2015). Peter Wallenstein (2015, 19) calls these cases "proto-desegregation," the first steps of "a process, a series of steps, not something that happened all at once." James T. Minor (2008, 863) defines desegregation as "dismantling infrastructure in public institutions that intentionally separates individuals on the basis of race, with the goal of ensuring the fair and equal treatment of every citizen regardless of ethnicity, sex, religion, or national origin." Desegregation is different than integration, or the individual choice to attend an institution in which a student is a racial minority (863). The process of desegregation involved what I call "desegregation enforcement," or monitoring of formerly segregated states by HEW under the 1964 Civil Rights Act. This monitoring had to be enforced by the courts, beginning in the 1970s when HEW failed to de-fund segregated university systems and was sued by the LDF in a series of cases called the *Adams* cases, beginning with *Adams v. Richardson* (1973).

Segregation, or the enforced separation of individuals by race, exists in two kinds: segregation as a legal practice (de jure segregation, or segregation by law) or a pattern of enrollment attributable to white supremacy (de facto segregation, or segregation in practice, literally by fact). De jure segregation was ruled illegal in *Brown*, and Title VI of the 1964 Civil Rights Act sought to enforce *Brown* by mandating that the federal government de-fund any institution discriminating on the basis of race. However, given resistance to desegregation, de facto segregation has persisted, most markedly in states that had segregation laws.[6] Laura W. Perna and colleagues (2006) found that enrollment and graduation rates are inequitable in most of the states involved in the *Adams* litigation. Further, these results are stratified across institutional tiers (that is, institutional level, based on selectivity of admissions), with Black students having the most inequitable outcomes in four-year HWCUs and public flagship institutions. Edwin H. Litolff III (2007) examined patterns of segregation, finding that resegregation has occurred since the 1990s and is worse in *Adams* states. In examining Mississippi and North Carolina, Minor (2008) found evidence of a "segregation residual" in enrollment patterns, attributable to desegregation-related admissions policies, transfer agreements, and decisions about where to place new academic programs.

Today, de facto segregation continues nationally and affects student outcomes. The Georgetown University Center on Education and the Workforce reported in 2013 and 2018 that the distribution of funding, admissions requirements, and institutional selectivity contribute to disparities in the enrollment and graduation rates of Black and Latinx students (Carnevale and Strohl 2013; Carnevale et al. 2018). Anthony P. Carnevale and colleagues (2018) found that whites are overrepresented in selective public institutions and have higher retention and graduation rates than Black and Latinx students. They attribute these trends to increasingly selective admissions processes. While racial disparities in SAT test scores contribute to segregation to some extent, there are enough Black and Latinx students with above-average test scores to have proportional representation in selective institutions. Furthermore, students with lower SAT scores have higher retention rates at selective universities, which provide greater funding for instruction and student support, suggesting that institutional resources and system funding practices matter.

Segregation in the History of US Higher Education

Existing patterns of segregation are connected to the history of segregation and resistance to desegregation. Early American colleges were primarily accessible to white men and supportive of slavery and segregation (Wilder 2013; Karabel 2006). African Americans attended and graduated from HWCUs as early as 1799, when John Chavis attended Washington and Lee University, and 1823, when Alexander Lucius Twilight graduated from Middlebury College with a bachelor's degree ("Key Events" 2020). The first postsecondary institutions to offer widespread admission to Black students, Black colleges founded during the mid-nineteenth century[7] were mostly controlled by whites, particularly abolitionists and religiously affiliated groups, through the early twentieth century (Rogers 2012). Whites sought to control Black colleges, either as vehicles to emigrate educated Black people to Africa or as white abolitionist colleges teaching assimilationist curricula (Rogers 2012; Royster and Williams 1999). By 1870, around thirty colleges and universities were open to Black students (Smith 2016). Some were integrated institutions founded during Reconstruction by the American Missionary Association, which believed that re-educating whites through the co-education of Black and white students could eliminate racism (2016).[8] However, early efforts at postsecondary integration fizzled out by the early twentieth century as segregation was codified in southern states and enforced through law, funding practices, or the dictates of external stakeholders, such as the American Medical Association (Smith 2016; Rogers 2012). During this time, competition for prestige among institutions and emerging ranking systems produced a racialized and stratified postsecondary system that discouraged early integration efforts (Smith 2016, 12).

From 1890 to 1935, higher education was segregated by law in seventeen southern states and mostly segregated by practice throughout the United States (Wallenstein 2008). Wallenstein (2015) argues that segregated HWCUs were specifically anti-Black colleges, having the strongest opposition to the enrollment of Black students while allowing limited enrollment of Jewish, Asian, Latinx, and Indigenous students. The federal government subsidized segregation under the 1890 Morrill Land Grant Act, which conditioned funding for land grant institutions in legally segregated states on the establishment of separate Black colleges (Chun and Feagin 2022, 8). The land and funding for land grant institutions came from the seizure and sale of Indigenous peoples' lands (6). State-funded Black colleges were often restricted to vocational or agricultural curricula, although some, including Savannah Sate, resisted and offered liberal arts programs (Wooten 2015; Brooks 2014). Many Black colleges were white-controlled (Rogers 2012). Although technically the 1890 Morrill Act prohibited the neglect of Black colleges, states routinely underfunded them without repercussions (Wooten 2015). However, starting around World War I, Black activists pushed for more control over Black colleges' leadership, faculty, and curricula; a surge in the enrollment of Black women happened during this period, with women constituting the majority of Black college graduates by 1940 (Rogers 2012, 21).

Despite growth, Black colleges were disadvantaged within a system measured by white norms. In the early twentieth century, accreditation agencies like the Southern Association for Colleges and Schools (SACS) were segregated (Williamson-Lott 2018). When they began to accredit Black colleges, their criteria were based on white colleges, resulting in some cases in the denial of accreditation or the use of a separate evaluation scale (Wooten 2015; Fester et al. 2012).[9] Black colleges were also disadvantaged by the GI Bill, which provided funding for veterans to attend college, under the administration of the Veteran's Administration (VA) (Herbold 1994–1995). While granting VA claims to white veterans, like my grandfather, the VA denied claims for Black veterans to attend HWCUs, and under-resourced HBCUs could not accommodate all Black applicants. Hilary Herbold (108) estimates that at least 20,000 Black veterans were unable to use GI funds at Black colleges. As Melissa E. Wooten (2015, 2) explains, "The racial dynamics of the United States that relegated black Americans to a subordinate class did the same to the organizations that sought to serve this community, making it difficult for black colleges to succeed in the areas that critics now use to judge their relevance." Limited funding, restricted curricula, and exclusion from policy formation contributed to stereotypes of Black colleges as inferior to white colleges.

*Resistance to Desegregation Post-*Brown

Higher education was an early battleground for ending legal segregation, as the LDF targeted graduate programs at HWCUs, which clearly violated the "equal" requirement in "separate but equal" (Brown 2004). As early as 1935, some states allowed white colleges to admit a few Black students and to invest in upgrading Black colleges to prevent litigation (Wallenstein 2015). In 1938, the LDF won its first case in the US Supreme Court against the University of Missouri School of Law (Williamson-Lott 2018). By the time of *Brown*, only five states remained completely segregated: Alabama, Florida, Georgia, South Carolina, and Mississippi (Wallenstein 2008).[10] Along with other Deep South states, Georgia's stance toward desegregation in the 1950s was characterized by "unyielding resistance" (Wright 1955, 4). Georgia's state legislature issued resolutions in favor of revoking the thirteenth, fourteenth, and fifteenth constitutional amendments and impeaching Supreme Court justices (Anderson 2016, 79). In 1954, Georgia adopted a constitutional amendment that allowed the state to direct money to individuals for private education ("Questions" 1954). Expressing fear that desegregation would lead to interracial marriage, some legislators proposed sex-segregated schools (Cook 1955). The Georgia Board of Education banned all teachers affiliated with the NAACP in an effort to oust Black teachers from white schools (n.a. 1955). State officials were willing to publicly resist desegregation through the 1950s and early 1960s. It was not until 1961 that the first Black students were admitted to Georgia Institute of Technology (Georgia Tech) and the University of Georgia (UGA), under court order at the latter (Pratt 2002).

After *Brown*, many southern states tried violence and resistance. For example, the admission of James Meredith to the University of Mississippi required a court order and the National Guard in 1962 (Wallenstein 2008). Court orders were required for the next two Black students admitted after Meredith, one of whom was later expelled (Wallenstein 2015). In 1963, Mississippi set a minimum ACT score requirement of 15 at its three flagship HWCUs—more than twice the average score of Black students at the time—against the ACT's own recommendation not to rely solely on test scores for admissions decisions (*United States v. Fordice* 1992). Other admissions requirements were used to prevent desegregation. For example, the USG passed a resolution in 1958 that required college applicants to submit proof of "good moral character" and "good reputation in the community," evidence of which included two alumni letters of recommendation or a certificate from a superior court judge (Armstrong College 1960, 11).[11] A law also formally restricted admission to students under the age of twenty-one, unless the student had served in the military or had proof of "ability and fitness" (General Assembly 1959, 20). Even after Georgia Tech had admitted its first students, the university was accused of using entrance exam scores to reject Black students ("7 of 8" 1961). By 1964, 64 percent of HWCUs in the South were still segregated (Minchin and Salmond 2011, 45). Further complicating this problem, white university systems began to establish or expand HWCUs in close proximity to Black colleges in the 1960s and through the 1970s, exacerbating segregation.[12] Armstrong, for example, was added to the university system, made a four-year college, and moved to a larger campus between 1959 and 1966 (Stone 2010).

Recognizing ongoing opposition to desegregation, the 1964 Civil Rights Act sought to enforce *Brown*, with Title VI requiring all institutions receiving federal funding to practice nondiscriminatory admissions. By this time, however, segregationist leaders in the states and higher education systems had implemented race-evasive policies that limited the scale of Black student admissions to HWCUs and placed programs that allowed for surveillance and remediation throughout curricula (Wooten 2015). ACT admissions requirements in Mississippi were defended through the 1980s as an effort "to redress the problem of student unpreparedness" (*United States v. Fordice* 1992). In contrast, Louisiana and Tennessee operated open admissions programs but adopted remediation requirements for enrollment or literacy competency tests and remained largely segregated (Greene 2008). These race-evasive policies were challenging to overturn because proponents justified them as upholding academic standards.

Resistance to desegregation caused overall Black college enrollment to remain low through the 1960s, both in the South and throughout the United States.[13] Reports by scholars and the National Center for Education Statistics (NCES) on Black postsecondary enrollment from this time place it at under 6 percent of total postsecondary enrollment, with more than half of Black students enrolled in Black colleges (Scranton et al. 1970; Hill 1985; Snyder et al. 2016). The 1965 Higher Education Act sought to improve resources to Black colleges, creating an official HBCU designation. HBCUs became important sites for desegregation activism in the mid-1960s, influenced by the Black Power Movement (Williamson-Lott 2018). Around 10 percent of HBCU students were active in protest movements, despite significant pressure from white trustees at state-funded HBCUs (93). These campus protests motivated the desegregation of HWCUs, but affirmative action and equal opportunity programs often came with remediation requirements (Karabel 2006; Lamos 2011; Kynard 2013).

It was not until the late 1960s that HEW began investigating whether formerly segregated states had adequately desegregated their university systems. In 1969, the OCR, a unit of HEW established to monitor civil rights enforcement,[14] investigated nineteen southern and border states[15] and cited ten of those states for having dual systems of higher education. During this period, many southerners shifted on segregation, as white politicians recognized the formation of a powerful Black voting bloc (Minchin and Salmond 2011; Kruse 2007). For example,

Georgia's investigations began under the term of Governor Lester G. Maddox (1967–1971), who campaigned on his infamy after brandishing weapons at civil rights activists trying to enter his restaurant, the Pickrick (Rice 1988, 196). The USG's desegregation plans, however, were written during the terms of Governors Jimmy Carter and George Busbee, who disavowed segregation to different degrees (Henderson and Roberts 1988). Kevin M. Kruse (2007) argues that southern white resistance to desegregation shifted to accommodate changing social norms into a conservative ideology of "white flight" that recast ongoing segregation as a matter of personal liberty, providing race-evasive justifications for segregationist practices. This ideology upheld claims that postsecondary segregation could be explained away as a product of student choice and meritocracy—individual achievement in academics, particularly in literacy.

Postsecondary Desegregation Goes to Court

In 1970, frustrated with HEW's failure to enforce violations, the LDF sued HEW in the District Court of Washington, DC, in a case known as *Adams v. Richardson* (1973). The court had to rule whether nondiscriminatory policies alone constituted sufficient desegregation when systems remained segregated in practice. For two decades, the courts and the federal government wrestled with this question. Following nearly twenty years of decisions and appeals, *Adams*[16] was dismissed from court in 1990 with the declaration that it was no longer appropriate[17] to bring litigation against the entire Department of Education (DOE)—the newly reorganized branch of HEW created in 1980—and that higher education desegregation must be enforced by district courts in individual states against specific institutions (Brown 1999). This ruling limited the power of the courts in postsecondary desegregation.

From the 1970s through the 1990s, district and appeals courts litigated not only the *Adams* case against HEW but other postsecondary desegregation cases in Tennessee (*Geier v. University of Tennessee* [1979]), Alabama (*Knight v. Alabama* [1991]), Louisiana (*United States v. Louisiana* [1989]), and Mississippi (*Ayers v. Allain* [1987]; *Ayers v. Fordice* [1995, 1997]). After ongoing appeals and little resolution in most of these cases, the US Supreme Court ruled on Mississippi's case, in *United States v. Fordice* (1992). *Fordice* established a precedent for postsecondary desegregation, remanding the monitoring of desegregation plans back to the district courts. The *Fordice* standard stated that a practice traceable to de jure segregation must be examined to determine if that practice continues to perpetuate segregation; if it does, then the courts must determine whether the practice is educationally justified and if it can be "practicably" eliminated.[18] The court specified areas of concern to examine, including admissions requirements, institutional missions, and the duplication of programs at nearby white and Black colleges.

Limitations of Postsecondary Desegregation Litigation

While *Fordice* did acknowledge that postsecondary desegregation needed its own standard, the ruling created two major problems that are relevant to this book. First, *Fordice* justified remedial education as an educational practice, particularly in Mississippi and Louisiana (Inman 2013; Greene 2008). Remedial programs in reading, writing, and math—even if they disproportionately enrolled Black students—were seen as having "sound educational justification," and the courts accepted them as necessary for Black student retention in HWCUs, without clear research supporting these claims and even if they limited the number of Black students gaining regular admission (*Ayers v. Fordice* 1997). In Louisiana and Tennessee, statewide open admissions programs that had been implemented in the 1960s were dismantled in favor of selective admissions and the relocation of remedial coursework to community colleges or lower-tier institutions (Greene 2008; *Geier v. University of Tennessee* 1979). Second, *Fordice* refused one of the many demands made by Black plaintiffs—the upgrading of HBCUs—arguing that enhancing HBCUs would constitute the creation of a "separate, but 'more equal'" dual system (*United States v. Fordice* 1992).

Scholars across disciplines argue that ambivalent desegregation outcomes contribute to racial injustice today. Ryan Tacorda (2003) argues that desegregation was limited by a reductive definition of the "vestiges of segregation"—a phrase intended to allow courts to redress racial injustices but subsequently used to limit intervention by requiring a direct link between a de facto policy and de jure segregation. Tacorda (2003, 1573) defines vestiges of segregation as any "phenomenon whose 'cultural meaning' provides evidence of unconscious discrimination that may not be observed directly but that is regarded with racial significance by society generally." This definition allows us to consider policies premised on anti-Black linguistic racism as vestiges of segregation, specifically the view that Black language and rhetorical practices are unfit for academic or professional use and that Black students need literacy remediation. While I do not pretend to make a legal argument here, my use of the term is intended as a heuristic for identifying histories of

racism that explain racist biases and racial disparities in higher education today.

Three critiques of desegregation provide a theoretical basis for
understanding the role of literacy in impeding desegregation and contributing to ongoing vestiges of segregation in LCR. First, desegregation was limited by the failure of the courts to allow for race-conscious
policies, that is, policies that acknowledge and seek to remedy the social
reality of racism. Many scholars have discussed this problem, including
Gloria Ladson-Billings and William F. Tate IV (1995), M. Christopher
Brown (1999), Jerome Karabel (2006), Shaun R. Harper and colleagues
(2009), and Anthony P. Carnevale and Jeff Strohl (2013). Early race-
conscious policies were undermined almost immediately. Affirmative
action rulings since *Regents of the University of California v. Bakke* (1978)
have limited consideration of race to the goal of achieving "diversity"
rather than remedying racial injustice, dismantling the processes put
in place to desegregate universities that acknowledged the racism Black
applicants experience throughout the admission process (Karabel 2006;
Olivas 2013). Similarly, *Fordice* did not support the enhancement or institutional upgrading of HBCUs. Race-evasive policies increasingly encouraged writing programs to eliminate race-conscious writing instruction,
which made remedying racial disparities an explicit part of the pedagogy or placement and assessment processes (Lamos 2011). As I will
show in this book, LCR scholarship and desegregation policies justified
race-evasive writing program curricula and policies by arguing that race-
conscious policies would promote segregation and disempower Black
students, turning the language of civil rights against itself.

Second, desegregation rulings focused too narrowly on integration
in student enrollment. Charles M. Payne (2004, 85) argues that desegregation rulings have been limited since *Brown* by defining racism as an
interpersonal problem, that is, a matter of how individuals feel about
one another, rather than a means of social and political exclusion. Tate
and colleagues (1993) describe how interpersonal solutions to desegregation resulted in plans designed to increase interactions between racial
groups in educational spaces. A key feature of these plans, they explain,
was a focus on "physically manipulating the students' school placement," a practice they describe as a "mathematical solution to a socio-
cultural problem" (259–260). In other words, desegregation became
about the student demographics of a school or college rather than
the transformation of racist institutional structures. As Carmen Kynard
(2013, 152) explains, this focus on "shifting demographics" avoided "the
more ambiguous questions that racial and educational justice demand:

What will we do with existing structures of oppression in which the participation of 'new minorities' will take place? Should participation have a transformative bent? What counts as transformative participation and who defines it?"

One example of how this "mathematical" approach undercut desegregation is the "program swap" between Armstrong and Savannah State described in chapters 3 and 4, which exchanged students and faculty from two high-enrollment degree programs. Teacher education went to Armstrong and was not offered at Savannah State; business went to Savannah State and was not offered at Armstrong. This approach literally transferred students of one race to the college of another race, and the decision was rooted in a claim that Armstrong had a superior teacher education program based on standardized test scores. In failing to address anti-Black linguistic racism, this plan reinforced concern about declining literacy at Armstrong that fed into an early WAC program designed to encourage all faculty to grade student writing. The repeated refrain of upholding literacy standards at Armstrong justified more literacy testing, writing assignments, and course requirements that established barriers to graduation for Black students.

A third critique of desegregation solutions is that they failed to account for ongoing anti-Blackness in education. According to Tacorda (2003, 1571), courts have failed to define academic disparities as vestiges even when plaintiffs have presented strong evidence that achievement disparities stem not from cultural or cognitive deficiencies but from teacher bias, low expectations for Black students, or disparities in Black and white schools' resources. *Brown* and other desegregation litigation perpetuated the idea that segregation left African Americans culturally deprived and educationally deficient, when many civil rights activists argued that segregation perpetuated belief in white superiority (Bell 2005; Crenshaw 1988; Prendergast 2003). Some historical scholarship in LCR has suggested that early basic writing programs at white colleges were "race-conscious" and promoted what critical race theorist Derrick A. Bell Jr. (2005) calls "interest convergence," racial progress accomplished when white interests align with Black activism (Lamos 2011). However, Bell (2005, 1066) argues that interest convergence cannot operate on *deficit* theories based on "the assumptions of white dominance and the presumptions of black incompetence." As I show in this book, deficit theories were pervasive in desegregation policies. Plaintiffs, such as those in Alabama's desegregation case, *Knight v. Alabama* (1991), were generally unsuccessful in arguing that "whites' underexpectations of blacks are precisely the attitudes of white superiority and black subordination" that perpetuated segregation. Blaming Black students' literacy deficiencies for ongoing segregation remained an acceptable defense in many states.

Finally, desegregation did not center HBCUs in the ways civil rights activists wanted. Wooten (2015) explains that the courts fundamentally misunderstood the rationale behind postsecondary desegregation litigation. Plaintiffs and other invested parties primarily wanted states to redress decades of funding and status disparities at Black colleges.[19] Without funding to improve facilities and programs and provide resources for students, Black colleges could not counteract the discriminatory attitudes white students had about attending Black colleges or about students coming from Black colleges. Instead, whites used academic standards to control the desegregation process. For example, Aldon Morris and colleagues (1994, 67), describing their experiences as witnesses in Alabama's desegregation case, state that Alabama justified its refusal to upgrade its HBCUs by claiming that "the top [HWCUs] earned their superior missions and deserve the prestige and resources they command," while "the missions of the two [HBCUs] should not be enhanced to flagship status because such enhancement would be educationally unwise and economically detrimental." Such arguments demonstrate the extent to which white self-interest maintained institutional identities despite desegregation (Tate, Ladson-Billings, and Grant 1993). As I show in chapter 3 of this book, fear of declining "literacy standards" was used to benefit HWCUs. Armstrong and the USG insisted that desegregation policies apply equally to white and Black colleges, requiring both Savannah colleges to set equal admissions standards and resulting in an over-enrolled and under-resourced Special Studies Department at Savannah State. In LCR, recent calls to center HBCU writing programs recognize that this history erased scholars from the field (Cheramie 2004; Spencer-Maor and Randolph 2016; Lockett and RudeWalker 2016; Ford 2016; Royster and Williams 1999; Kynard and Eddy 2009; Green 2016).

As I hope to show in this book, these critiques of desegregation can be illuminated by understanding how anti-Black linguistic racism became ingrained in the policies for writing programs that developed during desegregation. This analysis complements existing or proposed methods of examining or remedying racial injustices in LCR (Poe et al. 2014; Poe and Cogan 2016; Inoue 2015; Condon and Young 2017; Ruiz 2016; García de Müeller and Ruiz 2017; Clary-Lemon 2009; Gilyard and Banks 2018; Richardson 2003; Moss 2003; Villanueva 2006), including support for historical work designed to examine racial injustice (Inoue

2009; Hammond 2018; Lathan 2015; Epps-Robertson 2018; Kynard 2013). Scholars also call for articulating anti-racist practices for writing program administration (García de Müeller and Ruiz 2017; Perryman-Clark and Craig 2019b; Craig and Perryman-Clark 2011; Craig 2016; Green 2016). This work is vital given research showing that white WPAs continue to associate Black students with basic writing and lack direction for racial justice initiatives in writing programs (García de Müeller and Ruiz 2017; Perryman-Clark 2016). Institutional history can help WPAs and other faculty and administrators identify and dismantle pedagogies, policies, and programs that perpetuate anti-Black linguistic racism. While insufficient on its own, this analysis may provide a useful starting point for WPA activism, such as revising race-evasive policies, dismantling deficiency theories of literacy, developing race-conscious pedagogies, and transforming the rhetoric used to promote writing programs.

REVISING THE HISTORY OF DESEGREGATION IN LCR

LCR historians have already contributed to an understanding of postsecondary desegregation as an influential force in writing program development. Kynard (2013) provides an excellent history of the role HBCUs, the Black Power Movement, and the Black Arts Movement played in LCR during desegregation. Steve Lamos (2011) describes efforts to desegregate the University of Illinois at Urbana Champaign, which established basic writing as part of equal opportunity programs. Other histories of basic writing describe the role of desegregation in open admissions at the City University of New York (CUNY) (Horner and Lu 1999; Soliday 2002). However, only two article-length works on desegregation enforcement in the South currently exist in LCR history. Here, I review their findings to explain common themes and current limitations in histories of postsecondary desegregation, and I argue for a revision of this history grounded in the multidisciplinary critique of desegregation litigation reviewed above.

Rethinking Representations of Access in Desegregation

Nicole Pepinster Greene (2008) describes how desegregation litigation led to a statewide open admissions policy and the founding of basic writing in the 1950s at the University of Louisiana at Lafayette (ULL), a white college. Although most southern states did not implement statewide open admissions, Greene's history confirms that desegregation in Louisiana established and grew writing programs, beginning with basic writing and expanding into a writing lab, university-wide faculty writing workshops led by composition scholars, and retention initiatives for Black students. This growth in writing programs in white colleges during desegregation enforcement mirrors the trends I identify in Georgia.

Although Greene argues that basic writing facilitated desegregation, her description of the program suggests that basic writing did not offer Black students equitable access to ULL. The program employed a pedagogical strategy called "bidialectism"—a term used to describe literacy pedagogies that teach Standard English while also viewing other English dialects as legitimate, grammatical varieties of English.[20] Greene (2008, 74, original emphasis) describes how "the new students raised the faculty's interest in dialects. . . . In the remedial classes faculty encouraged students to use their 'natural mode of expression' in journals. These faculty wanted students to be able 'to communicate in *both* languages'—'standard' and 'nonstandard' English." However, "nonstandard" English was only allowed in students' journals, not in formal essays, presenting dialects deemed nonstandard as inappropriate or inadequate for academic writing—a form of anti-Black linguistic racism as Baker-Bell (2020) defines it. Furthermore, basic writing disproportionately enrolled Black students and failed them at higher rates than whites, information that was hidden from the desegregation enforcement monitoring committee to avoid scrutiny (Greene 2008, 75).

A 1987 review of Louisiana's progress found that segregation had worsened over the decade, a majority of students failed to graduate in six years, and the state's HBCUs had high attrition rates. The district court argued that these findings were due to open admissions' "fail[ure] to organize students by academic ability" (*United States v. Louisiana* 1989). If colleges admitted students on the basis of academic ability, then attrition rates would be lower and colleges would "forc[e] high schools to respond to the preparation challenge" (1989). The court ordered Louisiana to develop a tiered admissions plan, with remedial programs phased out at selective institutions beginning in 1990 (1989). Meanwhile, community colleges were tasked with providing "remedial education of those who might be excluded from the less accessible four-year college system, thereby helping to ensure a racially balanced system" (1989). This ruling cast remediation as an access strategy, while creating new obstacles—in the form of transfer—that displaced responsibility for desegregation onto high schools and community colleges.

I would argue that both Greene and the court misread the role of remediation in addressing racial inequality. For Greene, institutional racism in pedagogy, grading, and desegregation compliance is not presented as a serious obstacle to access. Instead, the termination of this basic writing structure, as Greene (2008, 93) puts it, "greatly affected the lives of many underprepared students in the area." In the context of desegregation, this remark codes under-prepared students as Black and remediation as genuine access for under-prepared students. Ironically, the court's termination of open admissions makes the same assumption, representing attrition solely as an academic preparation issue, even though ULL's program suggests that institutional racism was prevalent. Even more problematic, the court *still* cast basic writing as the solution, only it removed basic writing from most selective colleges. As critiques of desegregation have explained, focusing on enrollment demographics obscures larger institutional problems. For historians studying deseg-regation, access must be defined as what Adam J. Banks (2006, 45) calls "transformative access," which provides African Americans with "genuine inclusion in technologies and the networks of power that help determine what they become, but never merely for the sake of inclu-sion." Louisiana's history suggests that presenting basic writing as access for Black students ignores the system in which access is circumscribed through a racialized and racist system of instruction that allows HWCUs and white faculty to define academic standards and to prioritize their own role in providing access.

Shifting White-Centered Perspectives on Desegregation

Alongside rethinking access, desegregation histories require centering the demands of Black activists and HBCUs to understand how desegre-gation enforcement undercut transformational access. As I note above, orders to prioritize HBCUs in desegregation remedies were dismissed by whites who demanded "equal" treatment of HBCUs and HWCUs. Any history of desegregation must ask what HBCUs and Black students wanted desegregation to look like. How did their requests seek to dis-mantle segregationist ideologies about intelligence and cultural depriva-tion? What compromises were made by these parties? How have those compromises affected writing programs and perceptions of institutions and students?

These questions suggest an addendum to the history of basic writing in Joyce Olewski Inman's (2013) account of desegregation enforce-ment in Mississippi after *Ayers v. Fordice* (which went to the Supreme Court as *United States v. Fordice* and was remanded back to the district court for a settlement). As Inman explains, desegregation litigation dismantled open admissions at some colleges and mandated identical admissions and the formation of a summer remediation program across all Mississippi colleges and universities. She details the ways whites' appeals to race-evasive academic "standards" supported this summer remediation program, which consisted of a screening and Accuplacer testing in the spring and a ten-week summer program in reading, writing, and math—"taught both in traditional classroom settings and through computer-assisted individual components" (*Ayers v. Fordice* 1997). As in Louisiana and Georgia, desegregation enforcement centered on remediation policies, many of which required self-remediation (with computer assistance).

Inman (2013, 299) argues that this new non-credit remedial structure "ghettoize[d]" basic writing. However, there is a tension here in the way basic writing is labeled a ghetto primarily for its separation from the curriculum and not for its work as a remedial writing program. Does the segregation of basic writing from regular college coursework reflect, as Inman (2013, 314) argues, the state "not valu[ing] the educationally underprepared" or the separation of "student demographics perceived to be on the borders of white middle-class America?" Are basic writers demographically "other" in white institutions? Or are they underprepared? There is a real risk of misrepresenting the stakes of segregation when using the term *academic ghetto*, as Alexandria Lockett (2019) explains. Focusing on writing centers, Lockett describes how writing programs in HWCUs function as academic ghettos, spaces designed to "correct" literacy deficiencies by enforcing white mainstream literacy standards. The problem with the academic ghetto, Lockett argues, is not that its inhabitants are deficient but rather that such writing programs seek to assimilate students to white mainstream literacy in spaces physically separated from places of privilege, where inhabitants lack power to control the resources of the space. These two issues have been conflated in disciplinary discourse as HWCU-centered histories reiterate HWCUs' and states' arguments that Black students *need* remediation to access privileged white spaces—spaces where they are rarely granted the power of transformative access.

However, rereading this history to include HBCUs reveals that *Ayers* failed to center HBCU demands. As Inman (2013, 304) mentions, the plaintiffs in the original suit—Black citizens of Mississippi—asked for a desegregation plan that would raise the admissions requirements at HWCUs while making Jackson State University, an HBCU, an open-admissions institution. This request seems to defy representations of basic writing as key to Black students' access at HWCUs—an argument that often leaves basic writing's pedagogy and identity unproblematized.

In fact, plaintiffs pointed out that the summer basic writing program, which had not been tested for educational efficacy, would not simply segregate students; it would actually "significantly reduce the number of black students eligible for regular admission to the university system" (*Ayers v. Fordice* 1997). Furthermore, the plaintiffs argued that the courts failed "to consider the educational soundness of alternative proposals that would have excluded fewer black students" (1997). Although the courts denied the plaintiffs' request,[21] their proposal is an example of the ways HBCUs sought to circumvent the state's control over admissions requirements. The problem is not that a space is demographically other; it is that the demographically other is assumed to be under-prepared for white institutions and therefore is placed into a devalued, assimilationist space.

Forefronting HBCUs' arguments about admissions requirements in desegregation reminds us that admissions requirements and basic writing have never been neutral tools in desegregation; they have often been at the very center of efforts for HWCUs to maintain white identities and institutional power. While basic writing may segregate students, that segregation is a symptom of a larger structural exclusion rooted in a history of opposition and recalcitrant compliance in desegregation enforcement. HBCUs' proposals for desegregation reveal that white-controlled admissions requirements and basic writing translated the under-resourcing and racist perceptions of state-funded HBCUs to new spaces designated for remediation in HWCUs. These were not programs designed to transform anti-Black racism in higher education.

METHODOLOGICAL CONSIDERATIONS FOR INSTITUTIONAL CRITIQUE

Desegregation State seeks to revise existing histories of postsecondary desegregation enforcement by employing archival and interview methodologies for the purpose of institutional critique, that is, history with an investment in analyzing institutions to promote change (Lamos 2012a). Institutional critique examines the consequences of the systems that shape our institutions. As Ryan Skinnell (2016, 40) argues, writing program histories need more attention to the ways "non-disciplinary institutional exigencies" shape writing instruction, given that writing instruction has often been conscripted into political or institutional agendas. I see institutional critique as part of David F. Green Jr.'s (2016, 170) recommendation that WPAs use historical research to "invest in alternative composition histories that trouble discriminating attitudes toward linguistic and social differences" and to use that historical research to inform writing program development.

However, institutional critique does not inherently confront racism if I, as a white researcher, do not confront the role institutional racism plays in my position as researcher and in the composition of and access to historical records. As scholars have noted, LCR histories are prone to exclude or negatively portray Black students and writing programs at HBCUs and to depict white writing instructors and HWCUs as heroes in providing access and opportunity to Black students (Prendergast 1998, 2003; Clary-Lemon 2009; Kynard 2013; Craig 2016). Throughout this research process, I have asked myself why and how these histories reproduce racism, sometimes under the banner of antiracism. I think part of the problem lies in the tendency, or more aptly the desire, of white researchers to view ourselves as operating outside of institutional racism, even when reproducing the very genres and methodologies that emerged from this system. Ahmed (2012, 170) observes that white scholars seek to feel happy with our work, deploying antiracism for the purpose of "generating a positive white identity that makes the white subject feel good" about their scholarship while letting "racism . . . remain the burden of racialized others." The power of methodology is that it can be described for the purpose of feeling good about our research rather than addressing the limitations of research. Ahmed describes how her work with universities developing diversity plans is inextricable from a racist system, and to ignore that fact would be to gloss over what we can accomplish in these constraints. Here, I outline my methods, the processes I considered in determining those methods, and the limitations of this research.

Ashley Farmer (2018) details the ways archives are informed by whiteness, in terms of who has decided what gets archived and how the "normal" archival researcher is raced. Institutional archives contain records that powerful actors placed there and that institutions support through preservation (Royster and Williams 1999; Glenn and Enoch 2010; Masters 2010). Although the "Code of Ethics" for the Society of American Archivists now includes diversity and social responsibility as critical to its work, it does so in part because of a long history of "under-documented communities." Records of and by marginalized actors may be absent or limited, and resources directed toward preserving and cataloging materials differ across institutions. When I walk into the archive, then, it is something akin to when I walk into a classroom, enabled by a history of racist literacy practices that make my presence as a white person normal, capable of perpetuating white preservation practices or resisting the tendency to read absence or marginalization at face value. Part of this resistance involves what Jacqueline Jones Royster and Gesa E. Kirsch (2012, 84) call "strategic contemplation," making transparent how I, as the researcher, "process, imagine, and work with materials" to highlight archival inequities. My reading is an invested reading of archival records with a recognition of the social realities of racism. For example, institutional documents at Armstrong and the USG reproduce the stereotype of Black students as remedial. Recognizing that those institutional documents are selective representations recorded by those with institutional power means that I must read against the grain of these accounts, considering multiple ways of framing enrollment data and refusing to present absence from archives as absence from history. But, as Farmer (2018) argues, the structured exclusion of Black people (as archivists, researchers, and authors of records) is a larger problem than methodology can resolve. Resources need to be sent to faculty and institutions trying to remedy this problem.

As a white Armstrong faculty member, my affiliation with an HWCU also contributes to an inequitable power dynamic in accessing archival records and conducting interviews. Savannah State has been misrepresented by Armstrong and the white Savannah community and media for decades. Any attempt at reciprocity between myself as the researcher and historical or present-day participants is limited by what Katrina M. Powell and Pamela Takayoshi (2003, 418) describe as "a complicated process inextricably imbricated onto issues of power, control, and agency." Much community work needs to be done to redress the historical injustices against Savannah State, but that work cannot proceed without a revision of Armstrong's history of desegregation (reduced to an Armstrong-centric loss of a business degree, which it can now offer as Georgia Southern). In addition, there is more research to be done to recover the legacy of literacy and activism at Savannah State, research I hope scholars will take up.

One place where this limitation becomes apparent is in interviews, which I conducted to invite "multiplicity" into telling this history (Royster and Kirsch 2012). This decision, however, raised questions for me about how to negotiate the risks of asking participants about experiences related to racism: either a participant risks saying something racist, a participant says something that accuses the universities' or USG of racism, or a participant is asked to recall experiences of racism that are traumatic (particularly if uncertain about a white interviewer's position on racism). If I were going to ask participants about desegregation, I wanted, first, to disclose the argument of my project to explain my position; second, to allow participants to withdraw from the project after the interview without any material going public; third, to maintain their anonymity; and fourth, to avoid possible repercussions from either university. These considerations informed my decision to interview faculty no longer employed by either university, with the interview plan and consent forms first reviewed by the Institutional Review Board (IRB), instead of collecting public oral history archives (which I hope will one day occur). I worked with archivists and community connections to extend invitations to participate, both to establish some connection with participants and in some cases to allow people to refuse invitations anonymously. These decisions restricted the research practically, by limiting both the number of available participants in an already small pool of people and the ways participants might personally benefit from this research.

I selected prospective people to interview based on Brad Lucas and Margaret M. Strain's (2010, 261) recommendation to consider whose perspectives need to be represented. In archival records, I already had substantial archival comments from general faculty and students and a number of records of white faculty's perspectives on writing programs at Armstrong. Furthermore, I had written accounts that included faculty interviews from other histories of Armstrong and Savannah State, as well as accounts of desegregation in books by Armstrong alumnus, Savannah State faculty member, and Savannah mayor Otis S. Johnson (2016) and former Savannah State president Clyde W. Hall (1991). Given my existing resources, I ultimately decided to interview Black faculty involved in the literacy programs I study in this book. My decision did ignore that white faculty might have new perspectives that would be valuable to hear. My questions about literacy remediation and instruction also risk reproducing the dynamic Royster and Jean C. Williams (1999) criticize of white scholars delimiting participation to an identity participants did not wish to claim. When conducting the interviews, I explained what I had learned about racism in Savannah's desegregation process first, so I was transparent about my goal of critiquing institutional racism, and then I asked participants to describe their experiences working during and after desegregation. I did not limit their contributions to the topic of my study, and I allowed participants to define the direction of the conversation, often to concerns of teaching philosophy and career achievements—information that proved vital for understanding the events I describe in this book (Powell and Takayoshi 2003). I also shared chapters of this work in process to provide participants with an opportunity for feedback or to discontinue their participation if desired. Evelyn

Baker Dandy from Armstrong and Carolyn Warnock from Savannah State[22] describe their experiences as Black faculty teaching literacy courses during and after desegregation enforcement activities. I include their recollections and pedagogical recommendations as literacy educators who navigated the institutional environments and state policies that affected their work and their students. Their contributions detail the importance of Black literacy educators in creating educational spaces for Black students amid the challenges of desegregation and institutional racism.

One final concern, particularly given the recent nature of this history, is privacy. Writing institutional critique raises questions about how to name and represent historical actors whose actions or language are critiqued. J. W. Hammond (2018) argues that naming racism in historical research is not necessarily presentism, since sources show that critiques of racism have existed throughout the history of the United States. However, when describing recent history, Laura Clark Brown and Nancy Kaiser (2012) recommend exercising caution with respect to privacy, especially in cases where an individual named in the archives may still be alive. I take a hybrid-institutional approach to naming actors (Lamos 2009), delineating "what constitutes private, social, and institutional spaces" when talking about people and texts (Royster and Kirsh 2012, 150). I follow Lamos's (2009) recommendation that researchers consider the power and publicity of the person writing a particular document when deciding to protect privacy and omit names. I do not redact all individuals' identities from citations and references, but when describing institutional spaces, I focus on the documents as a reflection of institutional spaces without mentioning specific individuals. When describing public social spaces, such as comments made in public-facing documents, I typically reference names and titles, since those individuals are nearly always easily identifiable by the time period (for instance, the chancellor of the USG). However, in documents shared within smaller communities, as when students or faculty are speaking or writing for a limited audience, I omit names and instead refer to participants by institutional title (e.g., assistant professor of history, student government association president). These choices emphasize that institutional structures and individual choices uphold racist ideologies within a framework in which power, identity, and position matter.

As *recent* history, the subject of this project is still tender. This sentiment is perhaps best conveyed in the words of Mayor Johnson, whose advocacy for Savannah State during desegregation is well documented in the archives: Johnson served on the Savannah Community Liaison

Committee (discussed in chapter 3) and regularly advocated civil rights activism in Savannah State's student newspaper. In his memoir, Johnson (2016, 168) reflects on the fight to keep Savannah State: "This was a very difficult section of this book to write. . . . It pains me to know there are still political forces in Georgia that want to destroy black institutions of higher education. . . . Black institutions, especially state-supported ones, will be in constant danger because their funding is dependent on the good will of white-dominated state legislatures." I have kept Johnson's comments in mind while working on this book. There is pain and harm in university histories, and HWCUs and university systems must acknowledge that fact. I hope to explain the troubling histories behind the ways writing programs are supported on our campuses and how those actions have affected Black students and HBCUs. HBCUs have been central to the status LCR has attained as a discipline, in ways that have continually gone unrecognized and unrewarded, as Royster and Williams (1999) and Kynard and Eddy (2009) have already argued.

Despite being recent, this history is important for a moment in which universities are reconsidering the role of testing in admissions, testing organizations have proposed measuring student disadvantage, scholars are advocating changes to the uses of retention data, and WPAs are debating whether we have an obligation to teach Standard English on public listservs. This history is important for a moment in which the United States is experiencing a rise in hate crimes, state brutality against Black and Brown people, efforts to eliminate critical race theory from diversity training, and nostalgic calls from white politicians to return to a segregated time in our history. We have questions before us that demand action: Will HWCUs once again succumb to political pressures for race-evasive policies, or will they acknowledge the reality of racism and our need to take an active role in redressing it? Will policymakers and other stakeholders reconsider the ways they evaluate MSIs, and can their contributions rewrite white institutional norms for retention and student success? Can LCR rewrite a disciplinary history in a way that supports current arguments to rethink writing assessment and writing instruction for racial justice? Will we disinvest in the surveillance of correctness in writing and the penalties assigned to those targeted by this surveillance? Can the discipline commit to change students' and stakeholders' perceptions about what kinds of communication practices are valued and valuable? These questions demanded our attention long ago, and we must confront them now.

1

"TECHNOLOGIES OF THIS THEORY"
Desegregation as Remediation, Early 1970s

In 1972, several prominent social scientists—Martin Deutsch, Thomas Pettigrew, Kenneth B. Clark, and Hylan Lewis among them—published a collection titled *The Educationally Deprived*, devoted to exploring the "particular problem of improvement of higher education for Blacks" (Clark et al. 1972, v). Rather than arguing for postsecondary reform, contributors debated how programs for Black children—everything from remedial education to automated literacy learning machines placed strategically in supermarkets—might create equal educational opportunity. Noticeably absent were colleges themselves. College desegregation was, in many ways, focused on what happened before college. *The Educationally Deprived* illustrates how a theory of "cultural deprivation" became "an integral part of the controversy about the quality of education provided for Negro children in *de jure* and *de facto* segregated schools" (5). Remedial literacy programs, dubbed "the related technologies of [cultural deprivation] theory," were seen as key to equal opportunity, the solution to segregation (9).

Proponents of cultural deprivation theory considered racial gaps in academic achievement—and, by extension, segregation in colleges—a consequence of early childhood experiences. As historian Mical Raz (2013) explains, both policymakers and social scientists sought to explain why Black students on average scored lower on standardized tests than white students, without repeating by then outdated claims about biological racial inferiority. These parties, however, could not formulate a theory outside of anti-Black beliefs about racial inferiority. Enter cultural deprivation theory, which hypothesized that Black children living in "broken" homes in segregated, low-income neighborhoods lacked sufficient linguistic stimulation (2013). This theory equated segregation with isolation and borrowed findings from sensory deprivation experiments in psychology—which examined the cognitive effects of blocking a person's sight, sound, or touch for hours or days—to explain how culture and environment influenced learning (2013). This

https://doi.org/10.7330/9781646422036.c001

political misapplication of psychological research stigmatized Black literacy practices and communities, diagnosing the deprived[1] child as having "peculiar or bizarre language patterns; lack of verbal stimulation; absence of father or stable male figure in the home; and lack of books in the home" (Clark et al. 1972, 5). Although these "symptoms" made no mention of race, they were based on racist stereotypes about single Black mothers, who failed to provide sufficient linguistic stimulation for their children by abandoning their homes to work for a living (Raz 2013). It was a damned-if-you-do, damned-if-you-don't explanation that offered up remediation as a tool for enforcing social norms of race, gender, sexuality, and class through literacy. By locating deprivation in the childhood home, the policies that emerged from this premise also located the solution for college students outside the normal educational track, in remediation. Cultural deprivation shaped the very time line for how desegregation could unfold.

By 1972, the role of cultural deprivation theory in directing educational policy was well recognized, but debate over the concept in social science circles signaled the beginning of the end of the theory's academic acceptance (Raz 2013). Yet cultural deprivation already had, as Kenneth B. Clark and colleagues (1972, 6) wrote, "profound and widespread influences on educational policies and practices."[2] Just a few years later, Geneva Smitherman (1977, 202) observed that cultural deprivation had institutionalized "a framework of black pathology" in college-level remedial writing programs, which continued to present Black literacy practices as inappropriate in social interaction and workplace communication. For decades, even progressive publications, such as Andrea A. Lunsford, Helene Moglen, and James Slevin's (1990, 3) *Right to Literacy*, described how the "isolation, fragmentation, and dissociation" in families and communities negatively affected literacy practices. Through the 1990s, composition scholars referenced race euphemistically, using synonyms for cultural deprivation, such as "culturally disadvantaged" and "underprivileged" (Clary-Lemon 2009, W6). Why did a theory about childhood literacy development based in a misapplication of psychological research end up influencing college writing for decades? Cultural deprivation theory operated on a chiasmus: remediation facilitated school desegregation, and, in turn, desegregation remediated the cognitive deficits of segregation. When colleges began to desegregate, this theory outlined a process that placed very little responsibility on white colleges: pre-college, non-credit literacy remediation integrated Black students into white mainstream literacy norms to compensate for linguistic deprivation. Once Black students adopted these literacy norms, they could enroll as full students at white colleges with equal opportunity for social mobility. This was the path to desegregation in the white imaginary.

In this chapter, I describe how this redefinition of desegregation as remediation made linguistic stimulation and cultural integration the tenets of remedial writing instruction. Political and educational stakeholders blamed deprived students for de facto segregation. In its earliest versions of a desegregation plan, the University System of Georgia (USG) denied racial discrimination, stating, "All materials submitted in this document are prefaced by the specific observation that the University System is neither now nor has been in recent years operated in a manner discriminatory toward any minority group. . . . Students disadvantaged in either a material or educational sense are provided with financial aid and remedial studies programs designed to compensate to the greatest extent possible for their previous conditions" (Regents 1974, 2). Blaming de facto segregation on deprivation fed into anti-Black racism by presenting African Americans as culturally inferior and thus a threat to academic "standards" at white colleges. This threat was used to justify what Eric Darnell Pritchard (2017, 53) describes as the "regulation, policing, and surveillance" of raced and classed literacy norms in the form of technologies of literacy assessment, which began to exert greater control over admission to and graduation from college. Desegregation, both in US political discourse and the specific southern context of enforcement, established a set of policies and norms for literacy remediation that affected writing instruction for decades afterward.

REMEDIAL PROGRAMS AND THE
REDEFINITION OF DESEGREGATION

The influence of cultural deprivation theory resulted from its political popularity in explaining widespread protests against racism—in the streets and on college campuses. By the late 1960s, ongoing segregation was a recognized national policy failure and threat to civil order in the United States. Demand for an end to segregation and racism prompted hundreds of race riots in cities across the country in the late 1960s, spurring action to address ongoing segregation, seen as the root cause of racial inequality. President Lyndon B. Johnson, seeking to develop a policy response, formed the National Advisory Commission on Civil Disorders, better known as the Kerner Commission. Although progressive in its acknowledgment of white racism, the 1968 Kerner Commission's *Report of the National Advisory Commission on Civil Disorders,* or the Kerner Report, attributed violent protests to culturally deprived, segregated Black communities, drawing on research from the National Institute for Mental Health and social scientists' testimony (Raz 2013). "Civil disorder," the report claimed, was the outcome of a "culture of poverty that results from unemployment and family breakup," which left "Negro students . . . falling further behind whites" in "verbal and reading ability" (National Advisory Commission 1968, 7, 12). By connecting low educational achievement to participation in riots, the report fed support for compensatory education, specifically for programs enrolling Black students in white schools to cultivate "the image of a nonrioting citizen" (Raz 2013, 162).

The policy solution to racial unrest was integration. The Kerner Report explained, "We support integration as the priority education strategy. . . . It is indispensable that opportunities for interaction between the races be expanded" (National Advisory Commission 1968, 12). *Integration*, as the report defined it, might allow for the support of "ghetto enrichment" programs in the short term, but the long-term goal was "to encourage the integration of substantial numbers of Negroes into the society outside the ghetto" (10). Integration meant moving African Americans into white spaces. According to the report, accomplishing this movement would require remediation, specifically "intensive concentration on basic verbal skills"—judged to be the problem that affected "every other aspect of the later school program" (248). The Kerner Report's conclusions reflected a shift in justifying desegregation enforcement in a way that was more socially palatable to many whites: desegregation was necessary, not to remedy past segregation and racism but to create a more peaceful citizenry through exposure to white literacy norms.

Adopting white literacy norms was framed as the path to educational success for Black students in desegregation literature. One pamphlet for Georgia K–12 school administrators described Black students' "language skills" as the "first and often biggest hurdle" to desegregation—not because students couldn't speak or write but because white teachers had difficulty "understanding what many Negro students say" (Johnson and Hall 1968, 29). Thus, Black students must "acquire an *additional* method of speaking—i.e., 'Standard English,'" which should be taught "using methods resembling those for teaching foreign languages" (30, original emphasis). The assumption that desegregation would move Black students into white schools, without upsetting a racial order that prioritized whites, was critical to literacy remediation. This assumption supported a pedagogy called "bidialectism," an instructional philosophy that ostensibly validated all English dialects as legitimate but still stressed Standard English for professional and civic communication (Redd and Webb 2005). Some language scholars of the time criticized bidialectism for expecting Black students to integrate into white culture without any reciprocal effort to bring Black language and cultural practices to white students and schools (Sledd 1969; Kaplan 1969; Smitherman 1971; O'Neil 1972). Desegregation literature, however, justified bidialectism using arguments rooted in anti-Black racism. These arguments tried to define the possible audiences for Black literacy practices: white teachers in white schools, white bosses in white workplaces, and, by extension, white politicians, white juries, and white cops. The goal was to make Black students *legible* (not equal) to white audiences.

In 1970, a newly elected President Richard Nixon wielded these ideas to argue that the federal government should not intervene in de facto segregation except to provide educational remediation. Nixon's victory over Johnson in the 1969 presidential election was due in part to white backlash to busing in K–12 desegregation, which he promised to stop (Minchin and Salmond 2011). In a policy statement before the US Congress in 1970, Nixon fulfilled this promise by announcing that he would limit federal intervention by drawing a sharp line between de jure and de facto segregation. De facto segregation would no longer be constitutionally suspect, even where legal segregation once existed, and federal efforts would focus instead on enhancing the educationally disadvantaged, who were "isolated" in racially segregated schools and cities (Nixon 1970, 12). He explained, "It is not really because they serve black children that most of these schools are inferior, but rather because they serve poor children who often lack the home environment that encourages learning," such as subscribing to newspapers or owning books (17–18). Nixon represented Black literacy in the language of cultural deprivation: children in segregated black communities are isolated, deprived of stimulation, and stuck in a cycle of de facto segregation as a result.

This view of de facto segregation was a setback for desegregation enforcement, redefining segregation as a product of Black culture rather than anti-Black racism. This reframing blamed African Americans, but it adopted a race-evasive facade, as most commentators claimed that these problems had nothing to do with race but were a product of isolation also evident in other communities where people lived in poverty, including Latinx immigrant and rural white communities (Raz 2013). This race-evasive redefinition of segregation paradoxically prompted Nixon to direct resources toward educational programs, resulting in

$500 million diverted to "compensatory education for the disadvantaged" and other educational efforts in 1971—an amount doubled for the following year (Nixon 1970, 26). In 1970, college campuses had around 900 remedial and equal opportunity programs that stood to benefit from this new funding (Lamos 2011). Supporting the theory of cultural deprivation could, quite literally, pay off.

In contrast, accusations that white racism caused segregation were less successful, as evidenced by response to the 1970 report of the Commission on Campus Unrest, also known as the Scranton Report, commissioned to study campus protests after students were shot by law enforcement at Kent State University (a white university in Ohio) and Jackson State College (a Black college in Mississippi). The Scranton Report found that many campus protests were about racism.[3] According to the report, white colleges' failure to recognize Black history and culture was a chief cause of unrest at 59 percent of campuses and in 49 percent of protest incidents (Scranton et al. 1970, 109). The Scranton Report proposed two courses of action: founding Black studies programs at white colleges and enhancing Black colleges. This proposal rejected white mainstream integrationism, suggesting that integration "appears to many young Blacks to be a doctrine and practice of white supremacy . . . the destruction of all things black and the exaltation of all things white" (115). Unsurprisingly, the Scranton Report was not well received by Nixon (Rosenthal 1970).

The emphasis on remediation emerging during this time obscured the problems facing Black students in white colleges. Segregation did affect academic preparation for college; in some cases, K–12 schools had closed for Black students, and many Black schools lacked textbooks and other resources (Anderson 2016; Epps-Robertson 2018). However, recasting the effects of segregation as cognitive deficiency glossed over Black students' demands for instructional changes at white colleges and diverted attention from concerning trends in Black enrollment patterns. According to one survey of Black students in white colleges, some reported needing more college preparation, particularly in mathematics, although those data should be cautiously interpreted without comparable survey results from white students (Boyd 1974). Black students at Armstrong and elsewhere requested additional tutorial services as part of a set of larger demands for white colleges to support them ("ASC Submits" 1974).[4] Yet most evidence suggests that more Black students met college admissions requirements than could attend college, due to financial need (Semas 1974; Boyd 1974). Academically successful Black students were either unable to attend college or disproportionately enrolling in less selective institutions, particularly community colleges, even when qualified to attend more selective colleges (Newman 1973; Jaffe et al. 1968). When Black students did attend white colleges, around 42 percent reported experiencing discrimination from white faculty, in grading or in interactions during or after class (Boyd 1974). The persuasive power of cultural deprivation theory lay in its ability to downplay anti-Black racism and the broader needs of Black students affected by segregation. Yet the compensatory approach became so commonsensical that it was ingrained in desegregation criteria created by the federal government.

REMEDIATION IN POSTSECONDARY DESEGREGATION LITIGATION

Within cultural deprivation theory, remediation was "compensation" for childhood deprivation, a fact that did not make it an obvious policy to apply to colleges. But efforts to litigate college desegregation established its relevance there, warping cultural deprivation theory to fit the college context. The stage for this application was set by a 1969 US Supreme Court decision to uphold a district court ruling on postsecondary desegregation in *Alabama State Teachers Association v. Alabama Public School and College Authority* (1968), or *ASTA*. The *ASTA* decision permitted Alabama to build an extension campus of Auburn University in Montgomery, Alabama, where a Black college, Alabama State College, already operated. In effect, this ruling allowed white-controlled university systems to establish or enhance white colleges or branch campuses of white colleges in close proximity to (and competing for students with) Black colleges. *ASTA* set up the conflict that would make it difficult to develop desegregation plans for nearby white and Black colleges in Savannah and other cities, like Nashville, Tennessee, and Tallahassee, Florida.[5] This refusal to intervene in (or enabling of) college segregation was based in the argument that desegregating K–12 schools would "probably resolve" postsecondary segregation by better preparing students for college.[6] In effect, college preparation—not the efforts of white-controlled university systems to secure the status of white colleges—was blamed for college segregation.

After *ASTA*, the National Association for the Advancement of Colored People (NAACP) Legal Defense Fund (LDF) fought to bring college desegregation back to the courts, filing suit in 1970 against the US Department of Health, Education, and Welfare (HEW) in the US District Court for the District of Columbia. Importantly, the case included plaintiffs from colleges and universities alongside students from K–12 schools and taxpayers, lumping higher education in with other sectors to make it more difficult to separate postsecondary institutions as the Supreme Court had done in *ASTA*.[7] In its suit, the LDF listed ten cities operating proximate Black and white colleges, including Savannah State and Armstrong.[8] The LDF successfully argued that HEW had failed its duty to uphold Title VI of the 1964 Civil Rights Act by not withdrawing funding for ten states with recognized segregation. Although HEW had requested desegregation plans, the ten states had not cooperated, had not been properly notified, or had produced plans that were not being monitored (Panetta 1969; Haynes 1978, A-17).[9] The *Adams* litigation brought postsecondary desegregation to trial, but this time a Supreme Court decision in *Swann v. Charlotte-Mecklenburg Board of Education* (1971) enabled new possibilities. Citing *Swann*, Judge John H. Pratt argued in his initial opinion that the DC district court had the authority to oversee HEW's desegregation enforcement, since *Swann* granted that "a District Court has broad power to fashion an appropriate remedy" where "school authorities are in default of their obligation to proffer acceptable remedies to assure school desegregation" (Haynes 1978, B-12).[10] But *Swann* (1971) established a new threat to Black colleges by viewing any formerly segregated institution that remained racially identifiable ("one-race schools") as constitutionally suspect—and it was unclear yet whether this would result in the termination of Black colleges.[11]

Adams put Black colleges in a tough spot, and many opposed the ruling. To survive, Black colleges returned to the premise of *ASTA*, of arguing that Black students needed to be better prepared for white colleges. In response to the injunction order issued in *Adams* (1973), the National Association for Equal Opportunity in Higher Education (NAFEO), a group of 110 Black college presidents, submitted an amicus brief in support of HEW's appeal of *Adams*. NAFEO argued that Black colleges must remain until the "feeder" primary and secondary schools were "improved for black students" (Haynes 1978, C-23–24). At first glance, this argument implies that public Black colleges functioned primarily as remedial institutions. Yet NAFEO expressed a telling concern about white colleges' admissions. NAFEO made note of fifty-two anti-affirmative action cases working their way through the courts (C-24). If Black colleges were "assimilated out of existence" at the same time affirmative action was dismantled, their loss "would be tragic to the survival of Black people in a technological world" (C-25). NAFEO's amicus brief contributed to a modification of the original *Adams* order, adding a requirement for desegregation plans to favor Black colleges. But

NAFEO succeeded by adopting a talking point from cultural deprivation theory: that Black students were unprepared to enter white colleges without substantial remediation.

After the appeals court ruling, HEW was ordered to request desegregation plans within 120 days from the ten states in violation of Title VI (Haynes 1978). Plans were solicited in late 1973, ordering states (1) to eliminate program duplication at nearby Black and white colleges and (2) to redefine institutional missions on a basis other than race. In addition, HEW asked states to set numerical goals for faculty and student composition (1978, E-5). These goals were viewed by some as quotas, sparking criticisms of undue federal intervention and lowered admissions standards and fueling anti-affirmative action sentiment. In reality, these goals required all formerly segregated colleges to increase "minority" enrollment, including a proportional representation of white students at Black colleges—a requirement whose disparate effects on Black colleges I discuss further in chapter 4.[12]

What is important here is that HEW's criteria directed white colleges to create plans for the retention of Black students to help increase Black student enrollment. But the definition of retention returned to that old familiar talking point: college preparation. HEW told states, "If black students in predominantly white institutions show a significantly greater attrition rate than black students in predominantly black institutions, or than white students at predominantly white institutions, the plan must provide for implementation of appropriate *academic development programs* at the predominantly white institutions designed to eliminate the disparate attrition levels" (Haynes 1978, E-13, emphasis added).[13] In other words, academic programs were the only response if Black students dropped or failed out of white colleges. By suggesting that the attrition rates of Black students at white colleges might be higher than those at Black colleges due to academic preparation, the directive implicitly cast Black colleges as lesser institutions.

In response to this directive, remedial programs became the center of most states' desegregation plans. Georgia's plan proposed remedial education under the title "Retention of Black Students," as detailed in chapter 2 (Regents 1974, 211). However, during this period of ongoing investigations, Georgia was already developing remedial programs across its university system. These programs—remedial writing and reading courses and a literacy competency test called the Regents' Test—were predicated on cultural deprivation theory. The USG would simply modify these literacy programs and tests afterward and present them as compliance with desegregation enforcement. As I show later in this chapter, the origin of the USG's literacy remediation and testing in the late 1960s, during investigations of its institutions and university system, was not coincidental. The USG, however, was not entirely to blame: remedial writing scholarship nationally affirmed the idea that desegregation required literacy remediation, and it, too, was informed by cultural deprivation theory.

DESEGREGATION AS PLACEMENT IN COMPOSITION SCHOLARSHIP

Devoted to college writing instruction, the field of composition benefited from federal investment in writing instruction—including remediation—in the mid-twentieth century. Although composition and remediation existed in US colleges far earlier, the institutionalization of composition as a modern academic discipline is typically tied to 1949, the founding year of the disciplinary organization, the Conference on College Composition and Communication (CCCC), or to 1963, the year researchers Richard Braddock, Richard Lloyd-Jones, and Lowell Schoer published *Research in Written Composition*, a HEW-sponsored literature review of existing research on students' writing processes and errors (Mendenhall 2016). As Keith Gilyard and Adam J. Banks (2018) note, however, CCCC was predated by the College Language Association (CLA), an organization founded by Black language scholars in 1937 and a key site for the theorization of writing pedagogy (see also College Language Association 2020). CLA was publishing scholarship on writing process and pedagogy focused on Black students and Black colleges (Baddour 2020). But CCCC received the benefit of federal funding for writing research directed to its parent organization, the National Council of Teachers of English (NCTE), whose work the National Defense Education Act of 1958 sponsored in the early 1960s (Mendenhall 2016). This funding facilitated research on composition through the late 1960s and early 1970s, with an emphasis on experimental research into writing processes, writing errors, and the cognition of writing.

Histories of composition describe the foundation of the discipline as a response to unprecedented growth in US higher education that brought in students from historically underrepresented class, gender, racial, and ethnic groups.[14] These minoritized students were coded as "new" and remedial, "representative of a pedagogical dilemma never encountered before, despite the fact that [remedial] programs had existed for decades, even at elite colleges" (Kynard 2013, 117; see also Soliday 2002; Stanley 2010). According to this narrative, the arrival of new student groups on campus prompted an interest in the writing "process" and the nature of students' writing "errors," moving away from grading final written texts (the "product" of writing) to understanding why students produce errors (the "process" of writing) (Crowley 1998; Harris 1997; Faigley 1992). Less explored, however, has been the way desegregation influenced this research. As I show here, composition scholarship presented in mainstream, historically white publications or conferences supported cultural deprivation theory as a path toward "integration," providing suggestions for placing students in remedial courses that would attempt to compensate, through reading and writing stimuli, for the isolation of segregation.

In the earliest publications in the CCCC's journal, *College Composition and Communication* (*CCC*) (often simply reports on conference presentations), scholars discussed cultural deprivation theory to explain how linguistic stimulation and cultural background influenced writing errors. For example, a 1966 CCCC workshop on the "Culturally Disadvantaged" (1966) student articulated the effects of deprivation on remedial students' writing. According to this workshop, the "relationship between vocabulary and experience" determined what students could "verbalize" in their writing as well as their "logical understanding and conceptual understanding" (184). The goal of composition instruction, then, was to teach the disadvantaged student to "verbalize beyond his normal social level of experience" through exposure to stimulating reading and writing material (184). According to this theory, students possessed a discrete *level* of experience that constituted a skill level, and that level could be developed by exposure to reading and writing.

This focus on experience informed theories of dialect and literacy learning. Although most scholars in *CCC* acknowledged the legitimacy of all English dialects ("all dialects matter"), they viewed isolation as depriving some dialects of rhetorical resources, especially vocabulary and logic. Even scholars who affirmed the legitimacy of Black English dialects nevertheless argued that Black students had "the most intense problems" in writing classes (McDavid 1965, 257). But the problems in dialect extended to rhetoric. Edward P. J. Corbett (1969, 291–292) made similar criticisms of Black Power rhetoric, arguing that the "raised closed fist of the black-power militant" was emblematic of a new "non-verbal" and "fragmentary" rhetoric. Seen in light of the Kerner Report's representation of race riots as a product of cultural deprivation, Corbett's (1969, 295) analysis takes on new significance, revealing the racist underpinnings of arguments that classical rhetoric was "verbal, sequential, logical," while protests were a-rhetorical. As June Jordan (1981, 66) would write a few years later, the dehumanization of Black rhetoric reflected the "nationwide experience of Black life up against white English used to destroy us: literally accept the terms of the oppressor, or perish: that is the irreducible, horrifying truth of the politics of language."

To overcome language deprivation and its a-rhetoricality, composition scholars suggested remediation through stimulus: exposing students to vocabulary, reading experiences, or audio-visual content that would stimulate the writing process. For example, a workshop on the "Process of Composing" (1970, 286) recommended that students "must be exposed to the kinds of stimuli which will encourage them to write." Other stimuli included recording and replaying students' talk-aloud protocols (a methodology for studying the writing process by having students talk aloud while writing) or watching films to stimulate dialect awareness of imaginative writing (Tovatt 1965; Mullican 1971). Stimulus informed the writing process by providing motivation and content. Ironically, however, stimuli did not include material relevant to students' cultural experiences. For example, one CCCC presentation that recommended assigning James Baldwin in remedial composition courses was protested by audience members, who "concluded that teaching a plain, concise style was preferable, and that for this purpose having students read current magazines and newspapers, view pictures, and make personal observations, as stimulus to writing, would be most suitable" ("Freshman English" 1969, 250). Given that remedial scholarship racialized remedial students, I find it particularly upsetting that CCCC members argued to deny remedial students school-sanctioned access to writers like Baldwin, instead proposing magazines and pictures (likely from white mainstream publications) to stimulate the writing process. Was this not just another way Black writers were deemed illegible by white audiences, denied rhetoricity?

The concept of stimulus was connected to segregation in composition scholarship, including Janet Emig's (1971) foundational study of the writing process, *The Composing Process of Twelfth Graders*. After studying how environment, background, and task shaped the writing process of eight student writers, Emig presented stimuli (experiences or reading material) as critical to motivating the writing process. Emig implied that segregation affected students' literacy resources by listing the racial composition of each study participant's school and using this information to contextualize students' writing processes. Her representative writer, Lynn, attended the most desegregated school in the study (84 percent white, 16 percent Black), a fact that appears to inform Lynn's representation as best able "to verbalize the process of her thinking and writing"

(46). Bradford, the only Black student, also attended a comparatively desegregated school (83 percent white, 15 percent Black, and 2 percent "oriental"), and Emig identified him as the only student with a prewriting process and the only male student who engages in reflexive/personal writing (46). The two students from the most desegregated schools were presented as the most capable writers, having the best resources for the writing process. In contrast, students from segregated schools were isolated and overly focused on correctness. A Chinese American student (Victoria), described as "exceptionally hostile to adults," came from a predominantly Black school (4 percent white, 95 percent Black, and 1 percent "oriental") (80). Debbie, a (presumably white) student from a segregated white school (92 percent white, 8 percent Black, with the highest dropout rate at 35 percent), was the only student described as lacking parental involvement in her childhood literacy learning. Why does Emig go to such great lengths to discuss the racial composition of students' schools? Was she suggesting that segregation deprived student writers of writing stimuli? I'll admit that my reading here is speculative, but tracing Emig within a history of cultural deprivation theory's influence on the writing process suggests that there were unstated, perhaps omitted, ideas that desegregation—and its benefits for literacy—would resolve the nation's racial inequalities.

Composition research on process and error prompted debate about placement by skill level into remedial writing courses. Cultural deprivation theory's emphasis on "shared" cultural deficiencies seems to imply that writing skill levels may be shared. One *CCC* statement called for colleges to develop "placement procedures and several different freshman courses when they admit students whose home and school backgrounds vary widely" and who come from "home backgrounds in which little premium has been placed on a rich experience with language" ("Status" 1968, 81). The idea was that variation in cultural experiences correlated to variation in literacy skills—variation that might be measurable. A 1969 workshop called for "tests for placement for the unprepared freshman, for 'feeding' him to the proper place after his period of remedial study, and retracking him when he needs it" ("Composition Courses" 1969, 249). Thus, placement was contingent on home and school experiences that signaled a student's "proper place" in a writing course. Rooted in cultural deprivation theory, these placement proposals emphasized the need for a tracking apparatus, a kind of ongoing surveillance through assessment of writing.

Despite cultural deprivation theory's dismissal of remedial students' literacy resources, some scholars nevertheless appropriated its terminology to justify culturally relevant material in remedial classes. Nick A. Ford (1967), a member of the NCTE Black Caucus, published his research on the placement of "culturally disadvantaged" students into different sections of college composition. Ford supported instruction in Standard English and argued that Black students' "substandard dialect" reflected "the substandard living conditions that he and his parents are trying desperately to escape" (102–103). Articulated as a resistance to segregation, Ford used deprivation theory to stress that remedial writing courses should provide "reading materials and experiences" that reflected the experiences of marginalized students, including a unit on "Understanding Limitations and Opportunities of Minorities in the United States" (101). Similarly, Toni Clark Thornton (1972) described a pilot composition course in response to Black and Chicano student demands for ethnic studies courses in "An Alternative Freshman English Program for Minority Students"—an article that affirms Iris D. Ruiz's (2016) history of the influence on composition of the Chicano Movement alongside other civil rights activism. The pilot within the Equal Opportunity Program (EOP) at the University of California, Santa Barbara, was designed to provide "intensive, individualized help to overcome any educational deficiencies that might exist" for students coming primarily from "de facto segregated schools" (366–367). This work invited students to select course readings relevant to their experiences and backgrounds. Thornton found that students in these EOP courses outperformed their peers, likely due to the material's cultural relevance. These arguments made progress during a time when assigning Baldwin's work in remedial English courses was a controversial proposal at CCCC.

Not everyone, however, supported cultural deprivation theory in scholarship on remediation (Bosmajian 1969; Musgrave 1971). In a 1968 speech during the CCCC convention in Minneapolis, following the assassination of Martin Luther King Jr., Ernece B. Kelly (1968, 107) described how a segregated CCCC marginalized Black scholarship in the conference and prevented the field from recognizing "an image among Blacks which does not permit them to even bother with the question of whether or not the white man understands their dialect." Kelly (1968, 106) dismissed the idea that desegregation required Black students to concern themselves with their comprehensibility to white audiences, and she announced her plans to leave the conference, a symbolic abandonment of King's "dream of black and white people living and working together." She stated, "Ironically, because of the assassination of a Black advocate of non-violence, I am pushed further into a blackness which approaches violence" (108). In contrast to Corbett's representation of

Black protest as irrational, Kelly highlighted white CCCC members' unwillingness to understand desegregation.

In the years after, Black composition scholars advocated for disciplinary change to CCCC, an organization that functioned as "a kind of closed fraternity" for white academics (Davis 1994, 9). At the 1970 CCCC, "Black CCCC members forced the disruption and ending of sessions where White professors were badly handling the subject matter of Black literature and Black language patterns" (9). Black scholars came together that year to form the NCTE/CCCC Black Caucus and advocate for change, pushing to redefine desegregation apart from remediation. But ideas about segregation deeply informed the development of composition in ways that have made race what Catherine Prendergast (1998) describes as an "absent presence" in composition scholarship. The language of the "absent presence" signals that race was *present*. Race was present euphemistically through the terminology of cultural deprivation, through a collective white mainstream understanding of remediation as desegregation. By emphasizing cultural integration and writing remediation, the discipline normalized remedial pedagogies focused on vocabulary, speech, and logic. These arguments did not just have scholarly effects; they also had institutional effects. In the USG and in Savannah's colleges, these ideas informed policies and pedagogies that equated Black students and colleges with literacy remediation and emphasized integration into white literacy norms.

REMEDIATION AND EARLY DESEGREGATION ENFORCEMENT IN THE UNIVERSITY SYSTEM OF GEORGIA

The pervasive white mainstream view of desegregation as remediation was already at work in the USG as it responded to investigations of its segregation by developing remedial writing programs and a literacy competency test. Beginning in 1967, the USG piloted remedial writing courses and, simultaneously, began planning for a check on that program, a rising junior literacy test called the Regents' Test, which determined a student's eligibility to graduate from college.[15] These programs remained through later versions of the desegregation plan produced in 1974, 1977, and 1978 (see chapters 2 and 3) and survived additional scrutiny for racial bias in the 1980s (see chapter 4). Called Special Studies, the state's remedial program was described by the USG as "designed specifically to assist the poorly-prepared entering student" and key to recruiting and retaining Black students as part of desegregation efforts (Regents 1974, 27). Although presented as a desegregation

strategy, the program itself argued to be "in large measure race inde-
pendent, being primarily related to the educational and economic
background of the potential student" (51). This statement—the premise
supporting remediation—reiterated the political position that de facto
segregation was largely due to cultural deprivation.

The association of the USG's remedial writing programs with desegregation is widely enough recognized to warrant debate in histories of
the program. George H. Jensen's (1988, 30) history presents it as an
effort to conciliate "minority groups" who were "exerting tremendous
pressure on institutions of higher education to recruit more minority
students. Against this force were traditional academicians concerned
that a large influx of nontraditional students would lower standards
and dilute the quality of a college education." While Jensen links
the program to minority students' demands for desegregation, John
W. Presley and William M. Dodd (2008, 44) tie remediation to the
state's response to *Adams*. They argue that its political association with
desegregation caused Special Studies to be "labeled . . . as *bureaucratic*
rather than *academic,* subject to the winds of state and national politics and pseudo-politics" (48, original emphasis). Although correct in
their assessment that desegregation made remediation transitory and
unstable, Presley and Dodd overlook the political nature of all writing
programs, especially remedial programs that withhold full admission
and participation in college from certain students. How those students
are identified, the demographics of those students, the content of
the programs, and the failure rates of courses all pose or respond to
political questions. But in the case of the USG, a political view of the
state's remedial writing program is warranted, as the program anticipated desegregation and adopted the redefinition of desegregation
as remediation.

Georgia's first attempts to pilot, develop, and scale out remediation
occurred in the late 1960s, resulting in programs eventually formed
into Special Studies departments at all state institutions in 1974.
Offering reading, writing, and math courses, Special Studies developed
during a period of concern about what would happen with college
desegregation—between the initial proto-desegregation of white USG
colleges in the mid-1960s and HEW's investigations into postsecondary
segregation in the late 1960s. Special Studies was repeatedly considered
the heart of the state's desegregation plan and the solution to "the
problem of increasing minority student enrollment" (Regents 1974,
211). Later evidence shows that the USG believed HEW approved of
this approach to desegregation, which is no surprise given the influence

of cultural deprivation theory on HEW's criteria (Savannah Community Liaison Committee 1978, 244).

However, these remedial programs predated widespread enrollment of students of color. As Presley and Dodd (2008, 44) note, "White students were by far the majority, often comprising more than two-thirds, of the students in this program." The program's history suggests that Special Studies was developed to address what Jacqueline Jones Royster and Jean C. Williams (1999) describe as the literacy anxiety historically linked to the anticipated arrival of Black students to white colleges. Initially, in the late 1960s, the university piloted "Summer On-Trial" programs and other "short-term interventions," which enrolled students into *regular* college courses as an admissions trial (Jensen 1988, 31; see also Oxford et al. 1977, II:45). But in 1969, Special Studies courses began placing students into pre-collegiate, non-credit-bearing, semester-long courses (Presley and Dodd 2008; Oxford et al. 1977). In 1969, Black students constituted only 1.8 percent of total USG enrollment; by 1972, they made up 6.3 percent of total USG student enrollment (Board of Regents 1973, 2). However, this increase may have seemed larger because the total number of enrolled Black students had increased more than 14 times between 1950 and 1972 (from 454 students to 6,692 students) (2). In 1972, the USG planned to expand Special Studies (Oxford et al. 1977, II:46). This pre-collegiate, multi-quarter remedial program was considered "difficult and expensive" and therefore contingent on the availability of funding for "experimental programs" that promised to "find better ways to deal with these students" (Board of Regents 1973, 482). Private foundations and Title III grants offered funding for programs for low-income and minority students, further encouraging the association of remediation with cultural deprivation and the temporary task of desegregation (Ashmore 1972).

During this time, the USG developed a literacy competency test to ensure that its admission of more students would not be perceived as lowering academic standards. In fact, the USG Board of Regents described the test as "a corollary development" to Special Studies (Board of Regents 1973, 483). The newly developed Regents' Test provided additional insurance that all college graduates met the state's definition of academic standards in reading and writing. The test was required at the end of the sophomore year of college, at which point students had already taken admissions and (if designated as remedial) placement and exit tests. Like Special Studies, the Regents' Test was piloted in anticipation of desegregation enforcement. First proposed in 1967 and developed through the early 1970s, the Regents' Test's purpose was contradictory. On the one hand, it claimed to certify literacy standards for college graduation. Yet early descriptions called it "a fairly elementary test in reading and writing" (483) and an effort "to establish minimal standards of literacy for graduation from any of the thirty units in the System" (Owings 1974). According to the account of an Armstrong professor who was one of five faculty who contributed to designing the exam with the USG Testing Committee, the Regents' Test was designed to measure a tenth-grade reading and writing level, considered a "minimum level of literacy for a college student" (Dennard 1974, 3). Several accounts suggest that the test was a response to complaints from the business community and USG student body presidents about student writing (Watters 1979; Dennard 1974). These representations imply that the USG did not have *college-level* literacy as a goal; rather, the Regents' Test served to assuage primarily white stakeholders about academic standards—with literacy as symbol and arbiter.

In fall 1972, after a pilot experiment, the Regents' Test became a graduation requirement (Board of Regents 1973). All students earning degrees at USG institutions, including associate degrees, needed to pass the test to graduate (Fincher 2003). Developed with input from faculty across the state, the Regents' Test examined students in three areas: reading, writing, and grammar (the grammar test was eliminated in 1974 as unnecessary) (Dasher 1986–1987; Owings 1974). The reading portion of the test consisted of passages with multiple choice answers, graded using norm-referenced assessment, meaning that passing depended on how well a student did in comparison to an average score from a sample population (Dasher 1986–1987). The writing portion of the test was an essay exam that students completed in thirty minutes,[16] in response to an "expository or persuasive" prompt (13).[17] Students were given multiple prompts and selected one to write about (Watters 1979). Each essay had three raters, usually English faculty from Georgia colleges, who assigned a holistic[18] score between a one (failing) and a four (outstanding) based on comparisons to model essays (Owings 1974). Students needed to earn an average score of two to pass the exam (Owings 1974; Crew 1977; Dasher 1986/7).[19] The holistic writing assessment method reflected a trend in the 1970s of moving away from indirect writing assessment (objective testing) to direct writing assessment of a single, timed essay (Yancey 1999). As such, many viewed it as a more faculty-centered approach to writing assessment, although this representation raises questions about which faculty and which colleges were involved in developing and approving the test and whether those faculty had expertise in writing assessment. Unfortunately, I don't have answers to these questions, but the use of faculty expertise to validate different measures of literacy assessment remains a common theme in many justifications of writing policies developed during desegregation and a warning against decontextualizing disciplinary expertise when structures of participation in academic research are inequitable.

Further casting doubts on the validity of the Regents' Test is the fact that from the beginning students failed at high rates, blocking graduation and creating a burden for remedial programs that had to staff remedial courses for students who failed. One report stated that the failure rate for the USG was around 30 percent, with "as few as 10% failing on some campuses and as many as 85% failing on others" (Dennard 1974, 4). In reality, nearly 50 percent of students failed in the early 1970s, during the first years of implementation, and first-time pass rates remained below 70 percent through the mid-1980s (University System of Georgia 1996). Despite these problems, the USG maintained the Regents' Test as key evidence that it had raised standards for literacy instruction while providing increased access to students through remediation (see chapter 4). The Regents' Test would survive scrutiny from critical faculty, Black colleges, and the OCR, as later chapters will describe; it would also contribute to the growth in resources and identity for composition in the USG. However, the USG's remediation programs affected Black and white colleges disparately as Special Studies became increasingly centralized and subject to state oversight.

Piloting Remediation at Savannah State

The disparate effects of the state's interest in remediation and testing during this time are evident in Savannah State's early remedial program. The program's faculty viewed its work as central to the college's mission, and the program worked "in making education accessible to the underprivileged, in building a positive program image, and in preparing students for the standard curriculum" (Maynor n.d., 1). These goals were part of the college's larger mission. The oldest postsecondary institution in the city of Savannah, Savannah State, was founded in 1890 as the Georgia State Industrial College for Colored Youth with funding from the Morrill Act of 1890 (Brooks 2014). Savannah State's first president, Richard Wright Sr., had a broad vision of liberal education for the university that he maintained despite pressure from whites who believed "industrial education was the way blacks should be educated and subsequently guided to menial jobs" (44). Although its name changed several times (once losing its name to Georgia State College, a white college in

Atlanta that is now Georgia State University), Savannah State has always maintained its identity as a public HBCU, with a strong record of civil rights activism and support for Black scholars, as university historian F. Erik Brooks (2014) has detailed. This history of responding to white intervention with a broad, activist view of education is also evident in Savannah State's literacy programs.

The USG's remedial pilots in the late 1960s and early 1970s restricted Savannah State's autonomy over its remedial programs and writing instruction policies. Savannah State had decades of experience designing and teaching remedial courses, dating from the late 1940s. The 1948–1949 catalog lists English 99 as a non-credit-bearing course designed for "students whose training in the fundamentals is limited; who show by their speech and writing that they need intensive drill in the essentials of grammar, spelling, punctuation, usage, and sentence structure" (Georgia State College 1949, 73). Savannah State also piloted the state's remedial experiments in the 1960s (Maynor n.d.; Board of Regents 1973). It offered one of the first Summer On-Trial programs, granting students regular admission to the college conditioned on enrollment in two courses in the summer (Savannah State College 1968, 34). Successful Summer On-Trial students were eligible for regular admissions *with* credit for the courses they had completed in the summer (34).

Offered through the Division of Humanities, Savannah State's English 99 existed in some form through the early 1970s, when it was incorporated into the state's Special Studies program. Remedial English was renamed in the late 1960s to have the same name as the first-year English course, English Communicative Skills (Savannah State College 1968). All English Communicative Skills courses provided instruction in "(1) reading, writing, speaking, listening, and demonstrating; [and] (2) creative, critical thinking; precision of thought and expression through reports" (133). Students were placed into the remedial version of English Communicative Skills with a placement test, but remedial students with superior performance could move straight to the second semester of regular English Communicative Skills (Savannah State College 1968). These innovations addressed the stigma of remediation through naming and course credit opportunities.

A departmental report from the Division of Humanities (1970, H-10) described the writing pedagogy from this period as employing "effective methods" of teaching writing: "dialogues, group and individual reports, speeches, conferences, writing experiences, and close-reading analyses." The inclusion of collaborative writing assignments and conferences at this early date resisted the idea that students were deprived of linguistic resources and needed stimuli to write, recognizing the importance of collaboration and practicing writing in different genres. In English Communicative Skills, students took two essay exams per quarter. Students were given guidelines for successfully completing these exams, and all exams were graded using a collaboratively developed Grading System for Themes, compiled by English faculty. The department used its own placement and exit tests, and the faculty constantly revisited these tests, seeking "improved instruments for evaluation" and "ever more sensitive and realistic standardized instruments" (H-11). Savannah State faculty recognized the need to evaluate the ways writing assessment impacted students. The program's control over testing and placement policies suggests it had autonomy prior to the state's efforts to expand its remedial programs.

However, Savannah State faced new challenges in desegregation enforcement. In 1972, the department's research showed that its remedial pilot successfully prepared students for college, and at that time only 10 percent to 25 percent of incoming students were placed into remedial math, English, or reading courses (Maynor n.d., 1). However, remediation changed after the ruling in *Adams* made Special Studies the focus of USG's desegregation activities (1). According to the college catalogs, 1973 was the last year Savannah State offered its Summer On-Trial program and used its own placement tests (rather than SAT scores) for remedial placement. The mid-1970s then precipitated a period of "Great Panic" as remediation policies at the state overwhelmed the college (2). According to the USG's data, Savannah State's remedial student population increased five times between 1973 and 1974, and as figure 1.1 shows, this trend eventually led to more students enrolled in Special Studies courses than in the entire entering freshman class—a trend that would continue through the 1990s. The number of remedial requirements also increased as Savannah State now had to offer a new remedial writing course, English 200, to students who failed the Regents' Test (Savannah State College 1972). These changes, along with moving Special Studies into a separate department as required by the state, stigmatized Special Studies students and faculty within the college (4).

Changes at the state level occurred despite resistance to reductive testing at Savannah State, which is evident in faculty scholarship from the period. For example, in 1972, social sciences professor Isaiah McIver published "The Testing Movement and Blacks" in Savannah State's bulletin of faculty research. McIver (1972) argued that existing standardized tests (particularly the SAT) were not valid for use in admissions decisions. The SAT had only a medium predictive validity for first-year

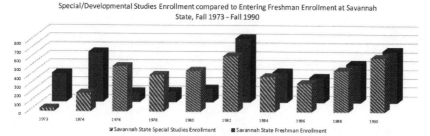

Figure 1.1. Special/Developmental Studies enrollment compared to freshman enrollment at Savannah State, fall 1973–fall 1990. Data compiled from reports by the University System of Georgia (1978, 1981, 1990).

students' grades, and those data were based on the College Board's sampling of primarily white first-year college students.[20] According to a study McIver cited by the National Scholarship Service and the Fund for Negro Students of more than 1,500 Black students across institutional types, Black students had higher retention rates than white students: Black student attrition rates were 18.9 percent compared to white attrition rates of roughly 60 percent (60). McIver argued that any application of standardized tests must consider racial disparities in results as well as the "personality and interest factors" that affect student retention (59). Critical to McIver's argument was his belief that retention predictions must account for the social meaning of a college degree. While the state's view of retention focused on remediating academic deficiencies, McIver suggested that attrition was a social and an environmental problem. As he explained, Black students were more motivated to persist in college because they faced "occupational limitations" and were held to higher credentialing requirements when applying for jobs (66). While white individuals at the time of McIver's report could find decent jobs without college degrees, "Blacks cannot. Black students persist more because of their racial role in society. If there is any room at the top for Blacks, they must be college trained" (66). McIver considered retention vital context for determining the validity of an admissions or placement testing requirement but only insofar as retention was understood as a social phenomenon, not merely an academic one.

Although McIver's argument did not change USG policies, it did reflect the tension between Savannah State and the USG's views of education. Savannah State's efforts to make remedial reading and writing instruction meaningful for college students were dismantled by the state's desegregation enforcement activities, placing them at an extreme disadvantage in terms of entering first-year students and full-time

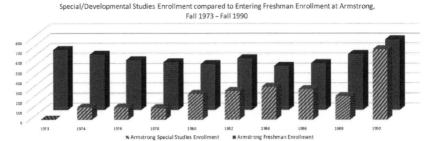

Special/Developmental Studies Enrollment compared to Entering Freshman Enrollment at Armstrong, Fall 1973 – Fall 1990

Figure 1.2. Special/Developmental Studies enrollment compared to freshman enrollment at Armstrong, fall 1973–fall 1990.

enrollment—especially, as figure 1.2 shows, compared to Armstrong. As Savannah State cooperated with the desegregation policy changes through the 1970s, state policies added additional instructional burdens the college sought to address with innovative course redesigns and peda-gogies. This response contrasted with Armstrong's remedial pilots at the time and the way state policies affected its identity.

Piloting Remediation at Armstrong

Investigations into segregation at Armstrong in the late 1960s centered on the college's failure to promote integration through affirmative action. Armstrong knew it was under investigation for segregation by 1968, when the college was required to submit a compliance report to HEW committing to nondiscriminatory operations (Panetta 1969). On May 21, 1969, HEW sent a letter to Armstrong's president, Henry L. Ashmore, requesting an observational visit to review the school's compliance with Title VI of the 1964 Civil Rights Act. Two men were sent for a day-and-a-half-long visit to the campus, followed up with an additional request for data on faculty, students, and institutional budgets (Dodds 1969a). On July 17, 1969, HEW wrote, "Although our review of Armstrong State generally indicated that Negro students are freely admitted and that students are treated without regard to race, we did find some indications of possible problems in relation to the requirements of Title VI of the Civil Rights Act of 1964" (Dodds 1969b). The letter made recommendations for recruiting, athletic scholarships, fraternity monitoring, tutoring services, pictures on recruiting materials, and other kinds of changes. HEW encouraged Armstrong to "under-take more affirmative action, beyond nondiscrimination, to attract and involve in the total life of the college, members of racial groups historically barred from the institution . . . extra efforts should be made to attract Negroes where they have been traditionally absent" (Dodds 1969b). HEW's visit made Armstrong aware of impending desegregation enforcement and the likelihood that Armstrong must take further action to desegregate.

However, Armstrong's president and other constituents felt Armstrong had satisfactorily desegregated. Between 1965 and 1970, Armstrong had doubled its overall student enrollment and its Black student enrollment, according to informal statistics submitted to a survey conducted by Indiana University ("A Study of Patterns" n.d.). In 1965, an estimated 36 of 967 students were Black, or 3.7 percent; by 1969, an estimated 78 of 2,200 students were Black, or 3.5 percent (n.d.). In 1969, these students would have encountered only one Black faculty member and one Black staff member. Armstrong also did not provide any "adjustments in admissions criteria [or admissions tests] for black students"; nor had it significantly altered its faculty. The college stated that it had "difficulty recruiting qualified black students" and that the college was "doing all we can or should do" to "meet the needs of black students" (n.d.). This assessment mirrored the USG position that nondiscriminatory admissions constituted desegregation and that denial of admissions was a matter of academic qualifications.

Yet racial desegregation was clearly in mind in Armstrong's remediation pilots in the late 1960s. The first pilot for remedial English was developed in 1968 and was called "Academic Skills." Academic Skills presented race as a critical component of its pedagogy. According to its first program report, nearly 40 percent of incoming first-year students were assigned to remedial English on the basis of receiving SAT verbal scores below 400 (out of 800) (Brown 1968).[21] These students, the report continued, shared similar error patterns (listed by frequency): punctuation, spelling, grammar, inability to connect ideas, and subject-verb agreement (Brown 1968). These errors could be significantly remediated by adjusting students' speech patterns, which fell into two groups: "the non-standard speech of inner-city ghettos, or the colloquial standards of the rural South" (5). Academic Skills pedagogy thus categorized language ability by race, class, and geography. Black students (identified euphemistically by the term *inner-city ghettos*)[22] had nonstandard *speech* while rural, presumably white students had "colloquial standards"— making evident the link between whiteness and standardness, even when whites did not speak Standard English (5). Consistent with cultural deprivation theories, culture was a product of race and geography, yet Black and white students' dialects were not judged equally. Black writing was described as more distant from Standard English than that of white rural students. By implication, Standard English was merely an abstraction—an ideology, as Rosina Lippi-Green (2011) argues—judged by its proximity to white mainstream (middle-class, suburban) speakers and writers.

By locating writing errors in speech, Academic Skills employed bidialectical pedagogy. According to the report on the Academic Skills pilot, remediation practices used speech practice to improve students' writing, claiming that even punctuation errors were a dialect and speech problem (Brown 1968). This approach to bidialectism is called dialect interference theory, and, although popular in the 1960s and 1970s, it was based on the belief that writing should not mirror vernacular speech, particularly for speakers of nonstandard dialects (Redd and Webb 2005).[23] This was an extension of cultural deprivation theory's assertion that linguistic stimulation in early childhood in the home determined literacy facility. In keeping with this theory, the goal of bidialectical pedagogy in Armstrong's program was to get students to move from their "current command of language to *a greater command*, from the student's own dialect to Standard American English" (Brown 1968, 4, emphasis added). This framing implied that dialects labeled nonstandard reflected *lesser* command of language, a command of language born out of supposed deprivation.

The pedagogy of speech-based writing errors supported assessment practices that treated writing as transcription, particularly the timed writing essay. If writing errors were located in speech and could be remediated through speech, then transcription was the primary skill necessary for good writing. Timed exams were used to place students into remediation, to assess student learning, and to test students out of remediation. According to the report on the Academic Skills pilot, student essays were completed in class and were graded based on "effectiveness" (Brown 1968, 8). The student essay pictured in figure 1.3 demonstrates the kind of short writing assignments completed in this early remediation program, along with the style of grading. The comments focus primarily on errors (typos, punctuation, homophone confusion) that have very little to do with speech, with the exception of the last paragraph, where the grader notes something as subject-verb "trouble" and a phrasing as "clumsy." Despite claiming to grade for "effectiveness," the grader did not mention the student's address to an imagined audience (as indicated in the last paragraph's address to a future student who "better spend at least two hours studying every night"). In addition, the rater did not comment on the student's command of rhetorical strategies,

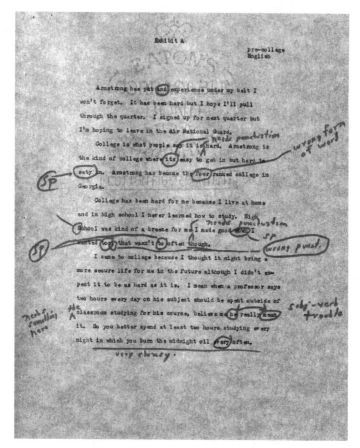

Figure 1.3. An Academic Skills student's marked essay (Brown 1968).

such as the metaphor of "burning the midnight oil." Effectiveness appears to equate to how the student deploys conventions for spelling and punctuation. I'll admit, the grading scheme here is puzzling to me, but perhaps its arbitrariness within the framework of bidialectal pedagogy is precisely the point. As a theory, it claimed to be "not racist" (or classist or disparaging of any dialect), but in reality its primary function was to police social knowledge of writing conventions. Its claim to logicality is contradicted in practice. But that claim to logicality was critical to its authority to determine a student's path through college.

As I read the essay (whose writer's race is not mentioned in the program director's report), I'm fascinated by the insight the student provides into retention. The student describes college as more difficult than expected, indicating plans to leave for the Air National Guard.

According to this account, getting into college was not the problem for the student; rather, the issue was the demands of college, made worse by the student's living situation, lack of instruction in study skills, and belief they did not belong at the "number four"-ranked college in Georgia. An often eloquent commentary on the disconnect between students' expectations of college and reality, the essay hints at inadequate counseling and advisement, as well as the way institutional identity affects a student's perceptions of their academic ability. With such a focus on error, remedial programs may have overlooked these reasons for student attrition. Perhaps unsurprisingly, Academic Skills did not effectively promote retention. Only five of sixty-eight students passed from remedial English into freshman English (Ashmore 1969a). Retention rates did improve in subsequent years, with 70 percent of remedial English students enrolling in first-year composition, although in total only 40 percent of formerly remedial English students ended up passing ("Remedial English at ASC" 1973) and only 12 percent of graduating students had taken remedial English (in contrast to the 40 percent of first-year students placed into the course) (Pendexter 1974). These high failure rates demonstrate that the pre-collegiate structure of remediation provided a place where entry to college could be determined through the enforcement of white mainstream literacy norms.

This early Academic Skills program demonstrates how theories about the effects of segregation informed bidialectical writing pedagogy. By racializing language errors, the instruction and assessment methods validated administrators' view that academic achievement explained the challenges Armstrong experienced enrolling Black students. This association between race and remediation was part of how the college promoted the program when arguing for grant funding. Remediation contributed to the retention of minority students—a key desegregation strategy. President Ashmore (1972) argued, "By sending our minority students through an initial year of remedial work, we have been able to increase our retention of such students by over 60%." A later reflection on the history of Armstrong's compensatory programs noted that it developed "one of the first compensatory education programs in the state" and described that early program as "an attempt to reflect society's growing concern with the problem of minorities and educationally disadvantaged students" ("1979–80," 2). Thus, the program forecast the USG's emphasis on remediation as key to desegregation.

An important contrast to the official representation of Black literacy at Armstrong, however, is the Black American Movement (BAM) on Armstrong's campus, a student-run organization founded in 1973

(Stone 2010, 177). The students who founded BAM were accomplished academics and activists. One history student, Twila Haygood, who served as president of the campus chapter of Phi Alpha Theta, helped collect an archive of oral histories of Black Savannahians[24] and later attended Boston University on scholarship for Afro-American studies. Haygood participated in a campus protest of an invited guest speaker, a supposed expert in "Ethnology, Ethno-Human Genetics, and Racial History," who delivered a lecture claiming that "African civilization was the result of the white man's work" ("Black Students" 1973, 1). Student government representative Ray Persons served as an English tutor and honor council president and went to law school after graduating from Armstrong (Stone 2010). These and other Black students accomplished significant academic achievements and participated in organizing protests, publishing about racism in the student newspaper, and organizing Black Awareness Week on campus. In one oral history collected by Haygood (1973, 4), a Black Armstrong employee named Madie Dixon described Black students on campus: "Well, I know just about every black students out here and from what I have seen . . . they are trying to study and get their degree and make something of themselves and they don't seen to whole any prejurices at all if any thing the whites are standing off from them. They don't seem to except the black." BAM called out this "segregative attitude" at Armstrong, including in the hiring of Black faculty and the "mistreatment of Black students by White professors" ("Blacks Express Grievances" 1974, 1). One wonders what desegregation in the USG and at Armstrong might have looked like if Black students and colleges in the system had designed it.

The late 1960s and early 1970s association of desegregation with remediation resulted in a particular set of assumptions about what remediation should do and who remedial students were. This view of remediation was institutionalized in the USG's consolidation of remedial courses into Special Studies departments in 1974, across the system's institutions. That same year, the USG submitted its 1974 desegregation plan to HEW and presented Special Studies as its official desegregation retention strategy. As I show in chapter 2, these efforts were enabled by a growing national and disciplinary concern with retention that considered student attrition a failure of integration.

2

ASSESSING POTENTIAL
Writing Placement as a Retention Strategy, Mid-1970s

When Evelyn Baker Dandy was hired at Armstrong State College in 1974, she was the first Black faculty member in the newly formed Special Studies Department, which offered remedial courses in reading, writing, and mathematics. Dandy had been encouraged to apply to Armstrong by Savannah civil rights legend and president of the local National Association for the Advancement of Colored People (NAACP) chapter, W. W. Law. After moving from Philadelphia during a teacher's strike, Dandy was concerned about living in the South. She explained, "When I moved from Philadelphia, I had an Afro. Big one. So I took the Afro out. I said, you know, I'm going to, because I had never lived in the South. I hadn't been to the South much at all, and I was kind of fearful of the South. So I changed my hair, and I put on a suit" (Dandy 2017). At Armstrong for an interview, Dandy was told by the head of the Languages and Literature Department that "not many Black people had gone through languages and literature, that they just couldn't meet the standards. Everything was a standard." The head of the Education Department told her she could not teach in that department without a doctorate, although at the time she had a master's degree from a well-known reading program at Temple University (2017).[1] Dandy then interviewed with the head of Special Studies, who offered her a position as an instructor. Congratulations followed from Armstrong's president, Henry L. Ashmore, who "said he was glad to have me on board, but he did not want to see me walking in any picket lines or doing any demonstrations in the city of Savannah" (2017).

Dandy's experience as one of the only Black faculty working at Armstrong in the mid-1970s was compounded by her location in Special Studies. In fact, as she described it, attitudes toward her employment in Special Studies were often intertwined with attitudes about her race. When she applied for her parking sticker, Dandy was told that "I wasn't an instructor . . . I was working in Special Studies, so I'm not really an instructor. So they weren't too sure whether they were going to give me

https://doi.org/10.7330/9781646422036.c002

a parking sticker. So those are some of the hurdles that I had to climb once I got here: you know, individuals who had their own way of thinking and had their own impression of whether or not they think Black people should come to this campus" (Dandy 2017). The obstacles Dandy encountered attest to the hostile environments of white colleges for Black faculty and students. Her recollections also reveal the ways Special Studies was associated with race and rhetorically separated from the rest of the college, as whites leveraged the program's remedial identity to exclude African Americans on campus. Although the Board of Regents may have presented Special Studies as facilitating desegregation, on white campuses it functioned to control the terms of desegregation.

Dandy's experiences reveal how white colleges appropriated remedial literacy programs to maintain the racial order of segregation in the face of desegregation enforcement. In contrast, policy at this time presented remedial programs as key to the retention of Black students. This contradiction was enabled by the broader political redefinition of desegregation as remediation that directed educational policy toward student retention in a push for more efficient admissions and remediation procedures. With this new interest in retention, remedial literacy programs became important to numerous stakeholders, paving the way for their acceptance by the federal government in state desegregation plans. The University System of Georgia's (USG's) *Plan for the Further Desegregation of the University System of Georgia* (Regents 1974) defined remediation as its plan for student retention and used this plan to exert more control over the structure and placement mechanisms of Special Studies, forming new Special Studies departments at all of its institutions. The strategy largely failed to consider that Black students' attrition might be affected by the exclusionary environment of white colleges or the burdensome remedial requirements now forced on public Black colleges.

As I argue in this chapter, recasting remediation as a key retention strategy embedded ideas about cultural deprivation and literacy deficiencies into official desegregation policies. The national discourse on retention echoed many of these ideas, emphasizing retention as a form of cultural integration that might help minoritized students at higher risk of dropping out. These automatic and commonsensical explanations for the underrepresentation of Black students and faculty in US higher education have consistently undermined desegregation and affirmative action efforts since this time period. As interest in retention informed new placement and testing policies, remedial writing classes grew into cohesive writing *programs*, governed by state guidelines. The centrality of literacy to retention efforts, buttressed by the structures of literacy testing used to predict student success, exacerbated racial disparities between Black and white students and colleges, forwarding racialized definitions of literacy standards used to legitimize white supremacy in higher education.

STATEWIDE PLANNING: REMEDIATION AND RETENTION IN MID-1970S EDUCATIONAL POLICY

In the mid-1970s, a growing body of scholarship and educational policy work on student retention emerged out of the scholarship on remediation. Tracking retention data and developing retention programs required a new level of state involvement in public colleges and universities. To facilitate this work, educational policymakers recommended that states coordinate the development of more efficient admissions requirements and remediation programs to ensure that students integrated academically at colleges. This new imperative for integration was implicitly racialized, in that Black students (or, more euphemistically, minorities) were described as having cultural backgrounds *more* inconsistent with the culture of higher education than other groups. The language of integration carried over into usage in desegregation plans, making retention a central focus of writing programs and rationalizing state standardization of such programs.

A philosophy for state coordination of policies and programs, statewide planning developed as a response to the increased access to and rapid expansion of higher education in the 1950s and 1960s that some government officials believed had made colleges inefficient. In a HEW report, D. Kent Halstead (1974, 130) argued that states, not colleges, were "best qualified" to make policy decisions that would *efficiently* improve access to higher education. To facilitate coordination with colleges, state university systems should supersede individual institutional governing boards and create regulatory boards (7). States could then monitor remedial programs, presented as key to helping "minority" students "compensate for, or overcome, the effects of indifferent or even hostile backgrounds" (130). Students' hostile backgrounds included a history of "absence of encouragement, isolation from cultural and academic experiences, and parental and peer-group indifference"—all euphemistic descriptions of cultural deprivation that identified Black students as less likely to fit in at college due to segregation (137). "Fit" could be addressed through admissions and placement policies organized by states to ensure that "student abilities and interests" were matched "to the level of existing educational practices and available programs" (130). This idea of fit normalized the notion that students had discrete skill levels related to their cultural backgrounds and that those skill levels could be used to place them in different programs and institutions.

Skill levels were not just about student performance, according to Halstead, they were also about *student potential*—a new buzzword that claimed to offer equal opportunities for culturally deprived students. As Halstead (1974, 133, emphasis added) wrote, "Genuine equal opportunity exists for minority groups only when they are equipped to compete fairly *on the basis of potential rather than on initial performance.* They cannot compete fairly when admission is based primarily on testing . . . and when institutions are insensitive to the wide variety of special compensatory services required to offset the effects of deprivation." By identifying students with potential, colleges could more efficiently remediate and retain students without wasting resources. Indeed, remediation, particularly in writing, was part of Halstead's (152) vision for accommodating the deprived student with potential, who should "gain proficiency in expression" and "be exposed to significant ideas with which to express himself." By providing stimulus for expression, writing was central to integrating the "minority" student.

Such arguments also appeared in emerging retention scholarship. Vincent Tinto's (1975, 90) landmark article, "Dropout from Higher Education," argued that postsecondary institutions had an "inadequate conceptualization of the dropout process," which reduced all dropout behavior to students failing courses.[2] Tinto (91) sought to theorize dropout behavior as more varied, related to students' cultural, familial, and educational backgrounds—which determined whether a student integrated into an institution's values, identity, and norms.[3] But unlike Halstead, Tinto (101) believed colleges could measure potential in the admissions process using the College Board's research on standardized tests as a prediction of "college persistence."[4] By promoting standardized tests as predictors of retention, Tinto provided a means of identifying the student with potential. And, like Halstead, Tinto (118) proposed that remediation would improve the retention and "academic performance of persons from lower social status backgrounds." Both Halstead's and Tinto's descriptions of minoritized students (typically referenced without direct mention of race) rationalized the problem of attrition by pointing to the effects of cultural background on students' ability to express significant ideas in writing and ultimately their integration into college. This concern with retention was premised on a model of student learning that emphasized stimulating deprived students to develop resources for expression, making writing remediation an integrationist project.

Early focus on integration in retention scholarship reflected the redefinition of desegregation as remediation that happened in the early 1970s. Even as *Adams* demanded that states submit plans for Black student retention, retention scholarship promised to resolve the problem of "integration." The prevalence of language about "minorities" and "cultural and home experiences" made race euphemistic, distancing desegregation from the work of redressing historical racism. Desegregation thus became a kind of data-collection process—a plan for developing the best measures to predict student persistence. The policies that resulted from this new direction for higher education resulted in a racialized and stratified system of higher education measured by what Gina Ann Garcia (2019, 3) calls "white normative standards" for colleges that articulated "indicators of prestige and effectiveness" based on norms that benefit historically white colleges and universities (HWCUs), including standardized test scores, institutional selectivity, and retention rates. In the context of retention, institutions could use selectivity to argue that they were improving access through student placement, by measuring the best institutional and programmatic "fit" for a student. As selectivity was tied to prestigious (and largely segregated) white universities, remedial programs were stigmatized as racially other.

WRITING PLACEMENT AS INTEGRATION IN COMPOSITION

Given national interest in remedial placement and retention, composition scholarship began to discuss its specific role in integration. Some scholars resisted the idea that writing instruction helped students of color integrate to white mainstream literacy norms, evidenced perhaps most famously in the 1974 National Council of Teachers of English (NCTE) resolution on "Students' Right to Their Own Language" (SRTOL). However, backlash against SRTOL doubled down on the view that literacy remediation was critical to integration and stressed the need for remedial placement policies to support this view of remediation. This backlash was rooted in anti-Black linguistic racism, arguing that acceptance of Black English in classrooms promoted a new kind of segregation. Redefining segregation as a failure to assimilate to linguistic norms, this backlash resulted in an inordinate emphasis on dialect in writing instruction—an emphasis that falsely oversimplified Black literacy practices.

One of the most historically significant resolutions in the discipline's history, SRTOL was drafted by the executive committee of the

Conference on College Composition and Communication (CCCC) in 1972 and adopted by CCCC members in 1974. The SRTOL focused not only on dialect but also on style, stating that the organization "affirm[ed] the students' right to their own patterns and varieties of language—the dialects of their nurture or whatever dialects in which they find their own identity and style." As Patrick Bruch and Richard Marback (2005) explain, SRTOL has alternatively been claimed as a landmark disciplinary victory for linguistic diversity and a conflicted compromise that resulted in little pedagogical change. However, Carmen Kynard (2013, 100) argues that the resolution established that "black styles are revolutionary, for the time and place in which they socially arise, when they move black working-class audiences to new levels of social awareness, solidarity, and political activism and push past the socially prescribed norms of being and thinking (and therefore, speaking and writing) under white rule." Kynard's description of the influence of the Black Power and Black Arts movements in the resolution highlights that some of the resolution's proponents wanted the field to acknowledge that Black language should not be evaluated by its suitability for white audiences.[5] SRTOL was not just about valuing language difference; it was about resisting integrationist white norms in defining which language practices and purposes were considered *appropriate*. It was, as Valerie Felita Kinlock (2005, 88) puts it, an effort to call on the "rhetoric of rights" to "rethink . . . the limitations of a privileged, standardized vocabulary used to theorize racial (in)equality, social (in)justice, and the learning practices of students marked 'disenfranchised,' 'remedial,' and 'underprepared.'" However, backlash against the resolution appropriated the language of civil rights, undermining SRTOL by arguing that it encouraged segregation.

Typically, the backlash against SRTOL has been presented as a public backlash, exemplified by the *Newsweek* article "Why Johnny Can't Write," in which Merrill Sheils (1975, 61) touted the socioeconomic benefits of basic writing skills and suggested that failing to teach Standard English was "itself a pernicious form of oppression." But Sheils was repeating popular talking points from composition scholars who promoted Standard English as key to integration, many of whom were published in the pages of *College Composition and Communication* (*CCC*). For example, William H. Pixton (1974, 252) argued that SRTOL denied students the "right" to learn Standard English, the most effective dialect for "attaining higher education and business success." In doing so, teachers "allow their students to remain linguistically different *and* deficient" (252, original emphasis). With an emphasis on deficiency, Pixton (269) implied that Black English usage reflected a "narrow consciousness of self" that lacked "intellectual maturity." Pixton represented Black English as deprived of linguistic resources.

Defined erroneously by scholars as a product of segregation (rather than traced in the development of a common language among enslaved Africans), Black language was argued to promote further segregation. Harvey Minkoff and Evelyn B. Melamed (1975, 311) argued that SRTOL would create "narrower segregation than ever before practiced in this country" by requiring students to be placed in linguistically "homogeneous" classrooms and restricting teachers' region of work to their dialect region. This argument makes no sense from a linguistic standpoint. Language speakers aren't homogeneous; speakers of different dialects of English are usually comprehensible to one another, and instructors can be trained to learn about dialects. The argument was, at its core, a reiteration of anti-Black linguistic racism, evident in the description of Black English as "understandably lack[ing] vocabulary and syntax for concepts that transcend localities," such as "intellectual vocabulary" like "electorate," "imagery," and "square root" (312). The language choices reveal how pernicious ideas about racial segregation as deprivation were: Black English ostensibly only had local terminology, as its speakers were isolated by segregation, and it lacked access to "intellectual" terminology (including, as its most ridiculous example, the notion of an electorate). What is perhaps most curious about the emphasis on a reductive notion of dialect as key to writing instruction is that these arguments coexisted with process theory, which advocated for less concern with students' final writing products. But as I discussed in chapter 1, process theory viewed linguistic experiences and vocabulary as stimulus for the writing processes. Deprived students lacked resources for writing. Thus, this theory of language offered a simplistic method for integration: Standard English, with its supposed "greater" resources. These kinds of arguments suggesting that Black English further segregates Black students have limited the potential of public advocacy for linguistic diversity by continuing to represent Black English as deprived, nothing more than a stepping stone to Standard English acquisition in, for example, the *Martin Luther King Junior Elementary School Children v. Ann Arbor School District Board* (1979) ruling and the Oakland Resolution (see Smitherman 1981; Banks 2006).

Disciplinary rejections of SRTOL argued that student placement into remediation would resolve racial segregation. Dorothy Margaret Guinn (1976, 349) argued for stricter placement practices by proposing that "segregation based on ability becomes the only way we can effectively teach" incoming students of varied skill levels. Guinn reiterated the idea that inadequate writing ability stemmed from a lack of resources in nonstandard dialects, not from the dialects themselves. She stated, "The problem is not that . . . blacks use multiple negation and 'invariant' *be*" but that incoming students have "limited" vocabulary because of "poor" reading skills (345, 347). She suggested, "They have been told too often that they have the right to their own dialect and not often enough that that right carried far enough separates people rather than unites them" (347). Black language was viewed paradoxically as lacking resources and having the power to create racial division. That is, language rights were restricted to preserve an imaginary racial unity that whites felt Black language threatened.

These arguments had more than pedagogical effects; they recommended writing program policies. Guinn (1976, 349) argued that writing programs should "resume or initiate screening procedures for entering freshmen and assign students to class sections based on ability." Placement by ability was not racial segregation since its *method* was ostensibly race-neutral, but in the end scholars were fine with racial segregation as its result. Seen as a pathway to integration, writing placement codified Standard English as an imperative, although what exactly that meant was vaguely defined as language resources and vocabulary in ways that positioned Black English as inferior. Whether these scholars intended for their arguments to stall or mitigate desegregation in practice is largely irrelevant to the fact that these kinds of arguments did play a role in how desegregation plans framed placement, testing, and remedial program policies that ultimately separated remedial students from collegiate identities and tested dialect, vocabulary, and logical reasoning throughout a student's education.

FROM PEDAGOGY TO POLICY: THE CONSOLIDATION OF SPECIAL STUDIES IN GEORGIA

The popularity of arguments for integrationist writing remediation legitimized this approach in state desegregation plans. At the request of the Department of Health, Education, and Welfare (HEW), Georgia submitted its *Plan for the Further Desegregation of the University System of Georgia* in 1974 (Regents 1974), and the plan was approved. Georgia was in many respects a national model of desegregation—and an indication of the underlying resistance that informed states' approaches to desegregation. With Jimmy Carter as governor from 1971 to 1975, the state complied with HEW's request, unlike Mississippi and Louisiana. But in Georgia many officials resisted desegregation and sought to mitigate its effects by emphasizing that Black students were not prepared for white colleges. The chancellor of the USG, George Simpson, expressed concern that desegregation would precipitate a "crisis of literacy" because "illiteracy is disproportionately high among blacks" (quoted in Winkler 1974, 6). He claimed that Special Studies was the only way white colleges could recruit Black students, to "help them compensate for their often-deprived cultural and educational backgrounds" (6). In keeping with the chancellor's concerns, the regents' 1974 plan (211) made Special Studies a key site of growth and intervention, presented under the section "Retention of Black Students." These policies reinforced the view among white colleges like Armstrong that attrition was evidence of Black students' academic deficiencies and remediation was an undesirable, temporary program; at Black colleges, including Savannah State, the policies failed to address what faculty and administrators there viewed as students' primary obstacles to completing a degree: financial needs and the exclusionary structure of remediation.

The 1974 plan enabled the USG to set new statewide requirements for admissions and Special Studies. First, the plan set statewide SAT score admissions requirements, which resulted in more students across the state being placed into Special Studies (Regents 1974, 211). The plan mandated that any student who earned a *combined* SAT score of 650 or lower[6] must take additional placement testing using the College Board's Comparative Guidance and Placement Program (CGP) (214).[7] Individual institutions were also allowed to set their floor scores *higher* than the 650 state requirement but not lower. According to the regents, this requirement would place roughly 3,500 more students into remediation—a number that would increase Special Studies enrollment by more than 150 percent (214). Furthermore, there was strong evidence that this SAT floor score would disadvantage Black students and Black colleges, based on previous years' data showing that between 75 percent and 90 percent of students at Black colleges had scored below 650 on the SAT (Winkler 1974).

At this point in the history of standardized testing, the Educational Testing Service (ETS) recognized and had begun studying racial biases on its tests—both overall test bias and item/question bias—in response to documented racial disparities in test scores (Cleary and Hilton 1966). The ETS identified item biases in the 1960s and 1970s, attributed to culturally biased test questions, but on the whole ETS research argued (and still does) that its tests have no clear racial biases and accurately predict first-year student performance (Cleary and Hilton 1966; Flaugher 1970; Letukas 2015). However, studies from the time found that the testing environment and the use of the test results were possible sources of discrimination, with early research strongly showing evidence of stereotype threat, or the negative effect of racial stereotypes about intelligence on test takers' scores (Flaugher 1970). ETS researchers argued that as long as the predictive validity of the tests held up, then any disparate outcomes were not racist. That argument, of course, relied on the spurious premise that college environments and assessment methods were not also racist. In fact, both placement exams and remedial writing instruction mandated in Georgia reinforced anti-Black linguistic racism through the same emphasis on dialect, vocabulary, and logic.

For placement into Special Studies, the regents' 1974 plan required the Comparative Guidance and Placement test. Like other standardized tests, the CGP was designed to "provide predictive information about performance in an entry-level course" (Educational Testing Service 1977, 8). The CGP further claimed that its content reflected the priorities of English teachers. The Written English Expression Test portion of the CGP tested for "sentence recognition," "sentence structure," "pronoun problems," "language and style," "verb problems," "logic," and "recognition of error-free construction" (8). All multiple choice, the largest section of questions was devoted to logic, and the other six areas of questions primarily tested Standard English usage and grammar. The College Board argued that scores on this test were as valid at predicting success in college writing courses as a holistically rated essay exam (8). These test areas did, in fact, correspond to the USG's guidelines for Special Studies writing courses, which were instructed to teach "grammar, spelling, word usage, sentence and paragraph structure and, when needed, speech," and reading courses were to teach "vocabulary, comprehension and speed" (Regents 1974, 211). Given the ways composition scholars framed dialect as evidence of intellect, this focus was primed to reinforce anti-Black linguistic racism.

The 1974 plan recommended that students placed in Special Studies receive a kind of diagnosis of their deficiencies through "develop[ing] and examin[ing] case histories to learn about each individual and problems which might cause the learning deficiency" (Regents 1974, 212). Special Studies students were depicted as having individual problems akin to a disability; thus instructors had to develop individualized teaching approaches and instructional media for each student (211–212). Special Studies programs were also supposed to coordinate with support services, including "individual and group counseling sessions, an orientation to college life, study skills, personal relations, and vocational and academic counseling" (212). These recommendations expanded remedial instruction beyond the classroom format, supporting the development of tutorial services that transformed into writing centers and media labs, which also became part of the state's recommendations for Special Studies later in the desegregation enforcement process (Simpson and Oxford 1978).

What emerged from the state's philosophy was a theory of literacy deficiency as individual pathology originating from the cognitive effects of cultural deprivation. The association of Black English with cultural and linguistic deprivation connoted disability. This pathologizing of remedial students recurs in Special Studies documents from the time period and eventually fed into support for individualized tutorial methods used in writing centers, making writing instruction an impossibly time-intensive exercise, with each student requiring a diagnosis and remediation plan. I am not sure how to reconcile this pedagogical approach with the seeming contradiction that testing could assess a student's skill level for placement into courses. However, my guess is that in practice the attempt to clearly group students by skill level fell apart; thus testing had to be followed up with this diagnostic work, doubling the labor of the writing placement process.

Insight into this contradiction between cultural and individual deficiency is found in the diagnostic method Mina P. Shaughnessy (1977) described in *Errors and Expectations*, often considered the foundational text of basic writing scholarship. As Shaughnessy (10, emphasis added) explained, "The issue of error is much more complex and troubling than it seems in theory . . . *the errors . . . students make cannot be neatly traced to one particular source, namely, the habitual preference of a vernacular form over a standard form.* Instead [the teacher] finds evidence of a number of interacting influences" related to media, neighborhood communication, and schooling experiences. This assessment of the ways vernacular alone does not account for writing errors hints at the problem with cultural deprivation theory's racialization of error, but it does not completely abandon the racialized geography used to explain writing errors as products of segregation. One wonders at the enormous amount of work required of teachers to follow Shaughnessy's (285) recommendation that they "must be prepared to make not one but many decisions," including charting students' different skills across several semesters like a medical practitioner. This time- and labor-intensive approach clashed with a growing emphasis on efficiency in higher education, setting up unsustainable remedial writing programs.

The unsustainability of the USG's remedial program is evident in the plan's directive that each USG institution must establish a Department of Special Studies. Students in Special Studies were not only required to pass each course they placed into, they also had to pass an exit exam to enroll in regular college coursework (Regents 1974, 212). The USG added to this workload by making Special Studies responsible for remediation related to the Regents' Test. Since the Regents' Test was required to graduate, students who did not pass had to enroll in a Special Studies course. The unsustainability of remediation, however, was not just about political investment—it was also about the form of pedagogy favored in basic writing scholarship.

A large enterprise, the Regents' Test became a driving force in defining college writing in the USG. West Georgia College professor Huey Allen Owings (1974, 1–2) argued that the test provided the impetus for transforming first-year composition from "a free-wheeling, literature centered course . . . to a highly structured composition and usage skills course, one in which each teacher is to follow scrupulously a prescribed syllabus that requires a certain number of exercises, a certain number of paragraphs of specified variety." Owings presented the Regents' Test as a force for standardization in writing instruction—requiring labor that other faculty were not willing to do. These changes were embodied in his caricature of the new composition instructor, "Miss Smythe," a "spinster cousin" of longtime literature professor "Dr. Smith, who never bathes and who never wears a change of clothes, who, though extremely knowledgeable in the field of composition, even its minutest details, sometimes forgets to discuss those details and to return papers" (9). Miss Smythe would "be able <u>To Prepare</u> her students for The Test . . . She will graciously accept the praise of the Department Chairman and the Director of Freshman English" (9). As Dr. Smith leaves to find another job, the "Misses Smythes from high schools from across America will flock to West Georgia for job interviews as a weary Department Chairman and an even wearier Director of Freshman English attempt to find replacements for that medieval scholar" (10). The transformations precipitated by the push for statewide standardization and assessment were felt as shifting disciplinary and gender power dynamics that changed not just *what* was taught but *who* would teach and *whether* it was associated with real college work. The composition instructor became a site of racial and gender norms, establishing the figure of first-year composition as a white woman—the nagging spinster who nevertheless upholds white literacy norms by doing work scorned by white men. The feminization of composition instruction boded poorly for investment in its instruction, but its racialization made it a site deemed useful for upholding white literacy norms.

Standardization in writing programs encouraged a new focus on assessment. According to Owings (1972, 2), composition now taught "usage, mechanics, the elements of the sentence, and aspects of the paragraph" to prepare students for passing the Regents' Test. But given the large scope of intensive work required for this kind of instruction, faculty across disciplines were brought into the project, as college administrators now required "all departments" to be responsible for teaching "good writing" and ensuring success on the Regents' Test (8). One later account of the Regents' Test confirms this impression, stating that implementation of the test in 1972 resulted in changes to course content, the addition of new courses, an increase in essay testing, and more faculty across the curriculum "teaching basic skills"—a comment indicating the vague role faculty in other disciplines would begin to play in assessing writing (Rentz 1979, 76). From the perspective of the beleaguered, spinsterly white composition teacher, having other faculty help out with writing seems a welcome boost to her identity. But for Black students in white colleges whose writing was now subject to multiple faculty members' critique, the scene probably looked less inviting.

The effects of these new remedial policies on enrollment and retention in the system are worth considering in evaluating whether Special Studies constituted a gate during desegregation—either admitting more students or hindering their retention. Nationally, Black student enrollment increased during the mid-1970s, although the data are unclear as to how many of these students were placed into regular college courses versus remedial programs.[8] Black enrollment also grew in the USG, from roughly 3 percent of total USG enrollment in 1972 to 15 percent in 1976, where it remained fairly stable through 1990 (Oxford et al. 1977, I:162–164). But enrollment gains were unevenly distributed across the university system, with the largest gains occurring initially in senior (four-year) colleges, which included the historically Black colleges in the USG (see figures 2.1 and 2.2).[9] By the mid-1970s, the gains had switched to junior (two-year) colleges and remained fairly stable at under 10 percent of university-level institutions.

The USG as a whole increased Black student enrollment during this period, but the enrollment increases alone do not give a full picture of the level of access Black students experienced within the USG or the level of segregation at its universities. As figure 2.2 shows, the state's flagship university, the University of Georgia, saw decreased Black student enrollment in the mid-1970s, sharply contrasting with the Black student enrollment at Black colleges like Savannah State and even with the

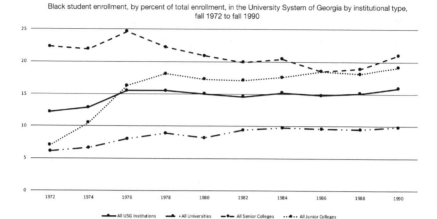

Black student enrollment, by percent of total enrollment, in the University System of Georgia by institutional type, fall 1972 to fall 1990

Figure 2.1. Black student enrollment, by percent of total enrollment, in the University System of Georgia by institutional type, fall 1972 to fall 1990.

moderate gains at senior colleges like Armstrong under the scrutiny of desegregation enforcement.

Institutional disparities in desegregation outcomes were concerning to the NAACP Legal Defense Fund (LDF). In 1975, the LDF filed a motion for further relief in *Adams*, citing Georgia and several other states' desegregation plans for "consistently declin[ing] to abandon or alter admission, retention, scholarship, and program elements at their prestigious white institutions, so as to achieve proportionate or even significantly increased black enrollment both at these schools and statewide" (Haynes 1978, F-7).[10] These problems were prevalent across all states' plans, particularly in North Carolina, Florida, and Georgia. For example, North Carolina had promised to study its current admissions requirements, but the state outright refused to create "tailored" admissions requirements for Black students, stating, "Higher education cannot and should not purport to function as a panacea for a vast array of social ills reflected by the seriously deficient student" (F-27). Similarly, Georgia was cited for failing to present evidence that the SAT, placement, and Regents' Test policies were "valid predicters of the performance of blacks in Georgia colleges" (F-54). The LDF contended that state plans failed to substantively address retention (H-6). North Carolina blamed attrition on the state being forced to admit "more high risk students," offering no real plan (F-61). Georgia's retention plan *was* Special Studies, which required more remediation, added new testing requirements for students, and allowed individual institutions to set higher bars for regular college admission—three policies

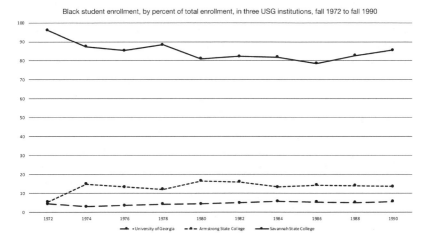

Figure 2.2. Black student enrollment, by percent of total enrollment, in three USG institutions, fall 1972 to fall 1990.

that created additional obstacles to regular college admission. The disparate effect these policies had on Black students is evident in that Special Studies disproportionately enrolled Black students (40 percent of students in Special Studies were Black, according to the LDF's data) and disproportionately consigned students at Black colleges to Special Studies programs (resulting in 45 percent of students in Black colleges being placed into Special Studies) (F-61). Finally, the LDF noted that all states treated open access institutions as "institutions which adequately serve disadvantaged and minority students as entry points for upward mobility throughout higher education," even though data on open access institutions suggested that Black students had higher attrition rates in those systems and were not enrolling in regular college degree programs there (F-54). In other words, the LDF found that state plans were inadequate because they treated remediation as a retention plan.

The 1975 LDF motion in *Adams* highlighted the problem with the ways retention efforts reduced attrition to academic ability. Even though the LDF brought HEW to trial again over these plans, HEW's acceptance of them had already built an infrastructure for remedial writing around racial ideologies of literacy and subsequently resulted in racial dispari-ties in student enrollment patterns. Institutions with a commitment to access had to accommodate a labor- and time-intensive remediation process, but institutions that wanted to become more selective could raise their admissions requirements and lower the number of remedial courses. This is exactly what happened in the case of Savannah State and Armstrong, as Armstrong's efforts to raise admissions requirements used verbal SAT scores to reduce the number of literacy remediation courses it had to offer.

THE UNEQUAL EFFECTS OF REMEDIATION AT WHITE AND BLACK COLLEGES

The Special Studies literacy programs developed in Savannah's two colleges in the mid-1970s illustrate the LDF's concerns that white colleges were using remediation as a catch-all solution for desegregation. Both Armstrong and Savannah State conformed to the mandated elements of the state's placement and remediation policies, but these policies affected the programs at both colleges differently. In response, both colleges sought to navigate the stigma of Special Studies and its impact on student attrition. Savannah State's Special Studies experimented with the state criteria to create forms of remediation designed to help Special Studies students connect with the rest of the college. Armstrong's program reflected concern that Special Studies negatively affected the college's reputation and needed to be reduced as much as possible.

During the mid-1970s, Savannah State and Armstrong cooperated to comply with desegregation. They were touted nationally as an "example of what can be done to ease the lines of racial separation when two colleges are in the same town" (Lewis 1974). National coverage of their efforts focused not on Special Studies but rather on the development of joint degree programs, which required students to attend courses at both colleges in pursuit of their degree. The theory behind this approach, according to USG vice chancellor John W. Hooper, was that having students attend both colleges would create "an intangible difference in attitudes" about race among students (quoted in Winkler 1974). However, HEW remained skeptical about cooperative programs because these arrangements did not require students to earn a degree from a college in which they were a racial minority. HEW's concern was justified: desegregation efforts had to navigate community perceptions about white and Black colleges. For example, a survey of Savannah State students found that many never seriously considered enrolling at Armstrong out of "fear of discrimination, loss of peer group, unfamiliar cultural environment" (6). On the other hand, Armstrong's president Ashmore presented desegregation as a zero-sum game, stating that efforts "to give funds to blacks" to attend college would mean denying admissions to white students: "Then you ask yourself, apart from any aspects of race, are you, in effect, taking money away from those who have some possibility of success and giving it to those who will never have a possibility of being successful" (quoted in Winkler 1974, 6). Like many racist remarks, Ashmore's comments were ostensibly presented "apart from any aspects of race"; yet the comment echoed the perception of the USG chancellor that Black students were illiterate and could not graduate from white colleges, stoking whites' fears that Black enrollment was reverse racism that denied whites opportunities.

These circulating beliefs about race and academic potential influenced Savannah State's and Armstrong's responses to the regents' plan's requirements for admission to regular college coursework. Prior to the 1974 plan, Armstrong and Savannah State set their own admissions criteria, and both required students to report their SAT scores for admissions without indicating any cutoff (Armstrong State College 1972, 31; Savannah State College 1972, 46). The statewide SAT floor score requirements officially raised regular admissions requirements at both colleges. Given racial disparities in SAT scores, this created a dramatic increase in both remedial courses and students at Savannah State, and Savannah State became concerned that Special Studies requirements would "stigmatize [it] . . . as a school only for the disadvantaged," according to the school's coordinator of Special Studies (Winkler 1974). This period of "Great Panic" resulted from applying the USG's new placement policies at Savannah State (Maynor n.d., 2). According to the data in the department's history, Special Studies enrollment increased from 1,193 students in 1975–1976 to 1,402 students in 1977–1978 (2). These numbers dwarfed the entering first-year student class (see figure 1.1).[11] Savannah State faculty were concerned that the additional financial burden and exclusion from regular college coursework would lead to high attrition rates. As table 2.1 shows, Savannah State responded by developing topical Special Studies courses across disciplines, which were designed to "provide 'high risk' students with a sufficient number of courses offering basic fundamentals of their fields of interest, thus staking an early claim on prospective majors" (2). This solution allowed students to maintain full-time enrollment to qualify for financial aid while connecting them to the regular college and their educational goals (2). The curriculum supported the retention needs of Savannah State students. However, after 1977, these courses were discontinued when the USG mandated that Special Studies departments only offer courses in reading, English (writing), and math that were "classified according to state regulations"—likely a result of the placement testing divisions into these subject areas (3). The policy definition of remediation as limited to literacy and math

Table 2.1. Changes in admissions, placement, and writing remediation at Savannah State College, mid-1970s

Bulletin	Regular Admissions	Conditional Admissions	Reading Remediation	Writing Remediation
Savannah State College (1974) Bulletin 1974–1975	Must have cumulative GPA of C or higher; composite SAT score of 650 or higher.	Composite SAT score below 650.	Basic Reading I and II: reading and study skills, with emphasis on "developing independence" and "communication skills" (234). Reading topics include courses in the humanities, social sciences, and natural sciences.	Basic English I and II: combined reading and writing instruction; "rhetoric of the sentence and paragraph," oral composition, reading comprehension, and "drawing inferences" (235).
Savannah State College (1977) Bulletin 1977–1978	Composite SAT score of 750 or higher.	Composite SAT score below 750.	Reading Foundations I and II. Topics include courses in social sciences, technology and graphics, home economics, biology, humanities (172).	English Fundamentals for Composition (ENG 97) and English Fundamentals for Reading and Writing (ENG 98): Integrated reading and writing instruction; "rhetoric of the sentence and paragraph," oral composition, reading comprehension, and "drawing inferences" (171–172).

skills worked against retention efforts designed to address the needs of Savannah State students. However, Savannah State faculty innovated in response to the exclusionary potential of Special Studies.

Armstrong was also concerned that the new Special Studies policies would create a larger, more visible remedial program that would negatively affect the college's reputation. Prior to the 1974 plan, the official policy for placement into Armstrong's Academic Skills Laboratory, for example, was referral from a faculty member or self-referral (Armstrong State College 1972, 28). After the 1974 plan passed, Armstrong increased its admissions requirements in an effort to reduce the number of students placed into Special Studies. In 1976, Armstrong implemented a requirement that students must have a minimum SAT verbal score of 300 to be admitted, even conditionally. This requirement allowed the college to discontinue offering one Special Studies course, English 098, and keep enrollment in Special Studies comparatively low (see table 2.2 and figure 1.2). Armstrong also began requiring regularly admitted students to earn at least a "1.2 predicted freshman grade-point average as determined by the College Prediction Formula" (Armstrong State

Table 2.2. Changes in admissions, placement, and writing remediation at Armstrong State College, mid-1970s

Bulletin	Regular Admissions	Conditional Admissions	English 98	English 99
Armstrong State College (1974) Bulletin 1974–1975	Minimum composite SAT score of 650.	Below composite SAT score of 650.	Review of grammar: sentence writing (119).	Fundamentals of Composition: paragraph structure and writing "clearly, logically, coherently, and correctly" (119).
Armstrong State College (1977) Bulletin 1977–1978	Minimum composite SAT score of 750 (verbal SAT 300).	Composite SAT score of 550–750 (required verbal SAT of 300).	Not offered; dropped due to admissions standards.	Fundamentals of Composition: paragraph structure and writing "clearly, logically, coherently, and correctly" (84).

College 1976, 57). Finally, Armstrong required all Special Studies students to get permission from the head of the Academic Skills Laboratory to enroll in any regular college courses (58), limiting Special Studies students' engagement with the rest of the college. There were also anecdotal reports of faculty refusing to give students a grade in a regular college class until they completed work in Special Studies at the instructor's demand (Dennard 1974).

Armstrong placed limitations on Special Studies out of concern that a higher number of remedial students would diminish its reputation. As Armstrong's head of Special Studies stated in a later defense of the increased SAT verbal requirement, "A college has no obligation to provide a program of study which any student can complete" (Savannah Community Liaison Committee 1978, 424). The head of Special Studies argued that college admission symbolized a contract with the student that "the college provides some program of study which the student has a reasonable chance of completing" (424). According to this line of reasoning, Armstrong had an "ethical" obligation to set the SAT verbal cutoff score at 300 (424). This rationalization highlights the way student potential was defined by standardized test scores at Armstrong. These arguments and policy changes turned retention into a judgment about academic potential, hinging on verbal ability—with retention paradoxically wielded to exclude students and courses the institution deemed a threat to academic standards.

REFLECTIONS ON SPECIAL STUDIES AT ARMSTRONG

When she began teaching Special Studies courses at Armstrong in 1974, Dandy (2017) encountered a very different environment than the one presented in official representations of Special Studies. According to her, most of the students enrolled in Special Studies during this era were "young people who came from the private schools in Savannah . . . built up to keep the children from going to the public schools, to keep them away from Black people." These students resisted Dandy's grading of their work, complaining to college administrators, "Who is she that she thinks that I can't pass this class" (2017). Dandy attributed these negative evaluations to the fact that she "probably was the first Black instructor they ever had, because they were coming from private schools" (2017) White flight from public schools after K–12 desegregation impacted the educational experiences and expectations of white students entering college. In the 1973–1974 school year alone, over 1,200 students left Savannah public schools, and a decade later, Savannah had the highest private school enrollment in the entire Southeast (Andersson 2006). Records of USG Special Studies enrollment show that even after desegregation efforts were implemented, Black students were never the majority of Special Studies students at HWCUs, although they were disproportionately placed into such programs (Hooper 1979).

In Special Studies, Black students encountered expectations that they would fail, according to Dandy (2017)—expectations that students recognized and that made them "afraid to come" to Armstrong. These expectations shaped faculty assessment of students: "The faculty would come with certain expectations for students. And a lot of times if students came and the faculty members had low expectations, then they would see to it that the students would meet those low expectations, and they'd try to get rid of them" (2017). This situation created additional work for Dandy, who took on a mentoring role for Black students on campus. She explains, "Any time Black students had a problem, they'd come to me. You know, I didn't really have time to counsel all of them, but I had to because I wanted them to stay" (2017). State and institutional desegregation plans denied the realities of what supported Black student retention in white colleges. Instead, as Dandy (2017) put it, "The question was always, will we lower our standards. So the idea was that, you know, those people are gonna lower our standards, and we don't want to lower our standards. . . . And here I was an African American on a predominantly white campus, probably only two or three of us on this whole campus, and they're debating about whether or not they want to connect with a predominantly Black school." Judgments of the academic potential of Black students coded anti-Black racism as "academic standards."

To put Dandy's reflections in context, one 1974 report by the National Scholarship Service and the Fund for Negro Students provided evidence that Black students' underrepresentation in higher education had less to do with academic preparation than with socioeconomic disparities. The large-scale survey of 80,000 Black graduates from 7,000 high schools found that 38 percent of Black high school graduates ranked in the top quarter of their class, with 16 percent holding a B+ or better average (Semas 1974). The majority of these students pursued academic (not vocational) studies and had the appropriate college preparation in lab science, algebra, geometry, and foreign language (1974). While income and socioeconomic circumstances determined college decisions, twice as many Black high school graduates were qualified for college than were admitted (1974). Indeed, another survey found that broad generalizations about Black students at white colleges were not supported by survey evidence, which showed that only a few generalizations could be made about Black students: most were graduates of public high schools, maintained at least a C average in their college coursework, made use of college resources to support their academic work, and met the required admissions standards for their institutions; however, many struggled to find financial support to pay for college (Boyd 1974, 5). The study further found that the majority of Black students at white colleges felt those institutions were unresponsive to their needs and needed to change (57).

Efforts to address retention comprehensively at white colleges, however, were dismissed. Dandy described how some Armstrong faculty treated the failure of Special Studies students as a mark of high academic standards. This attitude impeded Dandy's efforts to help students. When Dandy designed and proposed a study skills course to address students' non-content academic needs, faculty refused to count the course for degree credit, despite the fact that Special Studies departments at other USG institutions already offered such a course for degree credit. According to Dandy (2017), the faculty "went through years of going back and forth with that until eventually [they] did give us college credit." In 1982, Dandy became department head of Developmental Studies, formerly Special Studies. In that position, she "tried to get the Developmental Studies faculty to see how many people they could keep. And what would they do in order to keep them in class. . . . And the only people that I chose to teach in Developmental Studies were those people who were nurturing people, and people who believed, who had high expectations for [students]. So that was always a fight" (2017). Yet, according to Dandy, Black students continued to face obstacles in the way faculty assessed them at Armstrong well after formal desegregation efforts concluded—a problem she worked to address throughout her career.

After completing her doctorate at the University of South Carolina, Dandy moved to the College of Education at Armstrong, where she became dean and brought substantial grant money and national recognition for developing a program to recruit and train Black teachers. That program, the Pathways to Teaching Program, which began in 1993, changed faculty perceptions of Black students (Dandy 2017). It did so by teaching students how to ask faculty questions, where to sit in class, and "how to deal with a situation where the instructor might say a derogatory term" (2017). The program tried to create, in Dandy's (2017) words, the feeling of "a traditionally Black institution in a white institution" to make students feel "comfortable" on campus. Dandy (1991) further advocated for Black students in her book *Black Communications*, which explained the cultural, linguistic, and rhetorical differences of Black communication practices to teachers. *Black Communications* elaborated on the idea that teachers' negative expectations shape student performance. In her words, "The overwhelming consensus in current literature is not that the dialect causes problems in reading, but that *teachers' responses* to the dialect reflect low expectations about the abilities of those who use it in the classroom, setting up barriers between teachers and students. Expectations become self-fulfilling prophecies" (10, original emphasis). However, it is telling that Dandy needed to advocate for those changes more than two decades after higher education desegregation enforcement began and years after Armstrong was deemed in good standing with Title VI of the Civil Rights Act.

Savannah's colleges were shaped by the disparate effects of desegregation policies as well as their different admissions standards. Attitudes about the colleges would come to the fore after another ruling in the *Adams* case, *Adams v. Califano* (1977), which ruled in favor of the LDF's motion for further relief. As chapter 3 describes, *Adams v. Califano* required HEW to articulate more specific desegregation criteria, forcing Georgia to revise its desegregation plan and create a specific plan for Armstrong and Savannah State—with community, faculty, and student input from both colleges. Faced with a new debate over whether to merge or to relinquish key programs to the other college, Savannah's colleges would clash over the deterministic view of student potential the state's desegregation plan had implicitly forwarded. These negotiations between Savannah's two colleges and the state would make literacy standards even more central to defining institutional identity for Armstrong and Savannah State.

3

MEASURES OF CONTROL
Writing Programs and Institutional Identity, Late 1970s

The photographs in figures 3.1 and 3.2 are iconic images from the era of desegregation enforcement at Savannah's two colleges. In the first, a lone white man swings a mattock at a 1960s Chevy Chevelle parked on Armstrong's quad and spray-painted with the message "No ASU/ SSU Merger." In the foreground sits a mallet waiting for another person to join the activity, part of a spring fundraising event at Armstrong held in front of Lane Library (Stone 2010, 206). The image captures a sense of the white backlash against rumors that the US Department of Health, Education, and Welfare (HEW) would push harder to enforce desegregation in Savannah, merging Armstrong into Savannah State. In the second image, Savannah State students form a barricade, protecting the entrance to campus during a protest of the regents' desegregation plan, which transferred Savannah State's teacher education program to Armstrong. In the foreground are three police vehicles operated by a group of mostly white cops, shown huddled just out of frame in another photo of the scene (Lavoie 1979). These pictures provide a study in contrast of white and Black colleges' response to desegregation enforcement in the 1970s: white colleges did not want to be forced by the government to change—to risk losing white alumni or students' support through association with Black colleges. Black colleges were worried about losing programs or, in some cases, being merged out of existence.

The late 1970s marked a period of strict desegregation enforcement— and discontentment with desegregation—during the administration of President Jimmy Carter. HEW strictly monitored states' progress toward their enrollment goals and cited additional states for violations. A new ruling in the *Adams* case, *Adams v. Califano* (1977), forced states to produce new desegregation plans that specified actions for nearby segregated colleges. HEW prompted states to broaden their admissions requirements to meet enrollment goals, suggesting that colleges put

https://doi.org/10.7330/9781646422036.c003

Figure 3.1. Protest of desegregation enforcement at Armstrong State College, 1979. Courtesy, Georgia Southern University Special Collections, Savannah.

more emphasis on student potential—the key to predicting retention discussed in chapter 2. Forced to come together and develop a new plan for desegregation and shared admissions requirements, Armstrong and Savannah State clashed over the value of SAT and Regents' Test scores in measuring academic quality. Both colleges leveraged different definitions of literacy standards as they sought to preserve their identities. As I argue in this chapter, white backlash against desegregation enforcement made "academic standards" central to defining institutional quality and encouraged white colleges to limit remedial writing instruction. These events gave writing programs a central role in defining institutional identity, with remedial writing a mark of lower academic standards in political discourse and at many selective white colleges. Rather than unseating the theory of deprivation, this pushback against remediation further ingrained the idea that remediation should only be extended to students with demonstrated potential to integrate into college standards, and states increasingly restricted access through more stringent efforts to identify student potential with testing. The emphasis on potential and retention, originally part of HEW's directive to rethink college admissions, ironically became a means of further restricting admissions.

Figure 3.2. Protest of desegregation enforcement at Savannah State College, 1979. Photo credit, John Lavoie. Courtesy, Savannah Morning News.

"LODESTONE OF CONTROVERSY": DESEGREGATION
BACKLASH AND THE PUSH FOR ACADEMIC STANDARDS

In 1976, Jimmy Carter was elected president of the United States—a feat attributed to support from Black voters, who formed a powerful voting bloc in the late 1970s (Minchin and Salmond 2011). Whereas the administrations of Richard Nixon and Gerald Ford had limited federal intervention in desegregation and funneled resources into remediation programs, Carter's HEW secretary, Joseph A. Califano Jr. (1981, 219), pushed for "full speed ahead" on desegregation, endorsing enrollment goals and affirmative action. The Carter administration strictly enforced desegregation, even when doing so meant battling states, which happened when North Carolina publicly refused to cooperate.[1] However, Carter struggled to alter an educational landscape marked by setbacks to affirmative action and the heavy involvement of the courts (Minchin and Salmond 2011; Califano 1981). Nixon had strongly influenced the US Supreme Court, appointing four new justices by 1972, and subsequent Supreme Court rulings on desegregation signaled an end to the court's willingness to intervene in de facto segregation.[2] Carter's interventionism resulted in more backlash than change. Under Carter, HEW was "the lodestone of more controversy" than any other department (Califano 1981, 11).

This controversy intensified as HEW was forced to create updated postsecondary desegregation criteria after the court ruled in favor of the National Association for the Advancement of Colored People (NAACP)

Legal Defense Fund's (LDF's) motion for further relief against HEW, finding that HEW had accepted state plans with inadequate student retention plans, among other problems. HEW's desegregation criteria reflected an ambivalence toward admissions practices and Black colleges that was, as I will show, misinterpreted by states in desegregation plans. First, HEW directed states to specify both enrollment goals and clear timetables for reaching those goals, which were not quotas per se but were often viewed as such by critics (Califano 1981; Haynes 1978).[3] State-funded Black and white colleges were both subject to the requirement that they increase "minority" enrollment. This directive required nearby segregated colleges to work together to meet enrollment goals, and although HEW specified that Black colleges should be prioritized in this process (thanks to the National Association for Equal Opportunity in Higher Education [NAFEO]), it nevertheless required them to recruit more white students.

To encourage "minority" recruitment at other race institutions, HEW gave a statewide planning mandate asking states to revise the institutional missions within their university systems to eliminate any references to race, to ensure that "students will be attracted to each institution on the basis of educational programs and opportunities uninhibited by past practices of segregation" (Haynes 1978, L-13). HEW then tasked states with eliminating "educationally unnecessary program duplication" at nearby segregated colleges, adding or removing programs to encourage other race enrollment (L15). In other words, neighboring Black and white colleges with duplicate nonessential programs had to negotiate which college would keep which programs, so that students made a decision about where to attend college based on program offerings and not on the college's racial identity. This mandate intervened in curricula and in some cases relocated students and faculty. Furthermore, it ignored the reality of anti-Black racism in higher education: Neglected by states and disparaged by white communities, public Black colleges now had to abandon their mission to serve Black students and focus on recruiting white students who considered them inferior. In some cases that meant giving up the largest program on campus—the one that enrolled the most students—in order to send Black students to the nearby white college, where white students and faculty might assume that Black students were less capable of academic work and had only been admitted because of their race.

HEW anticipated that white colleges would raise concerns about academic standards in response to this directive to admit more Black students. HEW tried to quell these objections by asking states to rethink the way they measured academic standards and to adjust their admissions practices to consider student potential: "States' efforts under these criteria need not and should not lead to lowering academic standards. States may need to innovate in seeking out talented students who will profit from higher education. They may need to broaden definitions of potential; to discount the effects of early disadvantage on the development of academic competence; and to broaden the talents measured in admissions tests. But new and different yardsticks for measuring potential are not lower standards. They can be more valid measures of true potential and talent. Taken as a whole, these criteria seek to preserve and protect academic standards of excellence" (Haynes 1978, L-8). Drawing from the language of student potential that emerged from student retention policies, HEW's directive for states to view potential in new ways nevertheless provided rhetorical support for traditional "academic standards of excellence" in defining college preparedness.

The widespread rhetoric of student potential in higher education at this time drew from what Michael Omi and Howard Winant (2015) call the "race as ethnicity" paradigm popular in the late 1970s and 1980s. Omi and Winant describe how the theory of cultural deprivation, although out of favor with social scientists, increasingly appealed to neoconservatives who conflated culture, race, and ethnicity—comparing African Americans' so-called deprivation to the disadvantages of other ethnicities that had experienced but overcome hardship, particularly immigrant communities. Omi and Winant explain that this definition glossed over the ongoing effects of slavery and legalized racial exclusion specific to African Americans, viewing race as a disadvantage rather than racism as informing law and policy. Drawing on the language associated with the view of race as ethnicity, HEW's emphasis on student potential and academic standards framed race as merely another disadvantage among many. If race was similar to other kinds of disadvantages, the argument went, then race should not be prioritized over other kinds of disadvantage. Why, then, critics of postsecondary desegregation asked, should Black students or Black colleges be prioritized?

This was precisely the question asked in mainstream criticism of HEW's updated criteria. One *US News and World Report* article called the HEW criteria a "compromise" that reflected "conflicting demands by blacks" ("More Blacks" 1977, 69). The *Atlanta Constitution* reported that the criteria were "designed to accommodate two perhaps contradictory [HEW] policies: achieve swift and fair integration, while preserving the character and unique contributions of black colleges" (Field 1979, 1A). In Savannah, Armstrong constituents argued that the HEW criteria negated Black colleges' existence entirely, stating: "If one starts from the first HEW guideline—that each institution must redefine its purpose on a basis other than race—then it follows that there is no longer a black institution (in the abstract) to enhance" (Savannah Community Liaison Committee 1978, 417, original emphasis). When Savannah State reminded others that Black colleges should be prioritized, their advocacy was described as "deeply embedded in the black position" rather than a legitimate HEW requirement (417). These interpretations of HEW's updated criteria undermined protections for Black colleges and effaced the specific history of anti-Blackness in US higher education.

The race as ethnicity paradigm also informed litigation against affirmative action in court, even as HEW sought to enforce affirmative action. Public outcry over reverse racism used the concept of disadvantage to argue that race-based affirmative action should not single out Black applicants differently than applicants with other "disadvantages." The ruling in *Regents of the University of California v. Bakke* (1978)—the Supreme Court's first ruling on affirmative action—distanced affirmative action from reparations, establishing diversity as the only acceptable goal of affirmative action and eliminating any attempts to consider race alone (Karabel 2006; Olivas 2013). By reducing racism to disadvantage, *Bakke* validated standardized testing as a measure of student potential and an admissions requirement, with Justice Powell's decision in the case citing the Educational Testing Service's (ETS's) research in support of standardized tests as a predictive measure (Lemann 2000).[4] *Bakke* presented tables of GPA and MCAT score averages with little commentary on how they should be interpreted in light of racial disparities. Instead, *Bakke* (1978) conflated "disadvantaged" white applicants with "disadvantaged" Black applicants, flattening racial differences and suggesting that all cultural disadvantages were equivalent in determining whether a student merited admission to an academic program.

The validation of standardized tests as measures of potential undermined efforts to address anti-Black racism in white colleges. Political support for standardized testing grew, bolstered by the anti-affirmative action movement's arguments that test scores were the fairest, most meritocratic measure for admissions. But standardized testing was not universally popular and was criticized by many academics. The NAACP (1976) called for a moratorium on standardized testing in a conference with representatives from faculty, administrators, and the Association of Black Psychologists, based on concerns that objective standardized tests like the SAT and ACT were not valid and were racially biased. Amid this debate, some composition scholars agreed that objective standardized tests were not necessarily an appropriate approach to evaluating student writing for admissions and placement; however, many were compelled by the idea that standardized tests that directly evaluated student writing, if designed by writing experts, might provide a fair and race-neutral method of making placement decisions for contingent admissions, broadening access to college. Composition entered the debate over testing and its role in predicting student performance in college—a debate heavily informed by integrationist assumptions at white colleges.

COMPOSITION AND THE TESTING MOVEMENT

As political favor for testing increased, many composition scholars resisted objective tests but expressed interest in capitalizing on this trend to promote the discipline. The National Council of Teachers of English (NCTE) observed that standardized tests, particularly competency and proficiency tests, "appeared with dizzying speed" in the late 1970s, often in highly politicized contexts (Cooper 1981, vii). Public support for standardized testing was seen as an opportunity for English educators "to revitalize their remedial teaching" and promote their work (xii). As I will show, some composition scholars saw an opportunity for composition to take a larger role in standardized testing, particularly if the field could shift standardized testing away from objective tests and toward direct assessment of writing, such as essay exams. This approach was perceived to offer a fairer, yet still race-neutral, method of measuring student potential in writing.

In the late 1970s, interest in writing assessment grew substantially in response to resistance to objective standardized tests (i.e., multiple choice exams). Composition scholars pushed for evaluation of actual writing samples, particularly essay exams in which faculty readers would rate a timed essay exam, scoring it either holistically (a single score for the entire essay) or analytically (scoring several criteria) (Yancey 1999; Haswell and Elliot 2019). In 1975, the National Assessment of Educational Progress (NAEP) published its first report on writing and reading skills (Mellon 1975).[5] The NAEP was, according to Richard Haswell and Norbert Elliot (2019, 189), "the first attempt in the United States to collect national data about student proficiency, including writing ability." Subsequent research on the "evaluation" of writing appeared, such as Charles R. Cooper and Lee Odell's collection, *Evaluating Writing: Describing, Measuring, Judging*. In their introduction, Cooper and Odell (1977, viii) argued that standardized tests "are not valid measures of writing performance" but may be used "for prediction or placement," although placement decisions were best made by "a single writing sample quickly scored by trained raters." This argument presented direct writing assessment as better than objective tests but conceded that it might serve as an adjunct to such tests, emphasizing the need for composition scholars to be involved in creating and rating placement tests for writing courses. In these arguments, placement remained a primary goal, as did the notion that a test functioned to measure an ostensibly stable level of writing skill. Even those resistant to standardized testing did not completely dismiss the notion of using a single test to make predictive decisions for students.

In 1978, the *Journal of Basic Writing* published a special issue on writing "evaluation." The articles in this issue outlined two interrelated goals for assessment in composition: first, the need to become involved in standardized testing, either alongside or in place of larger testing organizations, and second, the need to address bias and subjectivity in writing assessment. Perhaps, contributors suggested, these two needs could be addressed simultaneously by developing expertise in writing assessment. Although the ETS was criticized in several articles, this scholarship expressed hope that faculty-developed tests could improve the accuracy and fairness of writing assessment, particularly for minoritized students. For example, Rexford Brown (1978, 4), a NAEP representative, opened the special issue by observing that the profession had "softened . . . up just a bit more toward the idea of measurement and the possibility that there are some shared units of quality upon which to build more accurate and useful systems of evaluation." Brown spoke to a growing concern in the late 1970s that writing assessment was subjective and therefore potentially biased, perhaps discriminating against racial minorities.

Other contributors proposed that composition should work with testing organizations like the ETS. These arguments typically expressed a desire to control the standards of evaluating writing. Composition faculty were involved in state-led efforts for placement tests that were competing with the Comparative Guidance and Placement test (CGP) and the Test of Standard Written English (TSWE), including in California, New York, and Georgia (Lamos 2011). White (1978, 19) described the English Equivalency Examination developed by the California State University and Colleges system as a victory of faculty who "gained control and retain control of the program by developing (with, I should add, the continuing good faith and assistance of the [ETS]) a considerable amount of expertness in essay testing." Composition scholars' involvement in writing assessment was based on the belief that they could *improve* the process, making it more fair and accurate. Indeed, Edward M. White (19) called for those developing tests to "demonstrate that a writing test in fact discriminates among students according to writing ability," not other factors. Yet the idea of faculty expertise in defining a fixed notion of writing ability was a double-edged sword, deployed to defend competency tests such as Georgia's Regents' Test in the 1980s (see chapter 4), as writing faculty often supported the test's validity by arguing that it had been developed by faculty and it increased the visibility of writing programs in the state.

Some scholars such as Rosemary Hake (1978, 39) embraced the idea of composition "teaching to the test" as a means of promoting equal opportunity and racial integration. Hake (43) viewed remedial writing as "a means of entry to the middle class" for students at her majority (65 percent) Black university. Given the stakes of this activity, standardized writing tests[6] could eliminate inconsistencies in grading that Hake believed might allow students "entering our required composition courses with serious writing problems" to "pass[] on through them with their deficiencies intact" (47). To provide common standards for evaluating writing, Hake (42) proposed a method of rating essay exams taken by students for placement into or exit from the remedial composition program, designed to ensure that students possessed "at least a minimal standard of competence in writing"—a phrase that echoes the justification of the Regents' Test described in chapter 1. In fact, this view of competence was based on the philosophy that "the vices or flaws [of writing] are capable of being classified and counted," including organization, paragraph structure, usage, and punctuation (47). The proposed method of writing assessment promised to help integrate Black students into "middle class" lives with "higher paying jobs," demonstrating how race-neutral assessments evaded issues of race that were present in test development (46).

In 1977, Geneva Smitherman warned about integrationist writing standards in *Talkin and Testifyin: The Language of Black America.* Smitherman (173) noted that portraying Black language as an obstacle to integration forwarded a reductive version of "correct writing," ignoring examples of ways Black English had been used profitably. She specifically condemned the use of tests to "predict the future of any individual test taker," and she advocated disciplinary activism against standardized tests, including the proposed moratorium on standardized tests to investigate racial biases and discriminatory applications of testing used to track Black students in special education and remedial courses (238). Smitherman (228) argued for a broader definition of communication skills, including "comprehension ability and reading skills, all of which are intellectual competencies that can be taught in any dialect or language," and for exposure to "materials written in other forms and reflecting other cultures." Specifically, white students needed to be introduced to Black communication—a theme she expanded later by studying white industrial workers' familiarity with Black English from their work environment (Botan and Smitherman 1991). Smitherman critically asked composition scholars to consider places where Black communication was both dominant and profitable; she resisted the presumption of white supremacy in workplace and other communication situations.

That is not to say that Smitherman was unconcerned with segregation's effect on literacy. In fact, she described how residential segregation brought white teachers from the suburbs to teach Black children—teachers who lacked proper linguistic training or familiarity with Black language. White teachers misunderstood Black literacy because of segregation. Reading Smitherman now, I think about how my own geographic movement from the suburbs of Atlanta to cities in Ohio and Georgia made me part of a larger problem of writing assessment that should cause us to look critically at what it means to value faculty expertise in writing assessment. Many composition scholars at the time agreed with Smitherman's opposition to the SAT and other standardized tests but promoted integrationist ideas in faculty-driven or locally developed writing assessments—tests that did not assess the broader, contextually situated notion of communication skills Smitherman proposed. This was another iteration of integrationist writing programs that promised to offer equal opportunity to Black students through bidialectism. But this time, writing assessment would provide a race-neutral measure of writing ability—the catch was that writing ability was defined primarily by white teachers from predominantly white communities.

Composition's ambivalence toward standardized testing reflects a tension we often see in the field today with respect to how much we should capitalize on political interest in writing to expand our discipline and access resources. Political investment in writing instruction may benefit the discipline materially, but it often forwards the ideological positions of those politics as well. Writing assessment scholarship probably did allow the discipline to gain some control over placement practices. However, this work often presented disciplinary knowledge as necessarily promoting fairer and more valid assessment practices, regardless of the faculty designing or rating writing assessments or the criteria used to evaluate a writing sample. This is why, critically, the form of the writing assessment is only part of the picture of racial injustice. As I will show, these efforts did expand the kinds of writing tests used in white colleges—as many composition scholars wanted—but as political trends made standardized tests more central to educational policies, these new writing assessments worked reciprocally with other measures of potential that gained political favor. New writing assessments were faculty-driven, but they were only allowed to the extent that they served integrationist ends defined by political actors in the state and university system. And when political favor shifted against remediation in favor of stratifying college admissions within a university system, these writing assessments became tools for institutional competition in ways white colleges deployed to maintain their institutional status.

"QUALITY OF INPUT": LITERACY STANDARDS IN GEORGIA'S DESEGREGATION PLAN

In 1977 and 1978, the University System of Georgia (USG) updated its desegregation plan, introducing placement and testing criteria that prompted debate over literacy standards at Armstrong and Savannah State. Following the ruling in *Adams v. Califano* (1977) and the revision of HEW's desegregation criteria, HEW solicited Georgia and other states for new desegregation plans designed to meet the enrollment and state-wide planning mandates of the updated criteria. In July 1977, the USG received a letter from the Office for Civil Rights (OCR), notifying the Board of Regents that it had sixty days to produce an updated desegregation plan that met the new HEW criteria (Oxford et al. 1977). The *Plan for the Further Desegregation of the University System of Georgia* (1977) described itself as an "interim document," essentially an updated version of the 1974 plan (Regents 1974)[7] produced under "severe time constraints" (I.1–2). State officials and the USG were described in the *Atlanta Constitution* as responding with a "'recalcitrant' attitude" (Reeves 1978). Their resistance is evident in the way the 1977 plan upheld academic standards by crafting policies designed to maintain the identity of the USG's most selective public white universities while emphasizing extensive remediation and testing requirements at the state's open access and four-year colleges.

The 1977 plan began by stating that the USG's "responsibility [to educate] cannot be abdicated in the pursuit of externally defined statistical objectives"—a phrase likely directed at HEW's required enrollment goals—and that its admissions practices were "predicated totally on academic criteria . . . without regard to race" (Oxford et al. 1977,

I.160–161). The plan then argued that "time will resolve the basic problem" of segregation in the university system, an argument that, not unlike *Alabama State Teachers Association v. Alabama Public School and College Authority* (*ASTA*), emphasized the need to remediate academic deficiencies in K–12 education to resolve the problems in higher education (I.184). The focus on K–12 educational deficiencies as the cause of postsecondary segregation continued to place Special Studies at the center of the state's desegregation plan. Still presented as the plan for Black student retention, Special Studies relied even more on the predictive power of the SAT in the 1977 plan. The plan maintained the composite SAT score of 650 as a requirement for regular college admissions at all institutions, as defined in the previous plan.[8] This cutoff score was based on the regents' "experience . . . that students below this level had little chance of success in college" (II.52). Below that score, all USG students were required to take a placement exam for Special Studies, which offered courses in reading, writing, and math. However, the 1977 plan changed its placement test, replacing the CGP with its own placement exam, the Georgia Basic Skills Examination (BSE), which the regents argued would "more accurately indicate the student's achievement level" (II.52). The Georgia BSE exam was designed to "correspond as closely as possible to the SAT total score of 650" in order to "minimize student classification errors due to error measurements in the test" (II.53). In other words, the 1977 plan placed most of the weight for admissions and placement on SAT scores' ability to predict student achievement. The placement exam was designed to confirm the SAT score.

In addition, the state allowed institutions to set higher admissions requirements than the state minimum and argued that transfer effectively facilitated access across the system. The 1977 plan stated that the USG's tiered system of institutions made the most selective and prestigious institutions (its universities)[9] accessible through admission to the lower-tier institutions (two-year junior colleges and four-year senior colleges) located throughout the state. The USG's thirty-two institutions (sixteen junior colleges, twelve senior colleges, and four universities) were geographically dispersed to ensure that two- and four-year degrees were available "within commuting range" of most citizens of the state (Oxford et al. 1977, I.8). Junior colleges offered the full core curriculum to facilitate transfer to a senior college or university. By emphasizing transfer as an access strategy, the 1977 plan promoted state control over "a coordinated core curriculum developed by all System institutions acting under the direction of the Regents' Office staff" (I.14). However, transfer was mediated by the Regents' Test, which, according to USG historian Cameron Fincher (2003, 74), was designed to ensure that transferring students met the same standards of minimum competency in literacy. Conceptualizing access through transfer justified institutional selectivity and placed testing as a guard at several levels of a student's college career—with the Regents' Test putting literacy competency, quite literally, at the center of college coursework. In this way, objective testing and direct writing assessment worked together to accomplish similar goals in the state.

The racialization of the USG's institutional tiers is evident in Black colleges' institutional identity as "senior colleges." While the USG did promise to upgrade funding, buildings, and programs at the state's three Black colleges (Albany State College, Fort Valley State College, and Savannah State College), the plan stressed that these three colleges should be treated "in keeping with their respective roles as senior college units" (Oxford et al. 1977, I.16). Not only did this mean that no Black college in the system would be upgraded to a university, it also meant that the regents would provide financial, building, and programmatic resources "on a basis comparable with those provided to the nine other senior college units which have similar missions" (I.16). Given that the USG proposed to distribute resources *equally* among all twelve senior colleges in the USG, this promise meant that no Black college would receive as much as a university-level institution.

The USG's approach to access was primarily defined through geographic location and transfer; although all institutions offered Special Studies, institutions were allowed to set higher admissions requirements than the state minimum, mediating the effect of Special Studies as an access plan. This definition of access helps explain why Special Studies was, for the state, a *retention* plan, not an access plan, a program to integrate students into college coursework for the purpose of ensuring an efficient system of admissions and placement. Yet the state's transfer and access policies, according to the USG's own account in the 1977 plan, originated in the 1960s when the state was actively impeding desegregation and many institutions were desegregating only under court order. Seen in this light, institutional selectivity, institutional tier (from junior college to university), and transfer policies were relics of resistance to desegregation that institutionalized USG literacy testing requirements.

RESISTING STANDARDS: OPPOSITION TO THE 1977 PLAN

The USG's proposal elicited some protest that Georgia was not adequately meeting HEW guidelines and instead was turning Black colleges into remedial institutions by reinforcing white academic standards. This opposition was articulated in a document titled *An Alternative Plan for the Desegregation of the University System of Georgia* (1977). The alternative plan (8), which remains anonymous and is archived digitally by Savannah State University, argued that the USG misrepresented system data to keep the "lily white" universities in the system largely exempt from desegregation intervention. According to the introduction, the alternative plan (1) was developed at a July 1977 workshop on the "Problems and Solutions to Problems of Poor People and Minorities in Higher Education in Georgia," held by "concerned educators, students, and other citizens of the state of Georgia."[10] Despite its unclear provenance, the alternative plan is worth discussing in some detail as a harbinger of contentious debates over institutional identity and literacy standards in Savannah.

The *Alternative Plan for the Desegregation of the University System of Georgia* (1977) first noted the limited nature of the system's geographic accessibility, explaining that universities were geographically inaccessible to those in the southern, agrarian part of the state, with all of them (with the exception of the Medical College in Augusta) clustered in north Georgia. In addition, the state had used geographic accessibility in the 1960s to establish three public white colleges (Armstrong, Albany Junior College, and Georgia Southwestern College) in close proximity to already operating Black colleges (Savannah State and Albany State), suggesting that geographic access was a segregationist plan. The alternative plan described this access strategy as "a deliberate effort to locate and expand white-controlled institutions of higher education in every large urban area of the state" (14–15). Meanwhile, universities maintained higher admissions requirements based primarily on the "culturally-biased" SAT (60). Repurposing the 1977 plan's data on test scores by institution, the alternative plan (60–61) noted that a 650 cutoff for regular college admissions would send roughly 75 percent of Savannah State College students and 80 percent of Albany State College students into remediation, as opposed to roughly 20 percent of Armstrong's students and 1 percent of the University of Georgia's students.[11] The authors feared that this mechanism created both "a new category of segregated students" in white colleges and a "dual system" in which Black colleges would become remedial institutions (60, 62). Given their higher admissions requirements, white universities would remain "untarnished and untouched by this responsibility [for remediation], with their obtuse, esoteric, and crypto-racist standards of 'quality' education rigidly in place" (62). The remediation and admissions standards were viewed as a racialized construction of institutional quality that promoted white academic norms.

The *Alternative Plan for the Desegregation of the University System of Georgia* (1977, 75) proposed instead that all USG institutions implement open admissions policies and allow students to choose whether to take remedial coursework—guided in this choice by "individualized evaluative counseling"—rather than a test designed to ascertain whether students felt they needed remediation. In short, the alternative plan proposed an early version of what composition scholars today call directed self-placement. The alternative plan also argued that all remedial courses should carry degree credit and that a student should not be able to fail the course but be allowed to repeat it until the instructor determined they were ready to exit. In addition to redesigning remediation, the alternative plan argued that white colleges should require all students to take Black studies courses in the core curriculum and to encounter Black perspectives in *all* relevant courses.

The *Alternative Plan for the Desegregation of the University System of Georgia* (1977) also singled out composition specifically for employing racial bias in the hiring process that influenced its curricula.[12] Hiring for composition, a "white-oriented discipline," might lead to discrimination against Black faculty (82). It is incredibly important, I think, that documents about desegregation enforcement viewed composition's disciplinary identity as white. The racialization of composition, according to the authors, was rooted in white colleges' definitions of composition expertise:

> Black applicants holding degrees in fields related to the Afro-American experience may be deemed less suitable candidates for positions in white-oriented disciplines than are white candidates with graduate work in fields of study more similar to those pursued by faculty members already employed. In fact, in the University System a candidate holding a doctorate in Chaucerian studies is more likely to obtain a position teaching freshman composition courses than is a candidate with a doctorate in Afro-American literature, even though neither candidate's graduate transcript indicates work specifically oriented toward the actual courses he or she will be required to teach. (82)

In other words, the lack of Black perspectives in composition allowed for hiring discrimination, as did composition's nebulous training requirements. By implication, composition was one of the key core courses desegregation activists felt should be redesigned to include Black perspectives on writing. While little historical scholarship examines composition's hiring practices as a means of perpetuating racism, this comment suggests that composition's disciplinary identity was racialized, defined by a disproportionately white faculty identity.

Although the alternative plan appears not to have been taken seriously by the USG,[13] its representation of desegregation demonstrates how visible writing programs became in the debate over desegregation—and the ways activists viewed writing programs as tools the state used to maintain de facto segregation through ideas about institutional quality and good writing. The alternative plan predicted, accurately, that literacy standards would result in the state prioritizing white universities in the desegregation process.

DEBATING LITERACY STANDARDS IN SAVANNAH: THE FOURTH SEGMENT OF THE REGENTS' 1977 PLAN

The problems with the regents' 1977 plan were obvious not only to its strongest critics but also to HEW, which rejected the initial submission of the plan and required the USG to outline more specific plans for its nearby Black and white colleges. The rejection of Georgia's plan seriously concerned the Carter administration. As the president's home state, Georgia needed to be seen as publicly cooperating with desegregation. Secretary Califano (1981, 248) described Georgia as his "top priority" in postsecondary desegregation. To address his concerns, Califano (1981, 248) set up a private breakfast meeting with Governor George Busbee, who came "armed with tables comparing SAT scores at the white and black colleges. He was worried that it would be impossible to integrate several of the white institutions without lowering admissions standards." From the start of these negotiations, Georgia used standardized test scores to measure institutional quality and control desegregation, an approach that influenced negotiations between Armstrong and Savannah State.

Eager to have Georgia publicly cooperate with desegregation, Califano and Busbee agreed that Georgia's plan would prioritize eliminating program duplication at nearby Black and white colleges. To craft recommendations for this process, three community liaison committees were established at Fort Valley, Albany, and Savannah. Savannah's committee, called the Savannah Community Liaison Committee, set up public debates and working groups in the spring and early summer of 1978, producing a report with recommendations to the USG. The report was then used by the USG to compose an addendum to the regents' 1977 plan, titled the "Fourth Segment of *A Plan for the Further Desegregation of the University System of Georgia*" (1978). The "Fourth Segment" included institution-specific plans for Savannah State and Armstrong, along with the other two Black colleges in Georgia—Albany State College and Fort Valley State College. In the process of debating their plans, Savannah State and Armstrong clashed over the role of testing and remediation in defining institutional quality.

The intense focus on institutional quality was prompted by the nature of the two proposed desegregation plans Savannah debated: either a program swap or a merger of the two colleges.[14] Although they represented different approaches to desegregation, either plan would affect the name of the institution listed on at least some students' diplomas—a fact that invoked students' attachment to their college's identity and community reputation. The first option considered by the Savannah Community Liaison Committee was a program swap, which would move one key program (either business or teacher education) from each college to the other but maintain separate institutional identities. The program swap would affect the institution listed on some students' degrees, but only students in those two programs would be moved to the other college. A program swap would affect only about 250–350 students from each campus who would be required to transfer to the other college ("Fourth Segment" 1978, SSC-14). The other option was a merger of both colleges into one institution (Savannah Community Liaison Committee 1978, 2). A merger would combine Armstrong and Savannah State into an entirely new institution, with that institution's name represented on students' degrees.

Both the merger and the program swap option required already admitted students at both colleges to move to the other college if they wanted to remain in the program. This swapping of students raised concern about academic standards in Savannah Community Liaison Committee meetings, which may help explain why the USG chose the program swap option that involved fewer students than a merger. As Gloria Ladson-Billings and William F. Tate IV (1995, 56) detail, desegregation plans prioritized white self-interest, giving precedence to plans that favored whites' choices and were designed to "ensure that whites are happy (and do not leave the system altogether) regardless of whether African-American and other students of color achieve or remain." In Savannah, this trend manifested in predictions that if desegregation required Armstrong students to earn their diplomas from Savannah State, which they perceived to be a lower-quality institution based on assumptions about test scores and remediation requirements, white students would drop out or transfer to nearby, predominantly white Georgia Southern College in Statesboro (Savannah Community Liaison Committee 1978, 387).

Fears of white flight were stoked by references to Armstrong's institutional quality, as defined by student achievement on standardized tests. For example, when debating whether teacher education should be located at Armstrong or Savannah State, Armstrong faculty prepared a report that used students' incoming SAT scores at Armstrong to develop *predicted* scores on the National Teacher Examination (NTE),[15] asserting that SAT scores were a direct measure of the institution's "quality of input," which could be used as "an indication of its expected outcome performance" for education students (Savannah Community Liaison Committee 1978, 170). Based on this interpretation of test scores, faculty argued that Armstrong's teacher education program had "a superior degree of program integrity" (236). The use of the NTE historically in support of white supremacy has been documented by Scott Baker (1995), who shows that NTE scores were used in K–12 contexts to justify higher salaries for white teachers despite no evidence of the NTE's validity in measuring teaching effectiveness. As Baker argues, the NTE fit with a trend after *Brown* (1954) to use standardized tests in the South to block desegregation and limit Black teachers. According to ETS data that Baker (64) cites, teacher testing increased 65 percent between 1955 and 1956. By the 1960s, many southern states, including Georgia, mandated the NTE and used it to get rid of Black teachers. Similar discussions of testing occurred during debates about the location of the business degree. Armstrong faculty predicted that only "probably 20 percent of the Savannah State students would be able to compete satisfactorily with Armstrong students," using national comparisons of test scores to argue that the academic differences of the two colleges constituted "an almost impossible barrier to integrating them in the same classroom" (Savannah Community Liaison Committee 1978, 291). These arguments suggest the extent to which white colleges used test scores to define their institutional identities and maintain control over programs during desegregation.

Comparisons of institutional quality using standardized test scores invariably invoked the recent change to Armstrong's admissions requirements (see chapter 2). Armstrong constituents justified the college's recently implemented SAT verbal floor score as a message to students about whether they could successfully complete a program at the school (Savannah Community Liaison Committee 1978, 424). The exclusion of students from Armstrong through this verbal SAT floor score signified Armstrong's quality. For example, one self-identified white Armstrong student commented in a student survey conducted by members of the Savannah Community Liaison Committee (1978, 389), "I know of people right now attending Savannah State, taking English because they could not meet the standards set at ASC. Armstrong has come a long way from the two-year college . . . I guess I am like most Americans. I want the best education I can get for the money I can afford, but I don't want to waste that money on a degree from a college with low standards and not respected as a qualified college." This comment indicates the extent to which white students viewed literacy requirements as symbols of academic standards that would, quite literally, pay off when employers evaluated degree credentials.

Other Armstrong students were less covert about implying the inferiority of Black students and Black colleges. One remarked, "I refuse to continue to attend a college which is willing to sacrifice its academic standards in order to integrate" (Savannah Community Liaison Committee 1978, 389). Another proposed, "I think we should keep our standards as they are and if [Savannah State] students can get in, good . . . I've found that the blacks in Georgia are slow to learn" (397). While not all comments by Armstrong students expressed such ideas, references to academic standards were overwhelmingly the most frequent objection to a merger with Savannah State. And while students valuing academic standards may seem positive, these comments were part of a larger community context in which, as Kelsey Kaylene Andersson (2006) notes in her study of Savannah's K–12 desegregation process, white Savannahians justified white flight from public schools under the auspices of the academic standards of private schools that not only lacked accreditation but often used the same curricula as the public schools. These comments valued academic standards defined through racial exclusion.

Given the centrality of literacy to defining white academic standards, it is no surprise that Regents' Test scores were used to measure institutional quality. Armstrong constituents cited pass rates on the Regents' Test to argue against the admission of Savannah State students to Armstrong. By the late 1970s, the Regents' Test had been publicly criticized as racially discriminatory, an accusation that would eventually result in additional Title VI violations against the state of Georgia (see chapter 4). According to one report, 37 percent of students at the state's Black colleges had passed the Regents' Test in 1974–1975, compared to 71.4 percent of total students (Crew 1977, 710). Students viewed the disparate pass rates on the test between white and Black colleges as evidence of academic standards, claiming that "many or most of the juniors and seniors at [Savannah] State have yet to pass the Regents exam whereas all students at Armstrong must take the exam and pass or upon their failures they must take additional courses before re-examination"

(Savannah Community Liaison Committee 1978, 405). Armstrong's Regents' Test scores and admissions requirements were evidence that Armstrong did not admit "people who are not functioning on a college level" (405). These comments further confirm Baker's (1995) findings that standardized tests functioned to justify white resistance to desegregation. Standardized tests efficiently validated anti-Black linguistic racism in defining college-level writing ability.

Savannah State constituents recognized that literacy ideologies were wielded to disparage the college's reputation. They sought to counter these negative representations by redefining literacy proficiency to include "proficient use of language in personal and professional operations," not just performance on academic tests (Savannah Community Liaison Committee 1978, 318). Faculty criticized the "comparison of quality programs" based on test scores as "subtle discrimination" (105). In keeping with their redefinition of literacy proficiency, Savannah State faculty argued for program assessments that measured program and institutional quality by student outcomes—"the progress and increments of growth experienced by its students"—rather than standardized tests (96). Measuring student outcomes accounted for both how students performed when they came to college and where they ended up—personally and professionally—afterward (71). These arguments assessed literacy achievement and program quality using contextual literacy practices.

Ultimately, however, negotiations in Savannah resulted in more conflict than resolution between the two colleges. By a vote of five (all Black) of ten of its members, the Savannah Community Liaison Committee favored a program swap in accordance with a plan presented by Otis S. Johnson, Savannah State's faculty representative (Stone 2010, 207). Johnson's plan proposed that Savannah State should offer unduplicated versions of all programs present in the 1964 catalog—the year when the Civil Rights Act was passed prohibiting discriminatory institutions from receiving federal funding and when the USG upgraded Armstrong to a four-year state college (207). However, the OCR and the Board of Regents made the final decision about which programs to move, resulting in the relocation of teacher education to Armstrong and of the business program to Savannah State (208–209). To facilitate this swap, the Board of Regents determined that the admissions standards at both colleges must be the same in the 1977 Plan's addendum, the "Fourth Segment." The submission of the "Fourth Segment" resulted in HEW's full acceptance of the regents' plan in 1978.[16] By requiring identical admissions criteria, the "Fourth Segment" eliminated the SAT verbal floor score recently implemented at Armstrong. The regents then raised the regular admissions requirements at both schools above the state minimum, requiring all applicants to have a combined SAT score of 750 for regular admissions; below that score, students would be admitted conditionally and tested for placement in Special Studies ("Fourth Segment" 1978, SSC-24). The goal of requiring the same SAT score for regular college admissions was to ensure that students could choose which college to attend based on programs instead of entrance requirements; however, instead of considering the concerns about the SAT's use raised by Savannah State faculty, the policy created a higher barrier for regular college admissions (see figures 1.1 and 1.2 for enrollment data). Furthermore, although Armstrong was no longer able to require its floor SAT verbal score for admission to the college, the college still determined its exit requirements for its Special Studies English courses, which it had recently increased. In November 1977, Armstrong faculty voted to require Special Studies students to pass an additional exit exam as well as the English exit test of the Basic Skills Examination to complete Special Studies (Stocker 1977).

Given the central role of test scores in arguments about institutional quality, it's worth examining the effects of SAT score requirements on students and the colleges. Overall, the USG Special Studies enrollment numbers show that Black students were disproportionately placed into Special Studies. In fall of 1977, 5,026 of 11,772 Special Studies students were Black (or 42.6 percent) (Nash 1978). In fall of 1978, 4,608 of 12,126 Special Studies students were Black (38 percent) (Hooper 1979). Perhaps more importantly, as table 3.1 shows,[17] Armstrong and Savannah State were disparately affected by placement requirements in Special Studies. Savannah State had nearly twice the proportion of Special Studies students as Armstrong had in 1977 and 1978, which meant it had to devote more resources to remediation—a program that was stigmatized and excluded from the regular college. Black students were overrepresented in Special Studies within the system as a whole and at both colleges. Armstrong was also generally able to maintain lower average class sizes in its reading and writing courses with these numbers. The reliance on testing resulted in disparate outcomes for Black students and Black colleges—placing an increased burden on both in the process of desegregation, counter to the *Adams* mandate.

Test scores became critical to institutional identity during postsecondary desegregation. It is unclear to what extent fear of white flight prompted the USG to adopt the "Fourth Segment" of the desegregation plan. However, the resulting increase in regular college admissions test

Table 3.1. USG Special Studies data, 1977 and 1978

	1977 Armstrong	1977 Savannah State	1978 Armstrong	1978 Savannah State
Total fall enrollment (% Black)	Total: 3,353 (14.5% Black)	Total: 2,641 (86.5% Black)	Total: 3,223 (12% Black)	Total: 2,229 (88.4% Black)
Total Special Studies enrollment, fall quarter (% Black)	Total: 404 (18.5% Black)	Total: 665 (93% Black)	Total: 361 (15% Black)	Total: 417 (98% Black)
Average class size, reading	15 students	31 students	15 students	17 students
Average class size, writing	21 students	27 students	25 students	19 students

score requirements at both colleges reinforced the importance of testing in predicting students' college preparation and exacerbated disparities in the impact of remedial policies. By 1980, when the desegregation plan was implemented, Armstrong's Special Studies student enrollment was about half the size of its entering first-year student enrollment; at Savannah State, there were three times more Special Studies students than entering first-year students (see figures 1.1 and 1.2). These numbers provide evidence to support Melissa E. Wooten's (2015, 60) argument that white institutions used testing and admissions criteria in desegregation as an attempt to maintain "the normative and cultural-cognitive dimensions" of segregation after *Brown*. When we consider the debate over institutional quality in Savannah, Wooten's theory seems to explain why literacy, testing, and remediation appear so frequently in reference to desegregation. Linked to reading and writing assessments used to validate anti-Black linguistic racism, test scores symbolized institutional quality for white colleges and mobilized white protection of academic standards. Even after the program swap, Armstrong continued to leverage its writing standards in ways designed to reinforce these perceptions about institutional quality and ward off a feared merger with Savannah State.

WRITING PROGRAMS AND INSTITUTIONAL POWER STRUGGLES AT ARMSTRONG

Concern about institutional quality prompted new writing program development at Armstrong. In chapter 4, I describe the program developments at Savannah State, as it was subject to far more federal scrutiny in the 1980s over Regents' Test failure rates, which resulted in changes to writing programs at Black colleges in Georgia. However, Armstrong's

writing programs grew in the years following the program swap, capitalizing off of concern about literacy standards. At the same time, interest
in maintaining Special Studies waned as many at Armstrong pushed to
raise admissions requirements. Because the program was tied to desegregation and stigmatized as remedial, Special Studies was considered
temporary. Armstrong's president explicitly associated Special Studies
with desegregation, stating that Special Studies and its associated tutorial programs "provide the essential individual help for the minority
students to adjust to this new environment" (Ashmore 1979). The temporary, minoritized, and separate identity of Special Studies lent support
to efforts to outsource remediation or limit its visibility on campus, contributing to the development of the writing center and a writing across
the curriculum (WAC) program to take on the work of Special Studies
and reshape Armstrong's institutional identity.

The fact that the USG viewed Special Studies as a temporary solution to a social problem is evident in an editorial by Cameron Fincher,
the director of the Institute of Higher Education, the USG's policy
arm. Fincher (1982) reported that the Governor's Committee on Postsecondary Education called for colleges to plan to phase out Special
Studies departments, which were renamed Developmental Studies in
1980. Fincher (1982, 3C) argued that to eliminate remedial instruction
in colleges, taxpayers needed to "spend more—not less—on developmental studies at the college level," but he prioritized new programs
that would "experiment with instructional methods and materials." The
USG funded alternatives to remediation as a means of phasing out such
programs. These events align with David R. Russell's (2002, 7) history
of WAC showing that such programs developed out of the "myth of
transience" of remedial writing instruction—the idea that eventually
students will come to college having already learned to write and then
remedial writing will no longer be necessary. This myth is tied to perceptions of writing skill as a reflection of social and cultural problems, such
as segregation and cultural deprivation, which require the assistance of
temporary programs—programs that are designed to be unsustainable,
requiring temporary assistance that from the outset is scheduled to end.
But in desegregation enforcement at Armstrong, we see how the myth
of transience is fed in part by the contradictory notions that writing
assessment can pinpoint a writers' skill level but that writing pedagogy
requires individualized diagnosis. Assessments were often supported by
writing faculty as means of disciplinary advancement, but they undermined advancement by capitalizing on political investment in perceived
cultural problems.

Both the USG and Armstrong supported experimental and "innova-tive" approaches to remediation that relocated remediation in different writing programs. Individualized tutorial instruction had existed since the earliest remedial pilots. For example, in the early 1970s, Armstrong operated the Academic Skills Lab, funded by Title III grant money, to support Special Studies classes (Ashmore 1972). In 1978, Armstrong had external evaluators for Title III funding recommend that the col-lege further develop the writing lab by expanding its instructional media so students could teach themselves—a promise that remediation could expand while also becoming less time- and labor-intensive (Ravan et al. 1978). At that time, the USG chancellor approved creating or upgrading writing laboratories at all USG institutions to assist with desegregation enforcement (Simpson and Oxford 1978). Writing centers were specifi-cally tasked with addressing the crisis of student failures on the Regents' Test that threatened the state's promise that the test supported deseg-regation through its transfer mechanism. Writing centers thus adopted the role not just of remediating students who failed the test but also of predicting and remediating "potential failures" on the Regents' Test (Bridges 1977, 26). Instructors were encouraged to refer students to the writing center, providing them with "sheets with their particular prob-lems noted" (26). Writing centers contributed to the surveillance of stu-dent writing based on faculty perceptions about who might fail the test.

Tasked with supporting the Regents' Test, the writing lab and an accompanying experimental WAC program grew at Armstrong in the 1980s, as the fate of Developmental Studies became uncertain. From 1982 to 1986, Developmental Studies experienced two department head resignations and a "change in tenure status for some faculty" (Burnett 1986, 21). Pass rates for students in developmental courses hovered around 40 percent to 50 percent, according to Armstrong's annual reports from that era (21). At the same time, Armstrong became increas-ingly concerned with its academic standards. Armstrong's president bemoaned an overall decrease in average SAT scores in the years imme-diately after the program swap (Ashmore 1982). In the 1982–1983 school year, Armstrong again asked to raise its SAT requirements, a request that was apparently denied (Burnett 1983, 4). The Department of Languages, Literature, and Dramatic Arts (LLDA) (1984) recommended elimi-nating English 98, based on the argument that "limiting the number of remedial students establishes and defines a new mission based on the premise that good students make good schools." The presence of remedial writing fed into faculty concerns about academic quality and demand for further use of the SAT to restrict admission to Armstrong.

These concerns about academic quality were specifically tied to student writing. A 1981 survey of Armstrong faculty, conducted by a fledgling WAC initiative, found that 67 percent of faculty felt student writing had declined in the prior decade ("A Survey" 1981, 1). One wonders why they even asked that question, since faculty almost always feel student writing is declining. Nevertheless, faculty cited the same error patterns found in the 1968 Academic Skills study: disorganization, faulty grammar, faulty punctuation, incoherence, incorrect diction, incorrect format, insufficient evidence, poor quality of thought, spelling errors, and vagueness (1). The 1981 faculty survey also found that faculty assigned mostly in-class writing and had not altered their assignments in recent years (1). But rather than address these pedagogical problems or educate faculty across disciplines about writing, the writing lab offered "individualized instruction and programmed texts" for students, who would work to "eliminate specific problems" in the lab "on their own initiative or following the directive of their instructor" (Nordquist 1982). These views of the writing center reflect Alexandria Lockett's (2019) theory of writing centers in HWCUs as an "academic ghetto" that is "a home for 'problem students,' whose performance of academic discourse has been evaluated by authorities as an obstacle to their self-sufficiency and social mobility." In the context of a white college with a history of resisting desegregation enforcement and racializing student writing abilities, the writing center's method of tasking faculty with reporting students as part of a temporary program of writing remediation echoes the Kerner Report's promise of "ghetto enrichment" policies as a stopgap measure until Black students could be fully assimilated into white spaces.

At the same time, writing centers provided a more welcome representation of the college's commitment to literacy standards than remedial courses did. When rumors circulated again that the two Savannah colleges would be merged, the department head of LLDA proposed expanding the writing lab, arguing that doing so would "place [Armstrong] in a good position to influence how communication skills ought to be taught" in the event of a merger (Crain 1982, 4). This argument reveals the significance of writing programs to leveraging Armstrong's institutional identity in desegregation. Along similar lines, concern over high failure rates on the Regents' Test at Armstrong became an opportunity for the writing center to enhance the college's status. Regents' Test failures maxed out Developmental Studies' resources, adding instructional costs and requiring last-minute staffing changes to cover ENGL 025, the remedial writing course for students who failed (sometimes repeatedly) the writing portion of the Regents' Test (Adams 1981). The writing center argued that it could improve Regents' Test pass rates and enhance Armstrong's standing in the USG by improving retention rates in the rapidly growing health services programs (Crain 1982, 3–4).[18] As a "low-budget, high-output" facility, the writing center was more efficient at doing this work than remedial courses were (Nordquist 1982). Furthermore, the writing center could adopt some of the work of other writing classes, including first-year composition, according to one department chair who increased course caps for writing classes on the premise that the writing center provided sufficient individualized writing instruction (Crain 1982). Faculty in the department observed that students were being "dumped" in the writing center instead of taking Developmental Studies courses (Languages, Literature, and Dramatic Arts 1984). In contrast, Armstrong's president felt the writing center had "blossomed into a valuable and well-utilized academic entity" (Burnett 1984, 20). The remedial spaces of writing centers reinforced not only white norms of "correctness" in writing but white colleges' institutional power as they sought to secure control over the desegregation process.

Similarly, the fledgling WAC program grew in an effort to address faculty concerns about a decrease in students' writing skills, in response to the 1981 study of faculty views on writing. The WAC program—an extension of the writing center—offered regular meetings, workshops, and a newsletter designed to promote WAC pedagogies to Armstrong faculty ("Writing across the Curriculum Newsletter" 1984). The WAC program earned broad participation across disciplines at Armstrong and was mentioned in the president's annual reports as a point of pride for the College of Arts and Sciences (Burnett 1984). As the program was described in its newsletter, WAC provided time-saving benefits. The newsletter assured faculty that "it was not the business of biology or art teachers to be teaching and correcting the basic mechanics of writing," but by assigning writing tasks, those faculty could improve students' writing "incidentally" ("Writing across the Curriculum Newsletter" 1984, 2). This representation of WAC validated faculty views about students' writing quality in the process of growing the program. Even though faculty were told not to correct writing mechanics, they were given responsibility for assigning tasks that would improve student writing. Such assignments increased campus-wide faculty oversight of student writing, adding to a culture of surveillance of student writing.

Following the program swap between Armstrong and Savannah State, the representation of institutional quality through literacy had tangible effects on the growth of writing programs at Armstrong, as Armstrong sought higher admissions standards and test scores. Elizabeth Bouquet's

(1999) history of writing centers notes that they grew as simultaneously remedial and technological spaces, designed to make students responsible for resolving their own writing deficiencies. The writing center methods of individualized tutoring and self-remediation represented writing instruction as a pathway to integration, offering equal opportunity to all students through individual efforts. As the writing center and WAC programs assisted remediation, these programs benefited from white educational norms used to define the college's reputation and the resources those norms afforded to white colleges through their higher pass rates on the Regents' Test and fewer remedial students. What literacy, composition, and rhetoric (LCR) scholars have to consider in this history is the ways the discipline has contributed to promoting the assessment of writing by more stakeholders—faculty across the curriculum, writing center tutors, and exam designers and scorers—without addressing the racial ideologies of literacy that persisted throughout desegregation. The field should be asking not how we can benefit from increased interest in writing instruction, but rather, how we can make up for the harm these programs may have caused by failing to transform literacy ideologies.

4

"WHO'S THE VILLAIN?"
Writing Assessment in Desegregation Policy, 1980s and Beyond

Before becoming a professor in the Department of Developmental Studies at Savannah State in the 1980s, Caroline Warnock[1] was a legacy student and alumna of the college. Recollecting the debates over whether to merge or swap programs to desegregate Savannah State and Armstrong in the late 1970s, she described her reaction: "As a citizen and as a graduate of Savannah State University I was not for the [program swap] in just a couple of senses. One was the fact that . . . they were taking education away from Savannah State University and putting business there. And we were in desegregation at a period where, if you're a white American, you wouldn't want to go to Savannah State anyway" (Warnock 2017). Warnock was skeptical that the program swap would desegregate both Savannah colleges, given the long-standing prejudices against Savannah State among members of the white community. She noted, "This was a period where you felt inferior at Savannah State University in a business degree, but then it didn't make education superior at Armstrong" (2017). Prior to the program swap, Savannah State's education program attracted Black students from across the state, but when the program transferred to Armstrong, it primarily attracted Black Savannahians who wanted to stay in the city and felt they "had no other choice but to go to Armstrong" (2017). Savannah State constituents recognized that racialized institutional identities played a key role in reputation and recruitment, regardless of whether HEW required institutional mission statements to remove references to race.

Like many Savannah State constituents, Warnock was concerned about desegregation's effect on the identity of her alma mater, and she particularly felt the impact of desegregation policies that required Black colleges to employ more white faculty (considered "minority" at Black colleges under desegregation enforcement). Black faculty had shaped Warnock's education, and desegregation changed that dynamic: "In the role that I played under African American professors, I felt they saw something

https://doi.org/10.7330/9781646422036.c004

in my interest to complete my degree, and they made that work for me. But then on the other hand when other ethnicities happened to come onto the campus, it was not the same" (Warnock 2017). Her recognition of the importance of faculty identity motivated her desire to return to Savannah State to teach. She explained: "All of my siblings attended the university. And I can tell you right now that I had fifty-four cousins and relatives that attended. It was just where we would actually have an opportunity, so it affected me becoming a faculty [member] there that I must have my wings cover these young people to become who they come to be. Not because you exhaust two or three terms in the Developmental Studies programs and go back home to whatever life is like in various areas throughout the state of Georgia, but to stay" (2017).

Warnock returned to teach reading in Savannah State's Developmental Studies Department in the 1980s, where she taught the Regents' Test—the reading and writing exam that became part of a national controversy over Georgia's compliance with its desegregation plan in the 1980s. Recognizing the obstacle the Regents' Test posed to students, she dedicated her efforts to improving their pass rates. According to her (Warnock 2017), pass rates in her courses went from as low as 30 percent to as high as 90 percent during her time there. Primarily a reading instructor, Warnock also attended workshops on writing instruction to improve her pedagogical approach when working with Developmental Studies students, shaping her holistic theory of literacy instruction.

Warnock's description of teaching at Savannah State in the 1980s and early 1990s reveals the ways Black colleges felt the inequitable effects of desegregation. By the mid-1980s, major newspapers warned of a Black enrollment crisis, with headlines like "Fewer Blacks Finding Way to College" (Richburg 1985a), "Declining Black College Pool Makes Desegregation Tougher" (Mitgang 1985), and "The Dwindling Black Presence on Campus" (Staples 1986). The media reported on the ineffectiveness of desegregation enforcement and the increased pressure it placed on Black colleges. Under President Ronald Reagan, Black colleges' desegregation progress was scrutinized. Adding to that pressure were threats in Louisiana and Mississippi to close or merge Black colleges to resolve contentious desegregation litigation. These threats became more worrisome following the court-ordered merger of the University of Tennessee at Nashville (a historically white institution) into Tennessee State University (a historically Black university), which resulted in a precipitous drop in white student enrollment from over 50 percent pre-merger to 7 percent post-merger (Warnick 1984).[2] In Georgia, white universities complained that Black colleges would prevent them from desegregating. The associate vice president for academic affairs at the University of Georgia stated, "I doubt that [desegregation] will make a great big difference as long as we have three schools in the state that are predominantly black. . . . Why would minority students come here when they would probably be more comfortable somewhere else" (quoted in Braswell 1983). Many Black colleges justifiably feared that they would be blamed for failing to desegregate and their doors would be shuttered. Black students would then be forced to attend white colleges where administrators openly stated that Black students would be uncomfortable.

This chapter describes how the intense scrutiny of Black colleges in the 1980s prompted new investment in writing instruction as a symbolic solution to the disparities between Black and white colleges. After a 1983 review of the state's progress, Georgia was cited by the Office for Civil Rights (OCR) for disparate failure rates on the Regents' Test. Interpretations of these disparities perpetuated the myth that Black students had literacy deficiencies and needed remediation during a time when selective universities increasingly sought to reduce or outsource remediation, adding to the stigma of large remedial programs at state colleges. Even though educational policy was moving away from support for remedial programs in most four-year colleges and universities, the agreement reached by the state and the OCR hinged on Georgia's promise to increase remediation requirements at Black colleges and to establish or enhance writing centers and writing across the curriculum (WAC) programs to support remediation. I argue that the disparate effects of desegregation policies on Black colleges' writing programs likely contributed to their underrepresentation in literacy, composition, and rhetoric (LCR) scholarship. As I show, remediation further racialized colleges, with white colleges raising admissions standards and establishing other writing programs, such as writing centers and WAC programs, to replace remediation. In contrast, state policies required remedial writing programs at Black colleges, favoring test-oriented curricula. Although Savannah State resisted this approach and implemented innovative pedagogy, the college's writing programs remained tied to remediation in official representations.

A "REAGAN REINCARNATION" FOR WRITING INSTRUCTION

In 1980, Ronald Reagan won the presidential election, in part by appealing to the backlash against desegregation and affirmative action that motivated white voters (Minchin and Salmond 2011). Many expected his administration to effect dramatic changes in the newly formed Department of Education (DOE).[3] Some hypothesized that he would eliminate the DOE entirely or slash its budget; others guessed he would end affirmative action and desegregation efforts. Many conservative supporters explicitly called for such action, including the Heritage Foundation, which published a report stating that civil rights remedies were "so far out of hand that it has become mandatory to discriminate in order to end discrimination" (quoted in Hasson 1980). This language reflected the growing belief that affirmative action disadvantaged high-achieving white students and constituted a form of reverse racism, validated by the *Bakke* (1978) ruling's rejection of race-based affirmative action. Feeding worries about academic decline, the DOE pivoted sharply on civil rights issues in education. As part of this shift, the Reagan administration moved away from remediation, supporting higher admissions standards and more testing, which it argued would motivate disadvantaged minority students to higher achievement.

The "Reagan reincarnation" of the DOE resulted in ambivalent outcomes for postsecondary desegregation (Connell 1981b). First, Reagan was unable to fulfill his promise to abolish the DOE, despite the stated intention of his appointed secretary of education, T. H. Bell, in his senate confirmation hearing (1981b). Once confirmed, Bell sought to "reopen negotiations" with states over desegregation plans to loosen the terms of desegregation (Connell 1981a). Following these renegotiations, North Carolina transformed from an example of resistance to a model of desegregation compliance (Stuart 1981, A1).[4] Supported by the newly appointed assistant secretary for civil rights, Clarence Thomas, North Carolina was allowed to keep some program duplication and abandon strict goals in hiring and student enrollment (A1). This hands-off approach was initially welcomed by some Black colleges, in the hope that it would stave off mergers or scrutiny over their unmet enrollment goals (A1). In contrast, civil rights leaders accused the Reagan administration of abandoning its duties to affirmative action, and their outcry helped avoid a complete reversal in policy. In 1983, the *Washington Post* reported that the DOE planned to comply with a federal court's ruling against states because, as Bell put it, the administration was "getting a pretty bad rap anyway about our civil rights record" ("Administration" 1983, C11). Caught between the push to end desegregation enforcement and public pressure on civil rights, the administration continued to monitor desegregation but maintained a hands-off approach.

This hands-off approach, however, appeared to worsen segregation and educational outcomes for Black students. The Black student enrollment rate remained flat (at around 10 percent of total college enrollment), even though college-eligible Black high school graduation rates rose roughly 29 percent from 1975 to 1981 (Richburg 1985a).[5] This stagnancy was attributed to many of Reagan's policies, including changes to affirmative action, rising admissions standards, a decrease in financial aid and federal funding to higher education, and a shift from federal grants to student loans that made students more reticent to attend college (Fiske 1982; Richburg 1985b). In addition, increasingly race-evasive policies perpetuated disparities in enrollment and funding. For example, between 1978 and the mid-1980s, white students received a nearly 8 percent increase in financial aid; in contrast, aid to Black students decreased by 4.7 percent (Richburg 1985b). Black students disproportionately enrolled in two-year colleges and in occupational rather than academic programs, and their attrition rates increased (Stuart 1984).[6]

Enrollment and retention declines challenged compliance with desegregation mandates, including for Black colleges, which competed for a smaller pool of Black students and struggled to recruit white students. By 1980, Black colleges enrolled fewer than 25 percent of all Black postsecondary students (Stuart 1981). As one report put it, there was an "intensifying . . . tug of war between black and white colleges for a dwindling pool of academically able black students" (Mitgang 1985). This situation exacerbated fears that state-funded Black public colleges would be "swallowed up by bigger, predominantly white state institutions" (Stuart 1984). These fears worsened when the US Department of Justice began to scrutinize Black colleges for failure to desegregate (Maeroff 1983). Prior desegregation litigation had focused on white colleges, but under Reagan, the Department of Justice's first desegregation citations were in Alabama, against HBCU Alabama State University, while nearby Auburn University at Montgomery remained predominantly white.[7] According to the *New York Times*, the suit was a response to "extended criticism by black groups over Mr. Reagan's record on enforcing civil rights laws," although its targeting of Black colleges likely did little to quell outrage (1983).

Debates over the dismal outcomes of postsecondary desegregation centered on whether the push for academic standards was racially biased. On one side of this debate were those like National Association for the Advancement of Colored People (NAACP) Legal Defense Fund (LDF) representative Jean Fairfax, who argued that "the whole climate of lessening concern for minority students" implied that "equality of opportunity was the enemy of quality" (quoted in Stuart 1984). On the other side were those like Clarence Thomas, who suggested that "it would service [Black] students if, instead of blaming the Reagan administration, we went back and looked at what is happening in grammar schools and high schools" (quoted in Richburg 1985a). These two perspectives on the Black enrollment crisis of the 1980s reflected the polarization over defining and measuring academic standards. As Kimberlé Williams Crenshaw (1998, 1383–1384) has observed, new polarization among African Americans portended the possibility of "the loss of collectivity among blacks" in response to newly formed class divisions, more "diffuse" and less overt forms of racism, and a strong belief in equal opportunity.

Faith in equal opportunity and socioeconomic mobility mobilized responses to "academic decline," evidenced by lower SAT score averages and literacy achievement indicators. The report of the National Commission on Excellence in Education, *A Nation at Risk*, decried high levels of "functional illiteracy" among "minority youth," whose illiteracy rates were postulated to be as high as 40 percent (Gardner 1983, 8). But instead of turning to the solution of decades past—remediation—*A Nation at Risk* called for educational institutions to emphasize grades, raise college admissions requirements, and develop competency tests or "rigorous examinations requiring students to demonstrate their mastery of content and skill before receiving a diploma or a degree" (19). These recommendations pushed for more testing at all levels under the belief that more academic competition would force achievement.

Following *A Nation at Risk*, the DOE, the National Assessment of Educational Progress (NAEP), and the Educational Testing Service (ETS) collaborated to publish the first ten-year study of writing skills—Arthur N. Applebee, Judith A. Langer, and Ina V.S. Mullis's (1985) *Writing Trends across the Decade, 1974–1984*. The NAEP reported on writing performance by nine-, thirteen-, and seventeen-year-old students across a ten-year period, finding inconsistent but generally low achievement despite increased emphasis on writing instruction over the decade.[8] Applebee, Langer, and Mullis (49) stated that Black and Hispanic students performed poorly "compared with . . . their White age-mates," but they noted that the study sampled too few students of color to generalize about race. However, they reported that Black and Hispanic students spent *more* time on writing instruction, on average, than white students (58–59). Still, the report concluded, students needed *more* writing instruction—so-called functional writing instruction (59). Interestingly, though, the report did not call for more remediation. Likely, remediation would not have been an amenable proposal for the new DOE. Reagan's educational initiatives proposed higher academic requirements and more testing at all levels. This approach deviated from the support for remediation of the 1960s and 1970s. Rather than strengthening remediation efforts, politicians cast doubt on their efficacy. For example, a Heritage Foundation report originally published in 1987 for conservative African Americans argued that colleges were "lured by federal money and by civil rights policies" to admit "students unable to handle rigorous academic training" (Gardner 1990, 46). These policies left "the traditional student population . . . deprived of the academic content and rigor a traditional college education historically has provided" (47). Remediation was effectively politicized.

Insofar as educational reports from this era promoted "basic literacy skills," they supported writing instruction; yet these reports made an about-face from prior decades by framing remediation as an ineffectual social program that should be dismantled. Instead, more strenuous academic requirements—more homework, competency exams, and higher college admissions requirements—would ostensibly encourage students to achieve. As scholars have observed, many public four-year colleges and universities that were previously open access raised admissions requirements and limited or eliminated basic writing programs in the 1980s (Lamos 2011; Soliday 2002). This was a complicated trend for states to navigate in the South, where remedial programs were mandated by state desegregation plans. The national shift away from remediation resulted in a disciplinary and institutional push for alternatives to basic writing, in which expensive remedial programs would be reduced or replaced through higher admissions requirements and other forms of writing support. Yet the *Adams* states had designed desegregation plans that presented basic writing as part of their major plan for Black student retention. By extension, basic writing programs and the institutions in which they remained were racialized. Writing program scholarship, torn between the ideal of access and the opportunity to expand the discipline, proposed new spaces for writing instruction that recast basic writing into writing programs for all students. This development largely reflected white colleges and white composition scholars, leaving a disciplinary gap in the knowledge of writing programs and racial inequities that scholars have since observed (Prendergast 1998; Jackson and Jackson 2016; Ford 2016; Lockett 2019; Burrows 2016).

WRITING PROGRAMS AS SITES OF INTEGRATION

With support for higher academic standards, the 1980s marked a period of growth for writing programs and faculty specializing in composition

(Mendenhall 2014). However, this disciplinary boom did not extend to basic writing, and fears about mainstreaming or outsourcing basic writing programs began to grow. Mary Soliday (2002, 110) argues that the era's increasingly anti-remedial political climate pushed remediation out of elite institutions and speculates that, in part, they moved into writing centers. Building on this narrative, Steve Lamos (2011) shows how the discipline shifted toward competency-oriented writing instruction and the mainstreaming of basic writing.[9] Both progressive and conservative voices in composition increasingly dismissed basic writing as either racist or ineffective. Many scholars consequently began to consider basic writing a form of segregation and called for "mainstreaming," or integrating basic writers into regular first-year composition classes (Adams 1993). Alongside such arguments for integration, however, a few voices suggested that basic writing had been unsuccessful at white colleges because they were racist. For example, William Jones (1993, 73, 76–77) described basic writing programs as "Jim-Crow way stations" for Black and Latinx students, but he argued for modeling new programs on Black colleges, which "have crafted programs of instruction and academic support that foster competence, balancing and juxtaposing course work, faculty mentoring outreach, and academic advising and individual support that may include peer tutoring and counseling by both professionals and peers." Jones argued that institutional identity mattered, shaping the way students perceived programs like basic writing.

Composition scholars did not broadly take up Jones's call to consider how writing programs functioned within a network of student support; rather, the push to mainstream basic writing and develop new approaches to writing instruction promoted the ideal of integration. These trends resulted in calls to "renovate" old remedial writing programs into new spaces that purported to integrate *all* students. In these renovations, writing programs maintained an uneasy relationship with external stakeholders' beliefs about literacy deficiencies and writing assessment, and their distance from concern for historically underrepresented student groups resulted in missing calls to investigate racial bias in writing assessment and ignoring racial disparities in the field's scholarship and labor.

Writing Centers as a "Growth Industry"

Although writing centers have a long history in US higher education (see North 1984; Lerner 2009), many writing centers developed in the 1980s—expanding or reinvigorating remedial labs established in the prior decade, often as an arm of the Equal Opportunity Program (EOP) (Greene 2008; Lamos 2011). Muriel Harris (1982, 1) labeled writing centers "a growth industry" in the *Writing Lab Newsletter* (*WLN*) but stressed that they were not yet "secure." To address this lack of security, other scholars, such as Jeanette Harris (1982, 1), proposed redefining writing centers in light of the fact that institutional support was swinging "away from concern for the basic student, the ESL [English as a second language] student, the reentry student, and the minority student and toward the traditional, adequately prepared student." She argued, "In order not to share the fate of basic studies programs that are increasingly being relegated to subordinate positions or actually abolished, writing centers must be integrally involved in a number of different programs" (2). In the 1960s and 1970s, funding for remedial efforts had supported writing labs as part of access initiatives related to open admissions or desegregation; amid concern about academic standards in the 1980s, writing centers recast their identities as spaces for integrated writing instruction to gain more security.

Disciplinary attention to writing centers was also growing. Started in 1976, the *WLN* gained wide circulation in the early 1980s. By 1981, the *WLN* had 900 subscribers, and the recently founded *Writing Center Journal* (*WCJ*) had 500 subscribers only a year after publishing its inaugural issue ("A Statement" 1981, 4). Articles in both venues expressed a commitment to basic writers but argued for resituating writing center work for *all* students. For example, Lou Kelly (1980, 11) stated that writing labs used to be "the slums of an affluent campus"—a referral site for students who failed exams. New writing centers were becoming sites for "individualized instruction . . . for any student who feels uneasy or hopeless . . . any student who feels inadequate when a professor hands out a writing assignment" (11). These students came "from diverse educational and cultural backgrounds and with a wide range of writing abilities" (12). Key to redefining the students served in the writing center was redefining writing itself, "not as a drudging academic requirement, but a fulfilling dynamic process . . . not as a product to be criticized and graded, but as a means of exploring and understanding their perceptions of the world" (19). The separation of the writing centers from the work of grading writing enabled an expanding definition of writing. Yet the argument for renovating the slums bears striking resemblance to the rhetoric of gentrification, taking a racialized space—Alexandria Lockett's (2019) "academic ghetto"—and redesigning it as a post-racial space for *all* students without considering how doing so reinforces inequities in resources, the normalization of white middle-class values, and the racialization of other spaces left out of or displaced by this renovation. Nowhere mentioned are Black colleges for which this redefinition of writing apart from "nontraditional" or "minority" students may have been neither possible nor desirable—a history that may help explain the lack of attention given to Black writing center directors and HBCU writing centers in the scholarship of the field (Valles et al. 2017; Jackson 2009; Lockett 2019; Burrows 2016).

The renovated writing center emphasized "individualized" writing instruction for all students based on redistributing the work of remediation to individual self-help tools. As Neal Lerner (2009) explains, the individualized method of writing centers swung between two polar definitions of individualization—that of experimental, hands-on learning and that of remedial clinics. Claims of integrated spaces blurred the lines between these two types of individualized instruction. Peggy Jolly (1980, 4) categorized the methods of individualized instruction as including "one-to-one tutoring," "self-paced instruction," and computer-assisted instruction. These pedagogies supported a "strict standard for competence in reading and writing," including two first-year composition courses and a five-part exit exam (4). Others similarly proposed that writing centers could build on their past successes with helping students pass writing competency tests by expanding to offer test preparation for exams like the LSAT and GMAT (Harris and Yancey 1980, 43, 46). As Marlene Cole (1982, 4) put it, the writing center provided "a place to go for special, individualized help," and the "remedial and developmental activities" helped support "a center to which all of our students can return time and time again for reinforcement and encouragement." While these examples certainly do not reflect all writing centers, they reveal how writing programs in several cases recast their historical role as designated spaces for the surveillance and testing of culturally deprived students into a new kind of self-help activity claiming to offer all students the tools to achieve equal status within this new space. In claiming to offer tools for success, however, the writing center was careful not to guarantee success, since its instruction was entirely separate from the grading and assessment of student writing elsewhere in the university.

Elizabeth Bouquet (1999) traces the ideal of integration in the history of writing centers to open admissions programs that offered instruction for nontraditional and traditional students together. As she explains, "If students did not need to be segregated—if a method were developed, in other words, which offered equal promise to both the strongest and the weakest student—then there would be no need for a separate site, no cause for treatments or cures" (472). Yet segregation is only by ability in this framing. Certainly, Bouquet gestures toward race by mentioning open admissions, a movement tied to demands by students of color for the desegregation of white universities. But the writing center's identity as an integrated site effaced racial differences in student writers at the same time nontraditional students (coded as non-white) were being pushed out of selective colleges and universities using the metrics that once placed them into remediation there. The stigmatization of historically underrepresented students' literacy would not go away with the changes in admissions; rather, those students would simply become more stigmatized as the writing center claimed to offer students equal access to writing instruction without acknowledging racial difference.

WAC as the Extension of Writing Centers

Alongside writing centers, WAC programs built identifiable spaces in scholarship and institutions beginning in the 1980s. In their history of WAC, Charles Bazerman and colleagues (2005) identify the late 1970s and 1980s as the early period of WAC growth, followed by professionalization in the 1990s.[10] During its early years, WAC scholarship appeared in writing center journals. Between 1985 and 1988, WAC was the most referenced program in the *WLN*, mentioned more than twice as frequently as first-year composition (Bell 1989, 2). As Bazerman and colleagues (2005, 25) note, "In many WAC programs, the writing center serves as the nerve center of the program, disseminating information to the university community and providing writing support and services to both faculty and students across disciplines." WAC programs helped writing centers distribute responsibility for writing instruction across the college curriculum. This placed the task of writing assessment in more faculty hands while distancing WAC and writing center administrators from grading and rating essays outside their spaces of instruction.

Like writing centers, WAC claimed to expand definitions of writing by offering instruction to all students in all spaces. Carol Peterson Haviland (1985, 25) described WAC as "an important extension of writing center activities." The growth of WAC in tandem with writing centers was "both cognitively sound and politically astute," because WAC "facilitates thinking/writing skills instruction throughout the university and establishes the writing center as an important resource for all students rather than as a narrowly-defined developmental resource serving only 'special' populations such as basic writers or non-traditional students" (25). WAC scholars argued that the integration of all students revived the instructional space for writing programs.

WAC similarly proposed a broader definition of writing. For example, Cynthia Stroud (1980, 1) described expanding the writing center's work across the curriculum by providing workshops for students that "dealt not only with basic skills—sentence structure, spelling, and punctuation—but with organizational skills as well." The center also provided WAC workshops for faculty, tailored to their departments' concerns about student writing. In these efforts, basic skills instruction and essay exams were a means to a redefinition of writing. Michael D. Chiteman (1987, 4) suggested that support for WAC programs often emerged from outside of English, "popping out of interdisciplinary curricular committees" that wanted more writing instruction. These committees' interests could serve as a basis for soliciting funding, describing the broader role of writing in the curriculum: "Our writing labs are no longer isolated islands in our universities. . . . When the student learns to write . . . he is learning to be successful in college and beyond" (4). These descriptions of early WAC programs distributed responsibility for writing among faculty and departments.

The expansion of writing across university curricula raised questions about the responsibility writing scholars had to ensure that linguistic discrimination and lack of knowledge of writing theory among faculty outside of composition would not harm students. WAC programs did provide an opportunity to change faculty ideas about writing, a fact discussed in Art Young and Toby Fulwiler's *Writing across the Disciplines: Research into Practice.* Young and Fulwiler (1986, 1) noted that WAC programs emerged from placement tests, competency tests, and other activities that required faculty across disciplines to participate in writing instruction. They stated that faculty across disciplines needed to understand that writing is a process and that students' writing problems stem from different factors, not just lack of knowledge. Indeed, Fulwiler, Michael E. Gorman, and Margaret E. Gorman (1986) found that WAC could change faculty attitudes about writing processes, usage and grammar, writing assessment, and other critical knowledge; however, this research did not examine race specifically.

The lack of attention to race in writing center and WAC scholarship in the 1980s was a systemic problem. Geneva Smitherman (1977) called for the field to address issues of racial discrimination in writing assessment in the 1970s. However, as Shirley K Rose (1999) found in her analysis of citations, Smitherman's work was cited only eleven times in composition journals (twice by herself) between 1977 and 1992; by comparison, Mina Shaughnessy's work on error received 199 citations in composition journals during the same period. Rose (200, original emphasis) concludes,

"To put this simply, we've preferred iterating Shaughnessy's concept of a logic of error or pattern of error to iterating Smitherman's description of the grammar of BEV [Black English Vernacular]. We've chosen to iterate Shaughnessy's description of the work we have to do as *teachers* analyzing *student* error to Smitherman's description of what we need to learn about the grammar and rhetoric, the history and politics of Black English." The focus on error in composition overshadowed a small but steady stream of research on race and writing assessment beginning as early as the 1980s but often published outside of mainstream composition journals (e.g., Spikes and Spikes 1983; Nembhard 1983; Powell 1984; Vasquez and Wainstein 1990; see also Brown 1986). In contrast, as analyses by Jennifer Clary-Lemon (2009) and Catherine Prendergast (1998) have shown, major disciplinary publications in composition referenced race euphemistically or metaphorically through the 1990s.

The few studies on race and writing assessment in the 1980s in mainstream composition publications largely reiterated the claim that faculty expertise in composition would solve the problem of racial bias. Roscoe C. Brown Jr. (1986, 106) reviewed research on racial bias and writing assessment, and he suggested that greater change for Black student writers would happen by "emphasizing quality education and quality teaching." Edward M. White and Leon Thomas (1981) published a frequently cited study showing that placement tests produced racial disparities. Comparing the English placement test developed by faculty in the California State system to the Test of Standard Written English (TSWE), a multiple-point usage test developed by the ETS in the early 1970s,[11] they showed that the TSWE was not a valid placement test for Black, Hispanic, and Asian American students because its score distribution patterns did not match the holistic scoring distribution patterns for racial minorities on the EPT (unlike for white students, whose score distributions did match). White and Thomas (1981, 282) argued that their method of direct writing assessment would be more "likely to produce more accurate distributions of scores, *at least in relation to faculty judgments of writing ability*" (emphasis added). They recognized that holistic writing assessment really only functioned as a valid prediction of faculty judgment of students. The question now was whether faculty judgment was itself racially biased.

Other scholars found that faculty evaluation of writing was racially biased. Research on racial disparities in writing assessment began to see wider publication in the 1990s (Ball 1993; Smitherman 1993; Redd 1992, 1993). One key publication that demonstrated faculty bias was Arnetha Ball's study showing that the organizational patterns of African

American students were penalized in holistic writing assessment. Ball (1993, 265) argued that these forms of assessment were "less than ideal" and called for ethnographic approaches to assessment, with "flexible" criteria and improved faculty training for assessment. Ball (1993, 265) viewed the recent push for direct writing assessment positively but argued that writing assessment must "define criteria and methods of assessment that adequately reflect diverse cultural and linguistic features as resources rather than liabilities." Ball's work represented an important move forward for writing assessment scholarship—one that questioned faculty disciplinary expertise alone as the solution to racial biases in writing assessment.

Perhaps it is unsurprising that today, work on anti-racist writing instruction flourishes in the field of writing assessment, given the role of placement practices, writing exams, and the evaluation of writing in debates over desegregation and affirmative action. Yet writing assessment scholarship on racial bias was not widely enough recognized by mainstream composition in the 1980s to inform the ways writing centers and WAC considered and responded to racist writing assessment practices, to provide the necessary tools for change. Instead, writing programs in the 1980s sought to renovate their identities in ways that did not equally benefit all institutions. As I show in this chapter, writing programs at public Black colleges in Georgia were penalized, as the state articulated new requirements in response to accusations of racial bias in the Regents' Test. The political context of this requirement further racialized writing remediation and the Black colleges that offered large remedial programs.

DESEGREGATION AND THE COMMITMENT TO COMPETENCY TESTING IN GEORGIA

In the early 1980s, Georgia faced problems that mirrored the national trends: downward-trending Black enrollment and stalled desegregation. By 1982, Georgia's overall college participation rates were the lowest of any southern state, a fact largely attributed to the low participation rate of Black and nontraditional students and poor high school graduation rates (Kiehle 1983). Georgia was 15 percent below the national average in enrolling Black students and 9 percent lower than the South's average (20). The state had projected that its university system would comprise 21 percent Black enrollment by 1982, but Black enrollment had stagnated since 1978, falling from 15.4 percent to 14.6 percent (Pounds 1983). Differences in the college entrance rates of white students

(38.9 percent) and Black students (18.2 percent) were stark (1983). Furthermore, enrollment was stratified by institutional tiers. In 1983, Georgia's overall public college enrollment was 81 percent white and 14 percent Black;[12] meanwhile, public vocational and technical schools were 72 percent white and 25 percent Black and for-profit colleges were 58 percent white and 33 percent Black (Marks 1983, 19). By 1990, Black enrollment in Georgia's public postsecondary institutions continued its decade-long downward trend, despite an increase in the number of Black high school graduates (Office of the Chancellor 1990). Georgia's desegregation efforts were widely judged to be ineffective (Al-Amin 1982).

These negative trends boded poorly for Georgia's scheduled desegregation progress review in 1983. In 1984, Georgia was officially cited for violating Title VI of the Civil Rights Act—again. In part, this violation was due to racial disparities in the state's Regents' Test pass rates. In an interview printed in the *Atlanta Constitution*, Reagan's assistant secretary for civil rights, Harry Singleton, described Georgia as "one of the most flagrant examples of not doing anything under the desegregation plan" (Sack 1984b). What Singleton meant was that a "lenient" Carter administration had allowed Georgia to overlook stark disparities in pass rates on the state's rising junior exam, the Regents' Test, which was required for all USG postsecondary students to graduate with an associate's or bachelor's degree (Sack 1984b). Developed in the late 1960s and early 1970s, the Regents' Test claimed to ensure that all Georgia college graduates possessed at least a tenth-grade reading and writing level (Schmidt 1984). However, students at the state's three public Black colleges disproportionately failed the test. Rather than redesign or dismiss the Regents' Test, the state and the OCR addressed these disparities by increasing remedial literacy requirements in Black colleges.

Although the Reagan administration's concern with racial disparities on the Regents' Test might seem inconsistent with its larger policy agenda, the Regents' Test was a competency test that fit the administration's preferred methods of raising academic standards. HEW was satisfied with leaving the test in place as long as it provided leverage for pushing Black colleges to "raise" academic standards. State and federal officials viewed the Regents' Test failure rates as a reflection of the literacy deficiencies of Black students and the failure of Black colleges' writing programs. New remedial literacy requirements and oversight added to Black colleges' concerns that desegregation enforcement consigned them to a remedial identity that hindered their growth and ability to recruit white students (as required by HEW). In contrast, selective white colleges were discontinuing open admissions, raising their admissions requirements, and moving remedial literacy instruction to alternative sites—reinforcing the disparities between Black and white colleges. The policies tasking public Black colleges with more remedial work may have contributed to their marginalization within a discipline increasingly moving away from an interest in basic writing.

Racial Bias and the Regents' Test Controversy

The Regents' Test had been accused of racism for years prior to the 1984 citations against it. Public controversy over racial biases in the Regents' Test began as early as 1977, when Louie Crew, a white professor (best known for co-founding the National Council of Teachers of English [NCTE] LGBT caucus)[13] at Georgia's Black college, Fort Valley State, published an article in *College English* detailing an experiment he conducted in which he took the Regents' Test. His essay for the test responded to an argumentative prompt: "'People who know too much are confused by their knowledge. It's the people who are not so smart who really understand what's going on.' Take and defend a position for or against this statement" (Crew 1977, 707). Crew (709) strategically mixed "poor white Southern diction and black diction" to show that essay raters lacked linguistic knowledge to rate the test reliably. The ratings, which ranged from a 1 (failing) to a 4 (outstanding), averaged to a passing grade but demonstrated a lack of inter-rater reliability on the exam (708). Crew (710) also critiqued the test's validity based on its inability to predict or correlate with other measures of writing of academic success. Crew argued that such tests might be used more appropriately to evaluate institutional effectiveness rather than individual writing competency. Using the test to evaluate individual students, he argued, continued a pattern of racist exclusion by denying students the right to graduate based on the results of an unreliable exam. Crew supported this claim by citing the director of the University of Georgia's Testing, Evaluation, and Career Counseling Center, who had publicly stated that "an increase of 1 percent in black enrollment is accompanied by a decline in mean total SATs by four or five points" (quoted in 1977, 708). Crew implied that the USG did not care about Regents' Test failure rates because Black student attrition benefited its white universities.

Pat Watters (1979) reported on accusations of racism against the Regents' Test a few years later. Consulted as an expert for the article, composition scholar James Sledd disparaged the test as racist and inappropriate; in contrast, the University System of Georgia's Special Studies director, Charles R. Nash (himself an HBCU graduate), defended the test. Nash argued, "If a large proportion of blacks need weaknesses corrected then they should be. It would be far more racist not to do that and just perpetuate the mess" (quoted in Watters 1979, 13). Complicating this interpretation of the Regents' Test scores, however, was the fact that so many college students failed the test, even though the test purportedly measured literacy skills below college level. From the beginning, failure rates across USG institutions were described as "discouragingly high," with a quarter of students failing on the first try and some institutions' failure rates as high as 85 percent (Fincher 2003, 74). Watters (1979, 10–11) reported that more than 30 percent of students failed on the first try and 50 percent of repeat test takers failed on the second try. In 1979–1980, the total failure rate was nearly 41 percent (Spikes and Spikes 1983, 111). Thomas E. Dasher (1986–1987, 13) identified similar numbers a few years later, with 25 percent failing the essay exam and 15 percent failing the reading section on the first try, although he noted significant institutional variation. These high failure rates were baffling to those who considered the test a minimal competency exam.

Limited evidence suggests that those failure rates did not correlate with other evaluations of writing performance. One institutional study at Armstrong looked for correlations and found that Regents' Test failure rates did not correlate with the number of courses taken at the institution (versus transferred in), SAT verbal scores, or previous placement in Special Studies (Stocker 1978). In fact, Special Studies students failed at the same rates (one-third of the population) as regularly admitted students (1978). The report also observed that "several students failed who by all academic indicators should have breezed through the exam. . . . The causes for the failure rate seem to be subjective. Some people who should have passed failed" (4). Such studies, like Crew's, highlighted the inconsistency of faculty rating, something subsequent research also found to be a problem (Lindsey and Crusan 2011; Johnson and VanBrackle 2012).

Evidence of disproportionate failure rates became public in 1983, when the OCR calculated racial disparities in pass rates. The *Atlanta Constitution* reported that the test disadvantaged Black students and Black colleges at alarming rates (Hansen 1983, 4A). At the state's three Black colleges, the pass rates were below 30 percent (19 percent of Savannah State students, 18 percent of Fort Valley students, and 26 percent of Albany State students passed). At the state's white colleges, students consistently passed at rates above 30 percent. For example, 81 percent of Georgia Tech students and 70 percent of University of

Georgia students passed. At Armstrong, 53 percent of students passed, and at Waycross Junior College—a small, predominantly white junior college in the state—the pass rate was 82 percent. Data also showed that "although black students are only 15 percent of students enrolled in the Georgia system, 57 percent of the students who have passed all requirements for graduation but the test are black" (1A). As a result, the Regents' Test came under national scrutiny for racial biases.

As evidence of these disparities became public, Black college representatives stated that they observed racial bias in the exam rating. The director of testing at Fort Valley State, W. Curtis Spikes, argued that test preparation or remediation had to focus on "teach[ing] the kids to write as if they're white. . . . We eliminate the kinds of things that identify they're black" (quoted in Hansen 1983, 4A). In contrast, state officials dismissed claims of racism. Chancellor Vernon Crawford insisted that the test was not "racially discriminatory" but instead was "educationally discriminatory. It discriminates between those who have the standard facility for English and those who don't" (quoted on 4A). It's unclear whether Crawford meant to say Standard English or whether he intended to say that Black students lack language facility, but either way, his comments demonstrate race-evasive understanding of writing and linguistics. Others cited the anonymous rating process, arguing that the exam could not be biased because it used a race-neutral scoring process to "judge the papers for spelling, grammar, sentence structure and organization," which ensured that readers had no knowledge of a student's race or a school's identity (4A). However, this assumption ignored research showing that essay raters infer racial identity from anonymous writing samples, associating Black writers with essays scored lower (Piché et al. 1978; Davila 2012).

Defenses of the test turned to its local and faculty-driven assessment. The director of the Regents' Testing Program noted that in designing the test, "the purchased national tests have been abandoned in favor of more topical, local material" (Watters 1979, 13). One after-the-fact reflection on the Regents' Test controversy pointed to the fact that "English faculty were directly involved in designing [the Regents' Test], determining the criteria, and establishing the testing procedure" (Dasher 1986–1987, 13). Furthermore, the test was defended based on the claims that students should "be able to use [the writing] process to their advantage given a time limitation even of sixty minutes" and that the Regents' Test offered "valuable opportunities to stress the need for Writing across the Curriculum programs on our campuses" (14). These defenses prioritized the test's role in promoting writing programs and faculty expertise over findings that the results had racially discriminatory effects. There is no question, however, that had the test widely failed that many students in white colleges, it would have been quickly abandoned.

The Regents' Test ultimately survived the scrutiny of the OCR, in part because Georgia viewed the test as politically important. Georgia's governor, Joe Frank Harris, felt so strongly in favor of the test that he publicly announced that he would take the OCR to court should it require the test's elimination ("Governor's Press Conference" 1983, 8). Members of the press pushed the governor on whether the test results were misapplied, asking if he would consider using the test as a diagnostic tool for improving programs rather than a competency test—a question that indicated public interest in program assessment (9). However, Harris argued that desegregation policy only required "removing any barriers that you have for white students to attend black colleges and black students to attend white colleges. . . . The Regents' Test applies to people after they are already in a system. That's not eliminating or prohibiting anybody from being accepted to go. That judges their ability, I guess, to be able to adapt to the situation after they are there" (13). Harris's remark reflected integrationist approaches to writing instruction, separating the system of assessment from its consequences and separating admissions from retention. In this view, attrition was always the students' failure to integrate.

Evidence suggests that Georgia officials may have known about validity and reliability problems with the Regents' Test. Unmarked meeting notes in Governor Harris's files from 1983 in the Georgia Archives indicate that someone expressed concern about the state's lack of evidence to defend the test (n.a. n.d.). The individual who transcribed the notes described the lack of evidence showing that the Regents' Test measured college-level writing abilities and the ineffectiveness of remediation for students who failed the Regents' Test to help them pass on subsequent attempts (n.d.). They also noted that Black and white students who had scored the same on the SAT had disparate Regents' Test scores, with Black students scoring lower and failing more often (n.d.). Alternatives to eliminating the Regents' Test were written down, including "institutional alternatives where disparate impact" was found (3) or conceding to the loss of federal funds and choosing to "clos[e] TBI's [traditionally Black institutions] and inject those funds into other institutions" (5). Although the notes lack identifying information for the meeting's participants, their inclusion in the governor's files provides additional evidence that the test lacked validity but had significant political support.

The state's defense of the Regents' Test speaks to the symbolic role of literacy in defining academic standards for politicians and white colleges at the time. The state government was strongly invested in maintaining the Regents' Test. Whether to impede desegregation, to enhance the perception of its white universities' academic quality, or to provide a metric for directing resources to its colleges, the intent matters less than the outcome. The effect of maintaining the policy was to consign more remedial work to Black colleges and Black students and to enact a high penalty on those who failed. What is perhaps most ironic about this fight is that Georgia was simultaneously involved in a legal battle after the University of Georgia, which routinely violated the state's remedial policies, allowed student athletes to stay enrolled past the number of allotted course failures, and passed football players who failed so they could play in a bowl game (Jensen 1988). A subsequent audit revealed that other white colleges—Columbus College, Kennesaw College, and Bainbridge Junior College—were also violating Developmental Studies policies (1988). The lax enforcement of remediation policies at white colleges contrasted sharply with the staunch defense of the Regents' Test and its remediation requirements, indicating that the test was not so much about literacy standards as about maintaining the existing racial order in higher education through surveillance and penalties disproportionately assigned to Black students.

Remedial Solutions to the Regents' Test Failure Disparities

With support for the Regents' Test from Georgia's governor and federal advocacy for competency testing, it is perhaps unsurprising that the OCR did not require the state to eliminate the Regents' Test. In its 1984 agreement with the state on the Regents' Test, the OCR concurred that "appropriate remediation" would be an acceptable solution to address racial disparities (Sack 1984b, 48A). As Singleton explained, postsecondary desegregation required "enhancement of traditionally black institutions," which he interpreted as adherence to the same standards as white colleges, stating that the Regents' Test failures reflected "the kind of education that kids are getting at the black colleges in terms of preparing them for the Regents Test" (48A).[14] This remark presented Black colleges as places where "these kids were being denied the same opportunities as the kids at the traditionally white institutions in terms of passing the test" (48A). The OCR viewed white colleges as the "standard" for Black colleges, a standard enforced through white literacy norms, as evident in the state's requirement for additional writing instruction for students who failed the Regents' Test and provision of $500,000 to the state's three Black colleges for compulsory remediation, writing centers, and WAC programs (Schmidt 1984).

Although the agreement emphasized remedial Developmental Studies courses, it also expanded the locations where writing instruction would be offered, providing new guidelines for first-year composition, writing centers, and WAC programs at Black colleges. The details of the plan are explained in a memo to Singleton from the USG executive vice chancellor, H. Dean Propst. Propst (1984) resolved that the state would now connect all forms of writing programs to the Regents' Test goals. Developmental Studies and first-year composition would coordinate to develop new "requirements for exiting developmental studies," aligned with the Regents' Test (12). In other words, the Regents' Test would shape the exit examination a student might take to pass out of Developmental Studies courses. Unlike the expansion of writing centers and WAC in composition scholarship and at Armstrong, the expansion of writing programs at public Black colleges was heavily controlled by the state and remained strongly tied to the remediation of Black students and the assumption that they came to college with literacy deficiencies.

The agreement further oriented other writing programs at the state's three public Black colleges toward the Regents' Test. In his history of the USG, Cameron Fincher (2003, 74) viewed the Regents' Test as a reason for "stronger emphasis to the basic skills of reading and writing in lower division coursework, especially freshman English courses." The extent to which those programs made significant changes at Black colleges beyond Developmental Studies is debatable, as I discuss below. However, Georgia's public Black colleges were tasked with developing shared "minimum guidelines" for first-year writing, including "types of writing experiences (timed in-class essays, long-term assignments), modes of composition, and number of required writing assignments per quarter" (Propst 1984, 16). The Board of Regents also promised to dedicate staff to work with Black colleges to develop more "standardized" writing instruction, "in line with the results of the literature relating to effective instruction in composition" (16). Ironically, this injunction represented Black colleges as places that lacked attention to composition scholarship even as it suggested that the state would enforce outdated composition pedagogies, such as teaching the modes of composition and assigning timed essay exams.

The remedial courses for students who failed the Regents' Test were required to coordinate with "reading and writing laboratories" (Propst 1984, 16). Furthermore, Black colleges were tasked with developing

WAC programs geared toward remediation, designed to support the "mastery of [writing] skills" and ensure that writing was "a responsibility integrated across disciplinary boundaries" (15). WAC programs were instructed to "teach the writing skills appropriate within their fields" and to grade writing "not only on the basis of content but also on the basis of effectiveness of form"—a directive that would take WAC programs in the opposite direction of mainstream composition scholarship (15). The state's directions indicated that Black colleges would be measured by the literacy performances of white colleges while paradoxically restricting writing programs at Black colleges to tasks selective white colleges were abandoning. At Armstrong, the writing center and WAC programs symbolized an escape from remedial identity (see chapter 3); at Savannah State, these programs were consigned to remedial status by state directives. This disparate treatment likely added to the insecurity public Black colleges felt during desegregation enforcement in the 1980s, as threats to merge or terminate them circulated. As white colleges renovated basic writing, Black colleges were forced to double down on remedial literacy instruction coupled with increased scrutiny, strict enforcement of rules, and lower valuation of their programs.

The funding directed toward the enhancement of Black colleges was attached to the development of specific pedagogies. The Regents' Test agreement provided publicity and funding opportunities for writing programs that favored auto-tutorial computer-assisted instruction for the Regents' Test. In its resolution with the OCR, Georgia announced a partnership with Control Data Corp,[15] which volunteered to donate thirty-six computers (worth $150,000) with PLATO software for laboratory instruction to the state's Black colleges (Sack 1984c, 1A). This "lend-lease program" promised to fulfill the need of "preparing black students for the Board of Regents' Test" (Bruning 1984, 2). The company anticipated that this partnership would result in "a long-term profit to be made by Control Data, by the state of Georgia, by the state university system, and most importantly, by those unnamed women and men who will profit from having the flame of intellectual curiosity fanned and fueled by our mutual lend-lease program" (3). That profit wasn't shared equally across those different stakeholders, particularly students.

The choice to provide computer-assisted remediation reinforced the notion that students were responsible for fixing their literacy deficiencies, an assumption that pushed self-remediation and devalued investment in faculty. Developed by the University of Illinois, PLATO programs were designed to "enabl[e] student 'self-teaching' of reading and writing skills" (Sack 1984c, 11A). The software offered a "drill-and-practice" approach to instruction, serving as a "medium for delivery of materials" to the student "in subject areas requiring knowledge of objective data" (Control Data Corp 1984, 2). One of the program's goals was to provide "individualized instruction for each student and remedial instruction when appropriate" (Murphy and Appel 1977, 20). However, one study of PLATO software showed "no consistent positive nor negative effects on student achievement nor attrition," finding that students used PLATO in classes less than expected and usage depended largely on the instructor (207). So, in sum, racial disparities on a test that lacked validity were resolved through a corporate partnership, using software without clear evidence in support of its usefulness for improving student literacy achievement. This resolution had the effect of increasing state ownership over Black colleges' literacy curricula and of seeking to do so in a way that pushed responsibility for literacy achievement further onto the student in the name of educational efficiency. Funding computers over faculty was a choice the state made in desegregation. Funding self-remediation over eliminating a dubious competency test was a choice. And these choices were premised on the depiction of Black colleges as places where composition pedagogy was lacking—a representation that was historically inaccurate.

STRATEGIES OF ADAPTATION IN DEVELOPMENTAL STUDIES AT SAVANNAH STATE

The Regents' Test controversy ultimately placed more pressure on state-funded Black colleges to conform to white literacy norms, forcing institutional comparison that cast doubt on the quality of literacy education they provided. These pressures continued to disadvantage Black colleges in the process of desegregation. Although cultural deprivation theory was no longer in vogue, it had firmly established the notion of race as ethnicity that, according to Michael Omi and Howard Winant (2015, 40), stressed assimilation to white norms through individual "bootstraps" effort. The pervasive view of Black literacy practices as insufficient for socioeconomic mobility framed Black students' failure on the Regents' Test as a failure of Black institutions—families, schools, communities, and language—rather than white institutions. The policies placed the onus for literacy achievement on a program for Black students to self-remediate, a temporary and politically volatile investment. These events fit within Melissa E. Wooten's (2015) overall analysis of the ways post-desegregation Black colleges were subject to the normative standards of white colleges that put their existence at risk; these pressures forced Black colleges to adapt their identities, programs, and missions to survive.

Savannah State dealt with pressures to accommodate the new remedial writing and Regents' Test requirements into the 1990s. At Savannah State, Developmental Studies adapted to state directives by resisting theories of individual deficiency and crafting spaces for community engagement within the program. As the Developmental Studies department addressed state policies, it crafted a writing pedagogy that emphasized social responsibility and community engagement with an eye toward addressing the retention concerns scrutinized by the state. This history suggests that writing programs at Black colleges may not be visible in the spaces where LCR histories have typically looked for WPAs or composition pedagogies. It also suggests that archival records of Black colleges' writing programs may be less robust than the programs actually were.

During this era, Savannah State struggled with the effect of desegregation policies on enrollment rates, which fell from 2,229 students in fall 1978 to 2,112 in fall 1980 (Cheek 1981). However, the college did successfully increase white student enrollment, which rose from 103 students in 1975 to 402 in 1980 (1981). Despite this success in meeting HEW requirements, Savannah State's enrollment and retention rates received significant scrutiny. In 1983, the Citizens Committee on Higher Education recommended turning Savannah State and Armstrong into a two-year junior college and a four-year senior college, respectively (McFarland 1983). The committee was concerned about "the large number of students who fail to complete a full four-year stint at [Savannah State]" (1983). Perhaps unsurprisingly, the committee made no mention of the Regents' Test's role in attrition. While public scrutiny blamed Savannah State for retention problems, several policies disadvantaged the college, including limits on the number of terms students could take Developmental Studies courses, requirements to sit out after repeat failures on the Regents' Test, and higher admissions requirements that flagged more students for remediation placement.

In the face of such challenges, Developmental Studies worked to improve retention and destigmatize placement into the program. Although faculty described a lack of recognition for the program in the 1970s, the 1980s marked a new era as a new department head sought to address the stigmatization of the program, which "consistently served over one-half of each in-coming freshman class" (Maynor n.d., 4–5). With the new department head's work, faculty in the program expanded "all over campus, participating in every facet of college life, serving on various committees and often functioning in key roles" (5).

The department's mission was explicitly social, committed to the college's historical mission "to encourage and assist the remediation of rising expectations among disadvantaged Americans" (8). The focus on improving one's writing extended beyond the notion of individual deficiencies. Developmental Studies pedagogy focused on mitigating the stigma of remediation by providing opportunities for students to participate in the discourse about their education and to write critically and creatively. As the English coordinator put it, an individual's struggle in writing depended on context: "Very often persons who are highly educated in one field find that they do not readily comprehend the jargon of another field. Each discipline seems to have not only its specialized vocabulary but also its own style of organizing statements. It is therefore not surprising that many students become very discouraged when trying to follow the ideas in textbooks and the lectures of their professors" (quoted in Pazant 1984, 1). Similarly, Warnock described how teaching awareness of disciplinary context was part of reading instruction in Developmental Studies. She recollected, "We would have [students] reading other academic readings. Like, if you don't have biology as your major, let me see how you might read a biology text. So we'd pull a biology text, we'd pull a history text, we'd pull narratives from classics, and so forth" (quoted in 1984, 1). These pedagogical approaches resisted treating students as individually deficient, acknowledging the contextual nature of reading and writing in the successful completion of literacy tasks.

Although the course bulletin during this time described Developmental Studies as focused on grammar, usage, and paragraph and essay development, the English coordinator described the program's pedagogy as a combination of rhetoric and writing theories, reflecting composition scholarship in the 1980s. The coordinator outlined five "writing competencies" taught in Developmental Studies:

> 1) The ability to conceive ideas about a topic for the purpose of writing. 2) The ability to organize, select, and relate ideas and to outline and develop them in coherent paragraphs. 3) The ability to write Standard English sentences with correct sentence structure, verb forms, punctuation, capitalization, plural forms and other matters of mechanics, word choice, and spelling. 4) The ability to vary one's writing style, including vocabulary and sentence structure, for different readers and purposes. 5) The ability to improve one's own writing by restructuring, correcting errors, and rewriting. (Pazant 1984, 1–2)

The first four learning outcomes corresponded to the rhetorical canons of invention, arrangement, style, and delivery; the fifth learning outcome integrated writing process knowledge, including the ability to assess, revise, and edit one's own writing.

In keeping with this rhetorical emphasis, Developmental Studies created audiences for students' writing rather than treating writing as an individual competence. A 1986 issue of its annual student magazine, *Impressions, Insights, and Images*, published poems about slavery, racial injustice, Black motherhood, class disparities, and inequality. The publication strived to "giv[e] students a voice to articulate concerns and an audience to listen" and was distributed at Savannah State and to "sister institutions" to provide students with a wide audience (Maynor n.d., 11). In addition to publishing student writing for this purpose, Developmental Studies also held meetings for students, staff, and faculty to come together "to address germane issues and to air grievances 'for the order of the good'" (11). These activities offered students an opportunity to interrogate their placement and define a role for their writing.

Retention remained a major focus for Developmental Studies, in an effort to deflect criticism of retention rates that threatened the existence of the college. In 1985, the department was recognized by the National Directory of Exemplary Developmental Programs of the Center for Developmental Studies at Appalachian State University (Maynor n.d., 8). From 1986 to 1989, students who exited the Developmental Studies program "performed just as well as the regularly admitted students in standard curriculum courses for which Developmental Studies courses are prerequisites, including English" (9–10). Furthermore, although first-year attrition rates of Developmental Studies students at Savannah State were similar to those at other USG units, the *multi-year* retention rates for Developmental Studies students were better than those at other USG units almost every year from 1985 through 1989 (9–10). According to the departmental history, retention efforts depended on "removing 'threat' from the learning environment" and creating "positive faculty-student interaction" (12). Faculty also understood that learning environments shape "students' self-efficacy," which "affects their acquisition of cognitive skills" and influences whether students "persist in and beyond the program" (12). These pedagogical emphases acknowledged that factors outside of individual cognitive ability affect student performance.

Prior to the Regents' Test controversy, many faculty and students at Savannah State felt that the test served a rhetorical and political function. An article in the student newspaper, *Tiger's Roar*, reported interviews with several students about their perspectives. One student argued that positive scores might serve as evidence to counter representations of Savannah State as "an inadequate school," a representation the student saw portrayed in "numerous articles written [stating] that Savannah State graduates can not write a decent sentence" (Glover 1977). This argument recognized the way literacy assessments were often used to disparage the educational quality of Black colleges. Other students critiqued the essay prompts, saying they were "not easy to write on because they are not in tune with the happenings of today"—a comment that hinted at possible reasons behind high failure rates on the test (3). Although views on the fairness and validity of the test differed, students agreed it should be used only to improve student learning, not for institutions "to gain a good record" and not as a goal for writing courses. In 1981, a study found that 87.5 percent of students felt the Regents' Test provided "motivation for improved writing" that was "beneficial" (Rayburn and Millege 1981, E-16). Thus, the test was viewed critically, with an awareness of its social meaning and uses.

However, state policies presented structural barriers to graduation. One report from 1990 noted that attrition rates for fall quarter entering students were as high as 39.4 percent (Douglas 1993, 24). Warnock (2017) noted the detrimental effect of the USG's policy that students who failed the remedial exit tests three quarters in a row had to sit out from college entirely, which caused their learning to "regress." Those students sent home went back to work. "Imagine how many will return," Warnock (2017) explained. "I live in a rural community. I need to help my parents. They sent me off to get into college to work, not to sit out a quarter." Warnock recalled one exceptionally persistent student who failed the Regents' Test twenty times until, finally, Warnock (2017) "gave her an ultimatum. Go back home to Ty Ty, Georgia, where she was from, or stay here and work with me." That student ultimately passed, but Warnock noted how the test blocked students not just from graduating but also from attending classes. She explained, "Now think about this, Annie. You're a young person. If you sat out, would you responsibly continue practicing and preparing yourself to be successful? That sitting out took them back to regress" (2017). For Warnock, strict testing policies detracted from students' learning; they did not motivate higher achievement.

According to one account, Savannah State increased its focus on getting students to pass exit tests as a result of pressure over retention rates and from "major corporations . . . raising questions about the quality of instruction" (Douglas 1993, 24). As a result of high remedial placement and attrition rates, the college increasingly relied on computer-assisted remediation to manage students' workload. However, the college encountered obstacles of access to and experience with computer technology. In the late 1980s and early 1990s, the effect of the state's agreement with Control Data Corp was minimal. Although PLATO programs were used at Savannah State (Testing Center 2017), Warnock did not recall computer-assisted remediation having much of a presence in Developmental Studies. Faculty offices were not equipped with computers, and her students lacked the experience with using computers that Warnock had. Her observations are consistent with research suggesting that HBCUs have historically been affected by inequities in digital and technological resources (Hill 2012). Spikes and Spikes (1983) similarly made no mention of computer-assisted remediation in their account of remedial writing instruction for those who failed the Regents' Test at Fort Valley State College, another public Black college in Georgia. First author W. Curtis Spikes is quoted above as stating that his program had to teach students to write white to pass. Spikes and Spikes note that repeat test takers at Fort Valley had high failure rates on the Regents' Test. Their program successfully piloted a method for Regents' Test remediation that quantitatively analyzed students' writing errors (using a corpus of Regents' Test essays) and then required students to take daily in-class writing exams. Thus, the Regents' Test promoted an error-focused pedagogy, even when faculty were aware of the racial biases in the test's assessment.

This error-based pedagogy influenced computer-assisted remediation when it was offered at Savannah State, as described in the *Journal of Developmental Education*. Michael A. Douglas (1993, 26) described computer-assisted remediation as "effective in helping developmental studies students learn how to decode a standardized English placement test and in helping the instructor to implement course objectives that require highly repetitive tasks inherent in the learning of basic writing skills, grammar, usage, and punctuation." This auto-tutorial method was as much a function of resources as of pedagogy: "Due to the large number of students enrolled in Developmental Studies English classes, program assistants and tutoring often cannot be made available at examination time for traditional one-to-one tutorials on test-taking skills or for the administration of practice tests and the timely evaluation of results" (25). Douglas's observation about the high enrollment in remedial courses indicates that the negative effects of desegregation policies on institutional resources at the state's Black colleges extended well over a decade after the initial implementation of the state's plan.

The development of the writing center and WAC programs remained either minimally visible or largely associated with remediation at

Savannah State in representations of the curriculum. Founded in 1979 as an addition to the existing reading lab (Maynor n.d., 5), the writing center was associated with remediation by students and faculty, who, in a 1981 survey, "rated the English Writing Center fair to good in helping students overcome their weaknesses in writing 'Standard English,' as did alumni who had used its services" (Rayburn and Millege 1981, E-16). Indeed, references to the writing lab in college materials focused primarily on remediation. Although the lab had a "technician" as early as 1981, its first mention in the college bulletin did not occur until 1989, where the writing lab was described as a component of ENG 098—a "laboratory oriented course," one of the remedial courses taken prior to first-year composition. ENG 098 included both classroom and laboratory time in its instructional methods (Savannah State College 1989, 237). A WAC program also merited brief mention that same year as part of a computer science course, Introduction to WordPerfect, a class offered to "help the student in writing across the curriculum" (196). The writing center and WAC programs remained less visible than the remedial requirements in institutional literature, perhaps because desegregation enforcement tied those programs to remediation, limiting the scope of their public identities.

Developmental Studies received greater attention in various public documents through the 1990s. In the 1998 *Bulletin*, the writing center was briefly mentioned for its relationship to the Regents' Test and remediation. The *Bulletin* noted, "All entering first-time freshmen are required to sit for the Writing Assessment. The Writing Assessment will be used to (1) determine which regularly admitted students need to be directed to the Writing Center for assistance; (2) to identify early test-takers of the Regents' Test, a comprehensive test of reading and writing skills which all students must pass (see Regents testing section of this document); and (3) to identify students ready for honors English (see Honors section). The Writing Assessment is also used to assess the entry level writing skills of students who place into remedial/Learning Support English" (Savannah State University 1998, 26). Another remedial course, READ 0099, referenced WAC in relation to the course's content but also emphasized that the course was geared toward helping students pass the Compass exam (the state's updated placement exam, also used as an exit exam). Furthermore, the course relied heavily on lab work, noting that 40 percent of scheduled class time would occur in the lab (246). The remedial courses may, however, still have found ways to engage students with community issues, noting that remedial students would write about "current events" (246).

As the discipline of composition argued to build identities for the writing center and WAC programs outside of remediation, desegregation policies influenced the continual association of such programs with remediation at Savannah State. Of course, the Developmental Studies program had crafted a valued institutional presence that used literacy to engage students in social and cultural issues and to teach rhetorical and writing process knowledge. In fact, Savannah State had tried very early on to implement WAC Special Studies classes as early as the late 1970s (see table 2.1). These early efforts may have followed the robust programs for WAC at Spelman and in other HBCUs since the late 1970s (Palmquist et al. 2020). However, the public identity of WAC and the writing center at the college was constrained by desegregation enforcement policies, which influenced the curriculum for years afterward. Even when faculty recognized racial biases in the Regents' Test, they had to focus on Standard English and mechanics to improve students' pass rates. The same policies that allowed white colleges to cultivate a robust disciplinary identity for composition beyond basic writing limited the ability of faculty and programs at public HBCUs to gain disciplinary representation with heavy workloads in remedial writing courses.

"HAVE WE REALLY PREPARED THEM?"

In reflecting on her career at Savannah State in the period following the Regents' Test controversy, Warnock indicated that these policies shaped the way she taught. Warnock (2017) recalled telling her Developmental Studies students to listen to the news to help them internalize Standard English for the purposes of passing their reading and writing exit exams. Yet she regretted this approach in retrospect, stating:

> I did wrong, because these youngsters are coming through from various places, prepositions, git, gat, whatever. And you hear all that and have no sense of Standard English. So why are we teaching Standard English? Can't we just teach English and it could be an amalgamation of Black English, Standard English, you know, whatever. Maybe, in this answer of responding here I want to tell you about the youngsters who came from a Gullah dialect, Gullah Geechee. They spoke Gullah Geechee in the home, but they had to code switch when they come to the classroom. So I had to understand that student. The Board of Regents and the legislators and all who pushed on this test, they are not there. They don't understand that, but I have to understand. And being an African American teacher, I certainly can appreciate assisting and taking patience. (2017)

Warnock argued that policymakers' curricular decisions were limited by their lack of experience working with students and their lack of knowledge of language and literacy.

Although Warnock (2017) increased the pass rates for her Developmental Studies students, she questioned the testing requirements—especially in writing—for the way they failed to reflect the processes of writing. She explained:

> Say if you had a candidate that was high in math, but because you couldn't get the reading and English[,] that hindered them from advancing. . . . If you are good at math, you are surely a good math scholar, but then when it comes to writing, you might have some little situations where you need to get a colleague or a friend or a peer to help you with your writing. And, you think back in 1890 at Harvard University they had developmental studies. But they worked at preparing the student to be successful, not worked it where it infringed on you continuing to get a college degree. (2017)

Warnock's comment hints at the different privileges afforded to remedial students in different racialized institutional contexts, contrasting the remedial obstacles at Savannah State with the belief of Harvard faculty that remedial students could be, as Kelly Ritter (2009, 96) explains in her history of the Harvard program, "groom[ed] . . . as gracious gentlemanly scholars who would represent Harvard to the academic and general public." In contrast, students in these programs were asked to pass a minimal literacy test, a feat that afforded no broader public identity and merely stood as a check on graduation. The ideas about the history of basic writing were critical to Warnock's holistic view of literacy instruction, which prompted her to enroll in workshops on writing, including one about Mina Shaughnessy's work and its applications for speakers of Black English.[16] Describing the importance of these workshops to her teaching, Warnock (2017) argued that typical patterns of responding to student writing were ineffective, stating: "When I red their papers—red, R.E.D.—all over and say nothing to you [about] how to correct that, who's the villain? It doesn't work when you're trying to help the students get into college." She connected this style of writing assessment to the entire system of curricular instruction that disadvantaged students on tests. She explained, "So we know that in the public sector in Georgia most often it was Comp Lit [composition and literature courses]. Where was the grammar? Grammar was on the Developmental Studies Compass test. Grammar was on the Regents' exit test. So here we are, saying that we are preparing them, but have we really seriously prepared them?" This question points to the alignment of pedagogy, assessment, and curricular structure that must occur for student success.

Warnock's experience contributes to the rich history of writing programs at HBCUs, which David F. Green Jr. (2016, 2019) argues the field should incorporate in its theories of pedagogy and assessment. Building on Geneva Smitherman's theory of the "push-pull" view of literacy among African Americans,[17] Green (2016, 154) explains that HBCUs historically taught students to be aware of "dominant, white language norms" even as they pushed students to use language for social justice and activism. Similar articulations of HBCUs' contributions to writing scholarship occur in histories of private Black colleges (Bell-Scott et al. 1991; Zaluda 1998; Cheramie 2004; Gold 2008; Jarratt 2009; Mendelsohn 2017). However, as a public Black college, Savannah State, whose existence has been frequently threatened by desegregation litigation and constrained by state policies that reinforce the norms of white colleges, applied its "push-pull" approach to literacy instruction to its programmatic philosophy—recognizing when state policies established harmful assessment norms and resisting those norms through critical pedagogy to support student retention. Hope Jackson and Karen Keaton Jackson (2016) detail similar trends in their account of another public HBCU, Cheyney University. Despite restrictions, public HBCUs like Savannah State have found meaningful ways to engage students in the social mission of the college, even though this work exacted a real cost on representation in LCR scholarship. The discipline has much work to do to enact remedies for these historical disparities.

CODA

Reflecting on desegregation at Savannah's two colleges, University System of Georgia (USG) chancellor George L. Simpson (1977, 8) declared in a letter to Office for Civil Rights (OCR) director David Tatel: "The long term inappropriateness of maintenance of this situation is evident; however, the short and immediate term interests of the Savannah State College and Armstrong State College constituencies must be considered." Simpson's remark foreshadowed decades of uncertainty over the future of Savannah State and Armstrong. Since the 1980s, rumors of a merger have circulated in Savannah. Those rumors were somewhat put to rest in 2018 when Armstrong was consolidated with Georgia Southern University in Statesboro, Georgia, roughly 60 miles away.[1] Maintaining its autonomy, Savannah State's enrollment has doubled in recent decades, from 2,199 in 2000 to 4,429 in 2017; however, sequential years of enrollment declines resulted in state budget cuts in 2019 (Meyer 2019). The fluctuating fates of Savannah's two public universities reflect the ambiguous achievements of postsecondary desegregation for formerly segregated institutions.

In 1988, renewed state interest in merging Armstrong and Savannah State prompted a feasibility report that found that both colleges' enrollments had not recovered from the program swap and that the number of Black teacher education students enrolled at Armstrong had declined (Propst 1988). What ultimately prevented a merger was the petition of Savannah State's alumni, who successfully persuaded Chancellor H. Dean Propst (5–6) that Black colleges were important historical institutions that provided "a social, a cultural, a political, and an intellectual oasis in a broader society that either did not or seemed not to care." Yet as with the many compromises demanded of Black colleges during desegregation, the USG justified Black colleges within its overall goal of providing students access through lower-tier, less selective institutions—the 1960s philosophy of institutional tiering that guided USG system development. Propst (27) wrote, "Standing at the center of our discussion of the consolidation is the individual student. . . . The richness of our University

https://doi.org/10.7330/9781646422036.c005

System is largely the result of the diversity of the students enrolled. . . . We have made conscious attempts to accommodate that diversity and to afford educational opportunity to a broad range of students from the less well prepared to the gifted. Our students can choose from among many types of institutions and pursue variegated academic interests. In such a context, there can be a place for the values of a traditionally black institution." As Gina Ann Garcia (2019) has shown, this very stratification—based in the ideals of choice, selectivity, and academic preparation—reinforces white institutional norms in defining the value and success of institutions, particularly through test scores, retention and graduation rates, faculty research, and institutional rankings. In turn, these features of institutional identity affect student recruitment and ultimately institutional resources, supporting the redirection of resources toward already privileged and typically historically white institutions (2019). The provision of more resources results in improved student retention, greater institutional reputation, and competitive student recruitment—feeding into a vicious cycle that contributes to ongoing segregation and racial disparities in higher education (Carnevale et al. 2018; Carnevale and Strohl 2013; Perna et al. 2006).

Writing programs have developed in ways that uphold these admissions and retention policies and contribute to racial injustice in higher education. This observation is not new. Mary Soliday (2002, 2) argues that writing programs historically marked institutional distinctions, functioning to "mediate the institutional and social class needs that tiering is designed to address." However, whereas Soliday attributes this function of writing programs to class, within the context of post-secondary desegregation, the racialization of these policies is apparent. Institutional stratification within a racialized system is defined by which institutions need to offer remedial writing programs, which literacy outcomes define general education writing requirements, how literacy standards are policed throughout the curriculum, and where students are graded for adherence to Standard English correctness and white literacy norms.

The significance of literacy as foundational to institutional identity is evident in the denouement of the Regents' Test, which remained a powerful symbol in the USG for many years. By the early 2000s, the USG Board of Regents continued to require the Regents' Test but struggled to develop a policy that did not disadvantage institutions or fail large numbers of students. In 2003, the USG voted to allow SAT verbal scores of 510 or higher to substitute for passing the verbal portion of the Regents' Test and a score of at least 650 on the SAT II writing test to substitute for the essay portion (University System of Georgia 2003). In 2007, the USG sought better methods of identifying students who were at risk of failing the Regents' Test and began to use SAT scores and scores on the Georgia High School Graduation Test to predict likely failures and provide them with earlier attempts to pass the test and "more individualized help" (University System of Georgia 2007). In 2010, the University System of Georgia (2010a) implemented a policy that provided an exemption to the Regents' Test requirement. To earn an exemption, institutions must demonstrate "institutional evidence of robust and effective student learning assessment and support for under-achieving students" by submitting an assessment report of their core area outcomes for first-year composition (University System of Georgia 2010b).[2] The competency test of the 1970s transformed into the program assessment of the twenty-first century, becoming another way of demarcating institutions through public perceptions about literacy achievement.

Of course, university and system administrators no longer reference cultural deprivation, and their policies have been revised to try to encourage support for Black and other historically underrepresented, minoritized students. However, these changes do not fully address the effects of racial ideologies on institutional structures of postsecondary education in the state, including institutional prestige, remediation requirements, expectations for writing program assessment, and ways of measuring and rewarding retention. As scholars have observed, whiteness is not the beliefs held by white people or the absence of people of color; rather, white institutional norms are institutionalized policies that occur as a result of the historical power of whites to define institutional commonplaces, publish research on higher education, and distribute resources (Garcia 2019; Gusa 2010). Good intentions cannot remedy the past. To address these complex legacies of racism and segregation, we must examine historical trajectories and transform our institutions and programs.

The Regents' Test's rebirth as program assessment is characteristic of Kathleen Blake Yancey's (1999) predicted new wave of writing assessment, in which program assessment followed previous assessment "waves"—from objective testing, to direct assessment of writing, to the evaluation of a portfolio of student work. Even though program assessment appears to transform the measures of student learning, waves may be "overlapping . . . with one wave feeding into another but without completely displacing the waves that came before" (483). We can see how the program assessment requirements I described above emphasized first-year composition as a check on graduation designed to ensure that all students possess "the minimum levels of collegiate reading and writing skill" (University System of Georgia 2010b). This language reinforces writing as a stable skill learned once and for all while also defining the USG's interest (and therefore investment) in writing programs. If this vision of program assessment drives state investment in writing, then it also precludes its investment in anything more than minimal literacy competency as demonstrated by one or two products of student writing, usually evaluated by faculty whose own racial biases and notions of correctness may pose ongoing challenges. Any writing program administrator (WPA) can see that asking for resources for a broader program of literacy instruction, particularly one that conceptualizes skills outside of the race-evasive framework proposed by the state and one that accompanies a transformation of the exploitative labor structures of first-year composition, will be a hard sell.

The symbolic role of the Regents' Test survived direct evidence of racial bias for decades. In 2012, more than two decades after Georgia's official resolution with the OCR in 1988, David Johnson and Lewis VanBrackle found that faculty raters of the Regents' Test lacked the linguistic knowledge to reliably rate essays from diverse English language speakers and disproportionately penalized student writing with features of Black English. In their experiment, they created three versions of three different essays that scored from a 1 (failing) to a 3 (high passing). Each essay in each set was then edited to include eight "errors" or dialect features. Three of the essays employed Black English, three had errors in Standard English, and three had errors associated with English language learners (ELL). At every level, the essays with Black English features were far more likely to result in a failing score. An essay originally scored as passing that was revised to include features of Black English was 7.6 times more likely to earn a failing score than an ELL essay at the same level and 6.1 times as likely to fail as an essay that had errors associated with Standard English (45). Johnson and VanBrackle (46) postulate that discrimination against Black English may be due to "an internalized derision" or a lack of knowledge of Black English. The Regents' Test defined college-level writing in ways that unfairly advantaged white students. The Regents' Test may be gone, but its elimination cannot give degrees to the students who were unable to graduate due to the test. Its elimination cannot undo the ways the Regents' Test formed the reputations of HWCUs and HBCUs in the state.

The Regents' Test is just one example of what Staci M. Perryman-Clark and Collin Lamont Craig (2019b, 21) argue is a tendency for the issues facing Black students (and, by extension, HBCUs) to be ignored in program assessments, student learning outcomes, and writing program policies. Tracing the iterations of these arguments within their racialized contexts provides a different way of upsetting the supposed "logic" of these beliefs about language, exposing their roots. Subsequent desegregation litigation furthered these ideologies of literacy in defining academic standards, student potential, and institutional identity. As I will show in the next section, postsecondary desegregation litigation rulings after *Adams* reinforced commonsensical beliefs about academic potential that have relevance for writing programs today.

LITIGATING STANDARDS: POSTSECONDARY DESEGREGATION FROM *ADAMS* TO *FORDICE* AND BEYOND

In 1990, *Adams* was dismissed from court, but several state desegregation plans were still being monitored or litigated, and reports on postsecondary desegregation progress at that time found failing plans and wider racial gaps (Vobejda 1987; Lawrence 1987).[3] Sufficient differences in lower court rulings resulted in the US Supreme Court hearing a case out of Mississippi and ruling on postsecondary desegregation in *United States v. Fordice* (1992).[4] Whereas the lower courts ruled that Mississippi had sufficiently desegregated its university system by implementing race-neutral admissions policies, *Fordice* overturned those rulings and stated that race-neutral policies were insufficient to desegregate postsecondary education. The Supreme Court then outlined a standard for postsecondary desegregation that acknowledged that admissions requirements, institutional stratification, and perceptions about institutional quality could contribute to ongoing segregation in higher education. In brief, the standard established in *Fordice* requires states to eliminate any practices traceable to de jure segregation, unless those practices no longer contribute to segregation, are educationally justifiable, or cannot be "practicably eliminated." As Albert L. Samuels (2004, 146) notes, however, "Exactly what standard courts should use to determine when a program can be 'practically eliminated' or lacks 'educational justification' remains unclear." *Fordice* identified four suspect areas for courts to examine: admissions standards (specifically, test score thresholds for admissions), program duplication, institutional mission,[5] and the maintenance of institutions operating during de jure segregation (Back and Hsin 2019). However, neither *Fordice* nor subsequent litigation addressed the definitions of academic standards used to create admissions policies and institutional tiers and in many ways reinforced deficiency-oriented and race-evasive definitions of academic achievement that disadvantaged HBCUs and increased the use of literacy assessment since the *Adams* era of enforcement.

Post-*Fordice* Desegregation and the Shifting Ground of Standardized Testing and Admissions

Fordice made admissions criteria suspect but reinforced myths about test scores as valid and useful predictors of academic success. At issue in *Fordice* was Mississippi's ACT requirements, which were set higher for white colleges than for Black colleges, maintaining a policy implemented in 1963 with the purpose of excluding Black students from HWCUs. *Fordice* (1992) overturned the lower court's ruling that the admissions standards were a response to "the problem of student unpreparedness," calling that explanation a "mid passage justification for perpetuating a policy enacted originally to discriminate against black students." Yet *Fordice* did not go so far as to suggest that ACT scores were invalid or inaccurate predictors of student success. Instead, the ruling suggested that their use violated the ACT's recommendations not to rely solely on test scores for admissions decisions.

However, when the district court took up the case to rule on a settlement, it emphasized the predictive validity of test scores at the expense of their consequential validity. *Ayers v. Fordice* (1995)[6] dismissed testimony that suggested that ACT scores had less predictive validity for Black students and students from "disadvantaged backgrounds." Instead, the ruling stated, "Regardless of whether the ACT is a flawed predictor of black student performance, the preponderance of opinion affirms that there is a clear correlation among success with standardized tests, the past degree of educational opportunity experienced by the test taker and preparedness for college work" (1995). The acceptance of historically segregationist criteria *regardless* of consequences for Black students demonstrates the ongoing preference for white educational norms. Furthermore, the ruling exposes the underlying problem with defenses of standardized tests used to ward off accusations of racial bias; such defenses emphasize predictive validity without considering that what is being predicted (i.e., the ability to earn certain grades in the first year of college) may actually be contingent on the environment in which academic standards are defined and enforced. In other words, are such tests predicting actual academic success or the effects of racist institutional structures?

Cory Todd Wilson (1994, 253–254) calls *Fordice* "a muddled jurisprudence" that favored defendants by allowing them to bring in "educational bureaucrats" to justify policies established during or contributing to segregation. But Wilson's observation also points to the importance of gearing literacy, composition, and rhetoric (LCR) research toward public policies, particularly for WPAs as our field's "educational bureaucrats." In the absence of awareness of the racialized history of predictive validity, WPA advocacy work has sometimes reinforced such measures or allowed them to continue. For example, recent movement in the field has supported directed self-placement for basic writing courses, in which students are involved in deciding whether to enter a basic writing course or a regular first-year composition course. Even when using directed self-placement, Emily Isaacs (2018) found that most programs use test scores (SAT and ACT) to identify students for additional placement procedures. Furthermore, Christie Toth and Laura Aull (2014) analyze the questionnaires designed for directed self-placement, showing that their validity and content lack consistency or sufficient research. The lack of disciplinary attention to race in these questionnaires may be an issue in cases where they ask students about their linguistic background or the diversity of their high schools—questions that may come across to students as a form of "profiling" by race and class and have unintended racial consequences (12). As this book has shown, substituting an objective test for a faculty-developed one will not automatically resolve racism in the structures and values of writing programs.

Racialized Perceptions of Institutional Quality

The *Fordice* standard has also been criticized for failing to consider the problems that have faced and still face HBCUs, which stem from the racial ideologies that inform beliefs about institutional quality. *Fordice* did note that institutional stratification was a problem in Mississippi, in the state's designation of only historically white universities as "comprehensive" institutions (University of Mississippi, University of Southern Mississippi, and Mississippi State University). Yet *Fordice* (1992) rejected plaintiff's request that the HBCUs be upgraded, stating that such a request was trying to perpetuate a "separate, but 'more equal'" system. The settlement of remedy funding to HBCUs in Mississippi was made contingent on their recruitment of at least 10 percent "other race" students,[7] with the narrow goal of increasing diversity for educational purposes rather than remedying the historical effects of segregation (Sum et al. 2004).

Much desegregation policy has failed to consider the problems with white attitudes toward HBCUs, which were raised in Savannah's desegregation negotiations (see chapter 3): white perceptions of HBCUs reinforce white norms in defining institutional quality, particularly white literacy norms. Paul E. Sum, Steven Andrew Light, and Ronald F. King (2004) confirm this problem, finding that white prospective college students in Mississippi overwhelmingly do not consider attending HBCUs as a result of anecdotal beliefs about their academic quality and the perceived negative effect a diploma from an HBCU would have on their job prospects. They note that participants could not provide evidence for these perceptions or distinguish between different types of HBCUs. Yet it's unsurprising that they hold these perceptions given that institutions are racialized, in part through rankings based on public reputation that favor HWCUs (Garcia 2019). Anecdotal beliefs about institutional quality dominate public perceptions of HBCUs and reinforce the academic standards associated with white institutions. Given that literacy requirements played a key role in associating some public HBCUs with excessive remediation, lower test scores, and higher attrition, these misconceptions will be difficult to overturn without actively reforming writing program policies and measures of institutional success.

Much LCR scholarship has shown that centering Black language and rhetoric in writing programs can improve student success, broaden the range of communication knowledge students learn, and counter deficiency-oriented ideas about writing skills (Richardson 2007; Richardson and Gilyard 2001; Perryman-Clark 2013; Perryman-Clark and Craig 2019a; Lockett et al. 2019). Yet it is imperative that HWCUs not hoard resources in developing their own writing programs, keeping the disciplinary center in HWCUs where faculty diversity currently remains low (Espinosa et al. 2019). If, as recent scholars have argued, WPAs should place HBCUs and other minority serving institutions (MSIs) at the center of writing program policy (Lamos 2012b; Green 2016, 2019), then our professional organizations need *resources*, not just attention, directed specifically toward MSIs and MSI faculty. This project should examine the systemic reasons HBCUs have been excluded from our scholarship. As Deany M. Cheramie's (2004) history of WPA work at Xavier University of Louisiana shows, histories of writing programs at HBCUs are complicated by the ways white norms have influenced these institutions. There is a real danger if white faculty at HWCUs simply "borrow" strategies and assume that borrowing constitutes anti-racist work. Placing HBCUs at the center of WPA practice and policymaking does not mean appropriating their practices or universalizing HBCU identities. We need better working histories of the racialization of higher education and its effects across a wide range of institutional types.

ROOT AND BRANCH

Geneva Smitherman (1987) has argued that writing instructors abandoned their duty to public policy and lost ground to reactionary forces.
Smitherman advocated that educators engage in "language awareness
campaigns," including defining effective and valuable communicative practice broadly and validating multiple dialects for communication and learning. As I reread Smitherman's (1977) history of writing
pedagogies in *Talkin and Testifyin* through the lens of failed desegregation enforcement, I hear a call for our field to remove the vestiges of
segregation—the "root and branch" so frequently referenced throughout desegregation rulings—by removing the policies and pedagogies
that extended from racist literacy ideologies. No matter how far the
branches have grown outward from cultural deprivation theory, they
still emerge from a historical racial dualism that Kimberlé Williams
Crenshaw (1988) argues positions white as *normal* and Black as deficient.
Historically, we have seen a push for race-evasive policies, a preference
for viewing literacy through a deprivation and remediation lens, and an
idealization of integration—none of which has served students equita-
bly. The recent attention to racial justice in writing assessment represents
one step forward, but I view Smitherman's call for language awareness
campaigns as asking us to *do more* to explain anti-Black linguistic racism
to students and policymakers and to argue that knowledge of linguistic
racism and language diversity is critical for many communication tasks
in our personal, professional, and civic lives. But this work cannot focus
solely on socioeconomic mobility, as it so often has. It must operate from
the understanding that, as April Baker-Bell (2020, 12) writes, "the policing of Black Language and literacies in schools is not separate from the
ways in which Black bodies have historically been policed and surveilled
in U.S. society."

I am not so naive as to believe that reimaging our representations
of writing and literacy in public and program policy will be easy, and
my experience has been that such work results in a recurring experience of being shut down or ignored. Based on my own experience, I
can guess what might happen: this work will be dismissed as political.
Administrators will respond to evidence that a particular placement
practice is an invalid measure of student writing by stating that they
don't care if the writing assessment is valid so long as it's useful for
placement decisions. Administrators will promise to "watch the data" to
see whether racial disparities really exist. Yet perhaps historical evidence
from our own institutions can provide a new way of framing policy decisions to audiences that generally do not want to support racism but

may not understand how such responses continue a history of white supremacy in higher education. To accomplish this kind of work, it is imperative that WPAs rethink existing race-evasive policies and practices in writing programs and call on institutional research to evaluate the impact of particular placement or testing policies on students of color (Poe et al. 2014); build knowledge of multiple Englishes and diverse rhetorical styles into learning outcomes and program assessment work (Comfort 2000; Comfort et al. 2003); develop writing assignments that require students to consider issues of racial privilege in the ways they find, cite, and relay information (Pashia 2017); engage faculty across the curriculum in unpacking and identifying racial biases in writing assessment; create criteria for evaluating faculty that recognize biases in student evaluations and value anti-racist pedagogies; visualize for administrators the impact of particular hiring policies on faculty diversity; identify the barriers to equitable rewards for faculty of color; and use research from faculty of color to construct policies ("Faculty Workload" 2019; Evans 2007; Turner et al. 2008). If desegregation has any lessons for WPAs, it is that race-evasive policies, white institutional norms, and a failure to consider past racial oppression on our campuses allow racial injustice to persist or worsen.

The focus on deprivation and integration in desegregation delimited possibilities for writing programs, with no public differentiation between the kinds of literacy practices valuable for different career paths, community work, or personal goals or even the radical potential of a future in which communication rather than correctness was emphasized in evaluating others in the workplace. Desegregation may therefore be one reason writing assessment has been, as Mya Poe, Asao B. Inoue, and Norbert Elliot (2018, 16) observe, so frequently reduced to "its constrained role as a tool used to support admission, placement, progression, and certification." Given how desegregation promoted writing programs, the field must examine the impact of cultural deprivation theory in the discourses surrounding historically underrepresented students, writing program marketing, and institutional self-definition—with an eye toward educating publics about language diversity and the scope of writing facility. As this history shows, we can learn from the way HBCUs and Black educators and scholars enacted literacy pedagogies with an eye toward social justice in the face of racist writing program policies. The challenge for LCR now is to think about how we can dismantle the ingrained systems that treat writing as correctness, not only from what we teach and how we grade but also from the design of our programs, the policies that inform them, and the gates that determine who enters and exits them.

NOTES

INTRODUCTION

1. I transcribe original documents as written. I do not use the conventional [*sic*] marker to note what I deem or what readers might deem an error.
2. I primarily use white and Black for racial distinctions, and I follow recently updated conventions for capitalization of Black but not white (Bauder 2020). The capitalization of Black recognizes Black histories and cultures as part of a shared Black racial identity, to which capitalization gives respect. Debates about whether to capitalize "white" remain ongoing, but I have chosen not to capitalize it here in keeping with recommendations that doing so would reinforce conventions of capitalization claimed by white supremacist groups.
3. I use the term *HWCUs* as suggested by Lockett and RudeWalker (2016, 175), who criticize the label "predominantly white institutions" (PWIs) for obscuring the history of segregation and "eras[ing] the cultural memory that created the need for HBCUs." They note that this term is also used in Cheramie's (2004) history of writing program administration at HBCU Xavier University of Louisiana. For the sake of readability, I follow Wooten's (2015) convention of using white colleges and Black colleges in historical analysis to include institutions founded both before and after the 1965 Higher Education Act, which officially designated Black colleges and universities as HBCUs. In addition, I use the term *Black colleges* specifically in describing Georgia's history because there were no Black university-level institutions. The failure to upgrade Black colleges to universities was a major criticism of desegregation enforcement (Morris et al. 1994). The terms *predominantly white institutions* (PWIs) and *predominantly Black institutions* (PBIs) are used only to label colleges and universities founded after 1964 that have majority white or majority Black enrollments. The PBI designation is an official term added in the 2008 Higher Education Act, to refer to institutions founded after 1964.
4. I use the terminology Pritchard (2017) proposes for the field, since it reflects the influences from these three interconnected disciplines.
5. I use the term *race evasive* instead of colorblind following Annamma and colleagues' (2016) argument that scholars should avoid using ableist terminology to describe institutional practices of ignoring racism and the racist effects of policies. Other scholars have labeled this dysconscious racism (Condon and Young 2017) or aversive racism (Davido and Gaertner 2004).
6. Much of the slow pace of desegregation is attributed to the ruling in *Brown v. Board of Education of Topeka* (1955), commonly called *Brown II*, which allowed for "all deliberate speed" in desegregating rather than specific deadlines (Bell 2005). As Rothstein (2017) recently argued, what is considered de facto segregation can in most cases be traced to specific laws and policies that intended to promote segregation and were often endorsed or allowed by government entities. Therefore, the remains of legal segregation and the de facto segregation that occurred in the decades following resistance to desegregation should be viewed as related phenomena.
7. Wooten (2015, 153) lists Lincoln University in Pennsylvania, founded in 1854, as the oldest HBCU, although she footnotes that Cheyney University in Pennsylvania

was founded first, in 1837, but that it did not begin as a postsecondary institution and did not become a college until 1913. Royster and Williams (1999, 573) point to the founding of Avery College in Pennsylvania in 1849, although it is no longer in operation. However, it's likely that these dates are further complicated by Lueck's (2020) research showing that many "high schools" or other educational institutes offered coursework comparable to colleges, but they were not labeled as colleges when their students were Black.

8. Oberlin College, Howard University, and Berea College were founded for the co-education of Black and white students (Smith 2016).

9. For example, Black colleges frequently offered extensive high school coursework to cover the segregated primary and secondary education that states neglected, and they were often limited to vocational and agricultural programs as a result of their connection to the 1890 Land Grant Act, as interpreted by white trustees (see Rogers 2012; Wooten 2015; Fester et al. 2012).

10. Louisiana, although it was also characterized as one of the most resistant segregationist states, desegregated just prior to Brown in an important legal win for the LDF in *Constantine v. Southwestern Louisiana Institute* (1954), which ruled that the state's HWCUs must admit Black students.

11. The resolution is printed in the *Bulletin of Armstrong College of Savannah, 1960–1961*. The district court decision *Hunt v. Arnold* (1959) ruled the use of alumni recommendation requirements as in violation of the equal protection clause of the Fourteenth Amendment of the US Constitution. The plaintiffs in *Hunt v. Arnold* were three women denied admission to the Georgia State College of Business Administration.

12. Other examples of this phenomenon include branch campuses of the University of Alabama in Huntsville and Montgomery, near HBCUs Alabama State University and Alabama A&M University, and the University of Tennessee at Nashville, whose expansion threatened Nashville HBCU Tennessee State University and prompted the lawsuit *Geier v. University of Tennessee* (1979). See Morris et al. (1994).

13. Federal data collection on race and ethnicity in enrollment did not begin until 1968 (Hill 1985). Rooks (2006) places total Black enrollment in northern colleges at 3 percent prior to *Brown*. According to Hill's (1985) enrollment data, total HBCU enrollment in 1953–1954 was 75,146 students, around 3 percent of total college enrollment that year. By 1970, there were 133,000 full-time Black undergraduate students in HBCUs and about 213,000 full-time Black undergraduates total, meaning that 62 percent of all full-time Black students were attending HBCUs. If we extrapolate based on total full-time undergraduate enrollment in 1970 as reported by the NCES, the number is around 4 percent of total enrollment. Scranton and colleagues (1970, 105) state that Black college enrollment was around 5 percent of total college enrollment in 1964 and 6 percent in 1969. Rooks (2006, 14) cites data showing that Black students constituted 8.4 percent of total college enrollment in 1971. In short, the numbers were quite small through the 1960s and into the early 1970s, although straightforward data are hard to find.

14. The 1964 Civil Rights Act established the OCR and began requiring states to report enrollment data by race, although the collection of this data was initially inconsistent and decentralized. The OCR was a branch of the Department of Health, Education, and Welfare responsible for overseeing HEW and ensuring that it did its job effectively with respect to civil rights.

15. The states involved in *Adams* litigation include Missouri, Delaware, Maryland, Tennessee, Arkansas, North Carolina, Pennsylvania, Mississippi, Alabama, Louisiana, Georgia, Virginia, Texas, Florida, Kentucky, South Carolina, Ohio, Oklahoma, and West Virginia. The original ten *Adams* states were Arkansas, Florida, Georgia,

Louisiana, Maryland, Mississippi, North Carolina, Oklahoma, Pennsylvania, and Virginia (see Haynes 1978; Litolff 2007).

16. As is the case with other desegregation litigation, the long period of time resulted in changes to the name of the case. *Adams* was originally filed against US secretary of education Elliot Richardson (who went on to become the attorney general who famously resigned after being ordered by Nixon to fire the special prosecutor investigating Watergate). The name changed based on the secretary of education. I refer to the entire legal battle as *Adams*; however, the two most important rulings to which I refer throughout this book are *Adams v. Richardson* (the first decision in 1973) and *Adams v. Califano* (the 1977 decision that mandated that HEW come up with more specific desegregation criteria and resulted in acceptable state plans).

17. In *Women's Equity Action League v. Cavazos* (1990), Judge Ruth Bader Ginsburg ruled in a joint brief with *Adams* that "Congress has not explicitly or implicitly authorized the grand scale action plaintiffs delineate." The district court was not authorized to serve as "nationwide overseer or pacer of procedures government agencies use to enforce civil rights prescriptions controlling educational institutions that receive federal funds." Brown (1999, 59) argues that this suit effectively overturned the work of *Adams* and the HEW criteria it created and "relegated Title VI compliance enforcement to the arena of racially neutral institutional policy statements and statewide attempts to operate in good faith."

18. Justice Clarence Thomas's opinion in *Fordice* (1992) states, "A challenged policy does not survive under the standard we announce today if it began during the prior de jure era, produces adverse impacts, and persists without sound educational justification."

19. In many cases, states were ordered to provide additional funding to Black colleges to compensate for historical neglect. However, in cases like Mississippi and Tennessee, those funds have never been adequately paid out in a way that provided additional compensation (González 2017; Gafford Muhammad 2009; Harris 2018). Some of the problems with funding were the conditions under which funds could be used. For example, Morris and colleagues (1994, 89) explain that Alabama's HBCUs were given funding for scholarship—attracting distinguished faculty, merit raises, and a lecture series. Additional funds were also provided specifically for the HBCUs to attract white students.

20. Although not a uniform pedagogical theory, bidialectical pedagogies used students' dialects as a strategy for teaching them Standard English (Kynard 2013; Lamos 2011; Fox 1999; Gilyard 1991). Historians of this pedagogy tie its focus on socioeconomic mobility and remediating speech patterns directly to cultural deprivation theories (Kynard 2013; Gilyard 1991). Young (2009) analyzes how code-switching pedagogies, which teach students to alternate between Black English and Standard English, are rooted in segregationist ideologies that treat Black English as separate and unequal. Baker-Bell (2020) describes these and similar approaches as rooted in anti-Black linguistic racism. See chapter 1 for additional definition and history.

21. Mississippi's series of litigation is especially long and complex, and after the 1997 ruling by the Fifth Circuit Court of Appeals, which I cite here, the case was denied a hearing again in the US Supreme Court. Jake Ayers Jr. was the first listed of the plaintiffs, who were Black Mississippi citizens, and Kirk Fordice was the governor of Mississippi at the time. The court of appeals upheld the district court's plans and denied the plaintiffs' appeal, with the exception of allowing individual institutions to offer their own remedial programs as well as the summer remediation plan.

22. Carolyn Warnock is a pseudonym used at the participant's request, in accordance with the terms of my informed consent documents. See chapter 4 for additional detail.

CHAPTER 1:"TECHNOLOGIES OF THIS THEORY":
DESEGRETATION AS REMEDIATION, EARLY 1970S

1.   As Raz (2013, 38–39) explains, cultural deprivation theory was often referred to by numerous euphemisms, even by researchers who employed the term, including "educationally deprived," "underprivileged," "disadvantaged," and so forth. Smitherman (1977) refers to linguistic deprivation theory, and Labov (1972) uses the term *verbal deprivation*, identifying the unique roll literacy norms played in defining cultural deprivation.

2.   Clark was involved in research cited in the *Brown* decision leading to desegregation. Clark's most famous study, conducted with his wife, Mamie Phipps Clark, involved using dolls of different colors to study the perceptions of racial identity in Black children (see Benjamin and Crouse 2002 for an overview). Criticized in later decades for reinforcing stereotypes of Black communities in *Dark Ghetto*, Clark's work and legacy has been controversial; however, some scholars argue that his legacy is more complex and has been misunderstood (see Phillips 2000; Matlin 2012).

3.   Anti-war protests were also a common reason for protests on many college campuses.

4.   Request for remedial coursework was also part of the demands in open admissions at the City University of New York ("Five Demands" 1969). Other demands included changes to admissions and the development of Black and Puerto Rican studies programs.

5.   Only a year earlier, in *Green v. County School Board of New Kent County, Virginia* (1968), the US Supreme Court had ruled against so-called freedom of choice plans that allowed K–12 students to choose whether to attend nearby white or Black schools. This decision appeared to contradict the *Green* ruling's assertion that "freedom of choice" (i.e., nondiscriminatory entrance policies) did not necessarily promote desegregation and might merely reinforce racial segregation when Black and white schools operated in close proximity. The *ASTA* ruling directly connected college admissions to freedom of choice, stating that "nondiscriminatory admissions in higher education are analogous to a freedom-of-choice plan in the elementary and secondary public schools" (*Alabama State* 1968).

6.   Justices Douglas and Harlan dissented on the per curium decision. In his dissent, Douglas asked, "Can we say in 1969 that a State has no duty to disestablish a dual system of higher education based upon race" (*Alabama State* 1969). What is perhaps most cruel about this ruling by the Supreme Court is that Alabama amended its constitution in 1956 to restrict property tax funding for K–12 education, stating that "nothing in this Constitution shall be construed as creating or recognizing any right to education or training at public expense" (*Knight v. Alabama* 2007). Plaintiffs tried to resolve ongoing postsecondary desegregation in Alabama through the courts and wound up in appeals court in 2007 arguing that property tax laws were vestiges of segregation that contributed to ongoing segregation in higher education. *Knight v. Alabama* (2007) ruled, "We cannot permit federal lawsuits to be transformed into amorphous vehicles for the rectification of all alleged wrongs, no matter how belatedly asserted, nor how unrelated to the underlying action."

7.   Kenneth R. Adams was the first of many plaintiffs, who were Black students and taxpayers in states accused of maintaining dual systems (Haynes 1978). Plaintiffs included taxpayers whose money was going to support education in states that operated segregated systems in violation of Title VI of the 1964 Civil Rights Act.

8.   Student enrollment was listed (no date given) for both colleges, with Armstrong State having forty-four Black students out of a total enrollment of 1,081 students and

Savannah State listed as having two white students out of a total enrollment of 1,898 students (Haynes 1978, A-16). These numbers seem to suggest, based on enrollment data I cite later in this chapter, that the data were from after 1965 but before 1969.

9. HEW did not dispute this evidence but argued that it had absolute discretion about when to pull funding from states (Haynes 1978). HEW had cited the states after an investigation of over 350 postsecondary institutions in formerly segregated states (Panetta 1969).

10. Judge Pratt issued an initial opinion on *Adams v. Richardson* in November 1972, but typically *Adams* (1973) is cited, with the amended decision including the injunction order. I rely on Haynes's (1978) collection of primary documents for citing various documents related to the *Adams* case in the 1970s.

11. To understand this threat, it's important to recognize that *Swann* reflected the influence of Nixon's newly appointed chief justice, Warren Burger, who replaced Chief Justice Earl Warren after his resignation in 1969 (Hoffer et al. 2007). Warren presided over what is widely considered the most activist and "revolutionary" court in US history, which backlash against *Brown* often rendered as unconstitutional and an overreach of the judicial branch (Powe 2000, 585). In contrast, Burger's goal was to eliminate all vestiges of segregation to end the court's role in desegregation (Hoffer et al. 2007, 378–379). Warren resigned in an attempt to allow President Lyndon B. Johnson to appoint the next chief justice rather than Nixon; however, Johnson's nominee failed to earn sufficient votes in the US Senate (Maltz 2016). Nixon campaigned on transforming the activist direction of the Warren court (Powe 2000). The backlash against the Warren court cannot be overestimated in Nixon's presidential win, as the Warren court's jurisprudence on race and criminal justice were both, as Powe (2000, 490) argues, specifically designed to dismantle the social norms built on white supremacy in the South, including norms that handed out death penalties for African Americans for crimes that did not involve death. For its rulings, the Warren court was accused of usurping legislative power from the legislative branch (490). After becoming president, Nixon launched investigations into two other justices, leading to the eventual resignation of Justice Abe Fortas from the court before Warren's resignation and the appointment of Justice Harry Blackmun to replace Fortas (490). Nixon appointed Burger to replace Warren as chief justice after his resignation. Nixon later appointed Justices Lewis F. Powell Jr. and William Rehnquist to the court.

12. White student enrollment was to reach one-third of Black college enrollment, and white colleges were to set the goal of increasing Black enrollment proportionally based on the percentage of Black students enrolled in twelfth grade (Haynes 1978).

13. While one might read "academic development programs" more broadly, to include other support programs, HEW's subsequent recommendation that no single type or group of institutions "assumes the major role of compensatory education" clarifies that the focus is on remediation (Haynes 1978, E-13).

14. College enrollment more than doubled from 1960 to 1970, going from about 3.6 million students to over 8 million, according to data collected by the National Center for Education Statistics (Snyder et al. 2016).

15. The term *rising junior* exam refers to the fact that the test was taken before the end of the student's sophomore year, between forty-five and seventy-five earned credit hours.

16. After 1978, students were given one hour to complete the essay exam (Dasher 1986–1987).

17. Johnson and VanBrackle (2012) provide rater instructions, sample prompts, and rating criteria from the early 2000s. Based on earlier descriptions, these documents seem similar to the forms used in the 1970s and 1980s, although the only prompt

I could find from that time was the one mentioned in Crew (1977). Owings's (1974, 16) essay examples appear to be written in response to the question "Does a generation gap exist today." Prompts generally asked students to take and argue a personal position on a topic, issue, or belief. I took the Regents' Exam as a student in a USG institution in the early 2000s and remember that my prompt was: "Given the choice, would you rather live in the mountains or near the beach? Discuss." I chose the mountains. A list of this and other prompts from 2004 is still available on Georgia State University's website.

18.   As Haswell and Elliot (2019, 4) note, holistic writing assessment is defined by its use of a single rating to score an entire writing sample (usually an essay, often written under timed conditions for the purposes of standardized testing) rather than using an analytic rubric or other tool to score individual traits of a writing sample. Holistic scoring dominated writing assessment from the 1930s to the mid-1980s (5).

19.   According to Dasher (1986–1987), two of three raters needed to assign the score a passing grade. Crew (1977) suggests that the three raters' scores are averaged. Model exams from 1974 are included as appendices to Owings (1974).

20.   For these data on the SAT, McIver cited the research of British mathematician and physicist Banesh Hoffman from his 1962 book *The Tyranny of Testing*.

21.   Records indicate that this placement number was still relatively consistent in subsequent years. A 1975 report also notes that approximately 40 percent of incoming first-year students took at least one Special Studies course (Hansen and McCracken 1975).

22.   As sociologist Elijah Anderson (2012) explains, the terms *ghetto* and *inner city* were widely associated with African Americans in the 1960s.

23.   Lippi-Green (2011, 19) argues that linguists' distinction between spoken and written language supports standard language ideology. Some of these distinctions include how meaning is clarified in written versus spoken contexts, whether variation is encouraged, and how they are learned (naturally versus instruction).

24.   This oral history archive is available to the public in the digital commons at Georgia Southern, Armstrong campus, under the name "Happiness and Hard Times."

CHAPTER 2: ASSESSING POTENTIAL: WRITING PLACEMENT AS A RETENTION STRATEGY, MID-1970S

1.   Dandy later earned her doctorate from the University of South Carolina while employed at Armstrong.

2.   This research actually began in 1973, when the Office of Planning, Budgeting, and Evaluation, a division of HEW's Office of Education, commissioned a study by Vincent Tinto and John Cullen. Tinto and Cullen's (1973) report synthesized existing research on student attrition. Thus HEW played a pivotal role in developing retention scholarship.

3.   Tinto has since discontinued use of the term *integration* and disavowed his earlier reliance on it (Ruecker et al. 2017). Rucker and colleagues (2017, 5) suggest that he has replaced "integration" with the term *sense of belonging*.

4.   The College Board began studying predictive validity in 1964, with the founding of the College Board Validity Study Service (prior to that period, colleges themselves were conducting the studies) (Schrader 1971). There was recognition at the time that these studies should divide up groups "on the basis of academic program and of sex" to be more precise (119). In addition, there was awareness that personality and motivation may play an important role in the correlation between test scores and academic success (Schrader 1971; Wilson 1974).

5. Richardson and Gilyard (2001) caution that some histories and responses to the "Students' Right to Their Own Language" (SRTOL) resolution have erased the differences among the document's creators.

6. The 650 combined SAT score was on the prior SAT scoring scale, in which scores ranged from 400 to 1,600. At that time, students received a verbal score and a mathematical score, which each ran on a scale from 200 to 800 (see Donlon and Angoff 1971).

7. The required CGP placement test, developed by the Educational Testing Service in the late 1960s specifically for community colleges, was an alternative to the Test of Standard Written English (TSWE). Both the TSWE and the CGP were part of a growing market for such tests during the era, and both separated reading and writing into two tests for two different remedial course placement decisions. The College Entrance Examination Board's CGP Program would be abandoned in favor of a state-created exam in the 1977 plan (see chapter 3).

8. According to Hill (1985, 45), the number of full-time undergraduate Black students went from 213,000 students in 1970 (with 62 percent enrolled in Black colleges) to 365,000 students in 1976 (with only 41 percent enrolled in Black colleges).

9. Data for figures 2.1 and 2.2 compiled from University System of Georgia (1981, 1990).

10. The LDF was correct that Black enrollment in white colleges was segregated by institutional tier. In 1974, for example, only 4 percent of students at ten major southern universities were Black (Minchin and Salmond 2011, 153–154).

11. The fall enrollment numbers pictured in figure 1.1 are lower than those in the Special Studies report cited here. However, the disparities are likely due to the number of Regents' Test remedial courses the college had to offer in the spring and summer terms in addition to pre-collegiate Special Studies courses.

CHAPTER 3: MEASURES OF CONTROL: WRITING PROGRAMS AND INSTITUTIONAL IDENTITY, LATE 1970S

1. North Carolina had documented disparities in funding to Black colleges and documented program duplication (Rich 1978; Califano 1981). Califano (1981) details the conflict in his memoir. North Carolina operated five historically Black institutions. The state had fifty-eight duplicated courses at nearby white and Black colleges that were not required core courses, and it approved new programs for white colleges at a higher rate than it did for Black colleges (an average of twelve at white colleges versus an average of eight at Black colleges). The University of North Carolina system refused to eliminate duplicative courses, set enrollment goals, or enhance the Black colleges. Califano was reluctant to pull funding for North Carolina out of fear that Black colleges would close without it. In 1978, North Carolina published a report arguing that all fifty-eight duplicative courses were "educationally necessary" and could not be eliminated, which was interpreted as a massive resistance to desegregation. The ongoing conflict caused fear that the district court would take over the state's university system and merge the Black colleges into white colleges, as had been done in Tennessee. The state legislature also threatened to increase minimum SAT score requirements in response to requirements that Black colleges be enhanced. North Carolina was in court until Ronald Reagan renegotiated the desegregation plans under his Department of Education.

2. *Keyes v. School District no. 1, Denver* (1973) established a limit to the court's interest in segregation, stating that "at some point in time the relationship between past segregative acts and present segregation may become so attenuated as to be incapable of

supporting a finding of de jure segregation warranting judicial intervention." The next year, *Milliken v. Bradley* (1974) further rationalized *Keyes*'s view of de facto segregation by ruling against busing students from Detroit city schools to the Detroit suburbs. In short, the court argued that a multi-district solution (that is, a solution involving both city and suburban school districts) could not be imposed if de jure segregation only involved a single district (the city schools), unless plaintiffs could prove that school district lines were *intentionally* drawn to create segregation. Validating white flight as a legitimate choice, *Milliken* not only made it harder to prove that segregation resulted from racial discrimination; it also threatened other racial remedies, particularly affirmative action (Hoffer et al. 2007).

3.   As part of desegregation criteria, Black colleges were supposed to increase white student enrollment. That directive included the caveat that such work should not negatively affect educational opportunities for Black students, and it should only occur *after* Black enrollment in the overall system and at white colleges was increased (Haynes 1978, L-18).

4.   The question of testing was more contentious in the Supreme Court's earlier ruling on affirmative action in *Defunis v. Odegaard* (1974). In a dissenting opinion issued on the case, Justice William O. Douglas, supporting affirmative action, had questioned whether standardized tests adequately measured academic potential. Douglas argued that two pools allowed for admissions to accommodate *cultural* differences associated with race, since the LSAT questions "touch[ed] on cultural backgrounds" and since "minorities have cultural backgrounds that are vastly different from the dominant Caucasian." Affirmative action, under this justification, provided exceptions for cultural background, allowing the "black applicant who pulled himself out of the ghetto into a junior college" a chance at admission: "That applicant would be offered admission not because he is black, but because as an individual he has shown he has the potential" (*Defunis v. Odegaard* 1974). This questioning of the validity of testing was not present in the later *Bakke* ruling on affirmative action.

5.   See Haswell and Elliot (2019) for a fuller discussion of the NAEP and its attitude toward the ETS as a motivator for developing writing assessment.

6.   Overall, Hake's (1978) method proposed analytic writing assessment, but the method also included counting flaws to compare to the rating as part of the process.

7.   The OCR rejected a 1973 plan, titled *A Plan for the Further Integration of the University System of Georgia*. HEW initially accepted the second plan, *A Plan for the Further Desegregation of the University System of Georgia* (1974), in July 1974. However, after the *Adams v. Califano* (1977) ruling, HEW was again forced to reject the 1974 plan. A letter from the OCR that year noted that Georgia's plan, along with plans from Arkansas, Florida, North Carolina, Oklahoma, and Virginia, were rejected because they did not meet "important desegregation requirements" from the newly developed HEW guidelines; further, the states did not demonstrate that they had made "significant progress" toward desegregation (Walker 1977).

8.   For reference, the mean total SAT score in the 1977–1978 academic year added up to an 897, or a 429 verbal and 468 math score (Snyder et al. 2016).

9.   The four universities were Georgia Institute of Technology, Georgia State University, the Medical College of Georgia, and the University of Georgia (Oxford et al. 1977, 10).

10.   The location of the workshop is not listed in the alternative plan. The inclusion of the alternative plan in the Savannah State archives, however, suggests either that some Savannah State faculty, staff, or students were involved in writing the document or that the workshop took place in Savannah. Although I worked with the Savannah State archives to see if anyone knew the authors of the document, our

efforts to find out more about its origins were unsuccessful. I did find reference to a Georgia Conference for Open Education, a group that appears to have worked with students at Georgia's HBCUs to produce "a joint declaration" that matches the demands of the alternative plan (Lovelace 1979, 13).

11.   I confirmed that the data on SAT scores were the same as those in the USG 1977 plan. See Oxford et al. (1977, 193) for the original data set.

12.   For reference, in 1976, less than 2 percent of university faculty in the USG were Black, roughly 14 percent of senior college faculty were Black (*including* those at Black colleges), and around 10 percent of junior college faculty were Black. Only 2 of 104 tenured senior college Black faculty members worked at HWCUs (*Alternative Plan* 1977, 79).

13.   Although the actual production and distribution of the alternative plan is unclear from the archives, the Savannah State College National Alumni Association made similar criticisms of the approach in a letter to HEW secretary Califano in 1979 (Brown 1979).

14.   Technically, there were five different options discussed in Savannah. See Stone (2010, 203) for an outline of the variations on the desegregation options in Savannah.

15.   The National Teacher Examination through the early 1980s included a section on "Written English Expression," as well as on general and professional education and tests in science and mathematics. Its validity and use were regularly criticized beginning at least as early as the 1970s. A review of studies by Quirk, Witten, and Weinberg (1973) found poor correlation between the NTE and teaching ability. Later, Moore, Schurr, and Henriksen (1991) found that it was less useful than GPA alone at predicting teacher effectiveness. NTE scores did, however, correlate with SAT and ACT scores (Egan and Ferre 1989).

16.   After being implemented in the 1979–1980 academic year, the plan was to be monitored annually and reviewed again in 1982.

17.   Data collected from Cheek (1981), Nash (1978), and Hooper (1979).

18.   The USG's support for health services at Armstrong was a point of contention between the two Savannah colleges. Savannah State argued to HEW that the USG Board of Regents had undermined desegregation by immediately placing "an impregnable fortress around Armstrong" by founding health programs on Armstrong's campus following the program swap (Brown 1979). The health professions programs, it argued, duplicated "one of Savannah State College's oldest programs by providing training for dieticians" (7).

CHAPTER 4: "WHO'S THE VILLAIN?": WRITING ASSESSMENT IN DESEGREGATION POLICY, 1980S AND BEYOND

1.   Caroline Warnock is a pseudonym used at the request of the faculty member. Faculty interviewed were offered the choice of using a pseudonym given the sensitive topic of desegregation in Savannah. The terms of the Institutional Review Board (IRB) approval also specified that faculty were no longer working at the institution. Some identifying information and dates have been removed to preserve the individual's anonymity.

2.   The 50 percent number refers to the combined white student enrollment at both Tennessee State and the University of Tennessee at Nashville prior to the merger of the two institutions into Tennessee State, which retained its HBCU status.

3.   The Carter administration split up the Department of Health, Education, and Welfare because of the large scope of work in which it was involved. The Department

of Education was established in May 1980, just prior to Carter's loss to Reagan in the 1980 presidential election (Wellborn 1980).

4.   Califano's 1979 resignation as HEW secretary was rumored to be due to his "insistence" that North Carolina follow a "strict interpretation" of HEW criteria (Richards 1979). His successor, Patricia Harris, entered office expecting higher education desegregation to be "one of her greatest problems," but she had less than five months in office before handing what was described as a "hot potato" to Reagan's secretary, Shirley Hufstedler (1979). With citations against Alabama, Texas, Maryland, and Pennsylvania, as well as litigation in Louisiana and Mississippi, higher education desegregation was described as a "politically touchy" subject in the 1980 presidential election, with many state governors "unsympathetic" to the cause (1979).

5.   In concrete terms, there was an 11 percent drop in the percentage of college-eligible Black students attending college (Richburg 1985a).

6.   One study attributed the higher attrition rates to Black students' feelings of isolation and the dearth of minority faculty and "non-Eurocentric" course offerings (Richburg 1985a).

7.   As described in chapter 1, the situation of Auburn University at Montgomery and Alabama State was considered by the US Supreme Court in *ASTA*, where the planned Auburn extension campus was thought to create potential for segregated postsecondary institutions in Montgomery. Interestingly, the two Alabama colleges were compared to the situations in Savannah and Nashville, with Savannah's program swap example presented as a more favorable option than the merger in Nashville (Maeroff 1983).

8.   The study employed a holistic assessment scale that rated longer writing more highly, with the highest rating (a 4 on a scale of 1 to 4) for "elaborated" and "extended" detail (Applebee et al. 1985, 13). The emphasis on writing length is a documented problem in these kinds of evaluations, with long writing tending to be valued simply for its length (Redd 2012) or resulting in a bias toward a higher score regardless of content (Kobrin et al. 2011).

9.   Mainstreaming basic writing refers to the trend of discontinuing traditional basic writing by moving it into alternative formats, including the stretch model (a student enrolls in a regular first-year writing course that is stretched over a longer period of time, such as two semesters instead of one) or co-requisite models (student simultaneously enrolls in a regular FYW course and a support course that is usually only one or two credit hours). See Adams (1993); Otte and Mlynarczyk (2010, 117–118).

10.   The first WAC conference, the National Writing across the Curriculum Conference, was held in 1993, and the first journal, the *Journal of Language and Learning across the Disciplines*, was published in 1994 (Bazerman et al. 2005).

11.   See Educational Testing Service (1975) for background on the TSWE.

12.   This number includes Georgia's three public Black colleges.

13.   See Marinara and McBeth (2011) for an interview with Crew on his experiences.

14.   Singleton resigned from his role in the Reagan administration in 1985 after criticism that he mishandled resolutions of Office for Civil Rights cases (Twomey 1990).

15.   Control Data Corp was an IBM competitor founded in the 1960s that invested significantly in social responsibility programs designed to facilitate public-private partnerships to cover the loss in federal funding for such programs in the 1980s under Reagan's policies (see Hart 2005; Carroll 1983; Rankin 2015).

16.   Maher (1997) chronicles Shaughnessy's interest in theories of Black English in her biography, *Mina P. Shaughnessy: Her Life and Work*. Although not a part of *Errors and Expectations*, Shaughnessy's famous work on student writing errors, Warnock's recollection may support a broader reading of Shaughnessy's legacy.

17.   Smitherman's (1981, 15) push-pull definition applies W.E.B. DuBois's notion of double-consciousness to language. The "linguistic push-pull" as defined in her work is "the push toward Americanization (i.e., decreolization) of Black English counterbalanced by the pull of its Africanization." See also Smitherman (1977).

CODA

1.   Armstrong and Savannah State were upgraded to university-level institutions in 1996. Armstrong was at that time renamed Armstrong Atlantic State University and in 2014 was renamed Armstrong State University. The Armstrong campus of Georgia Southern University is still restricted in offering the full suite of business degrees that are available in Statesboro. Savannah State's teacher education program was returned to the university in the 1990s, and Savannah State has founded a distinct program—a nationally recognized marine sciences program—on its campus.

2.   In 2020, the Regents' Test requirement was officially removed from USG policies.

3.   Judge Pratt dismissed *Adams* in 1987 (Goldstein and Butner 1987). See introduction note 18 for more information on its final dismissal after appeal.

4.   *Fordice* came to trial after decades of refusal to agree on a desegregation plan in Mississippi. Mississippi initially refused to submit a desegregation plan to HEW, and then the state's Board of Trustees overseeing the university system refused to fund it. Originally filed in 1975 as *Ayers v. Allain*, failure to reach a settlement resulted in additional legal battles. Both the district court and the appeals court ruled in favor of Mississippi, arguing that it had done its duty by eliminating discriminatory policies. The Supreme Court ruled otherwise and sent the case back to the district court. The state finally reached a settlement with the plaintiffs in 2001, which promised enhancements to the state's HBCUs and made some additional funding contingent on the institutions reaching at least 10 percent non-Black student enrollment. See Wilson (1994) and Sum et al. (2004) for an overview.

5.   Institutional missions were a concern in *Fordice* (as well as other desegregation litigation) because they might be used to give white and Black colleges different missions and therefore different funding levels and program offerings. As *Fordice* explained, in Mississippi, the three flagship HWCUs had been reclassified in 1981 as comprehensive and given the most extensive program offerings; one of the Black colleges was classified as urban; and the rest of the colleges were classified as regional colleges.

6.   Although the Mississippi settlement was not reached until 2001, the admissions standards outlined in the 1995 ruling were upheld in 1999 and remained in place. An early version of the remedial summer course program pilot was implemented in 1996 (Healy 1996). The first pilot of the summer program resulted in a dramatic drop in students attending the remedial courses (200 rather than the anticipated 2,000 students) (1996).

7.   The Supreme Court's ruling in *Fordice* remanded oversight of desegregation back to the district court. The decision to make funding remedies contingent on 10 percent other race enrollment is based on the ruling in *Fordice* specifying that diversity should be the goal of any remedies.

REFERENCES

Adams, Joseph V. 1981. Memo to Robert Burnett, March 13. Box 60.1, Folder 1A. Lane Library Special Collections at Georgia Southern University, Savannah.

Adams, Peter Dow. 1993. "Basic Writing Reconsidered." *Journal of Basic Writing* 12 (1): 22–36.

Adams, Peter Dow, Sarah Gearhart, Robert Miller, and Anne Roberts. 2009. "The Accelerated Learning Program: Throwing Open the Gates." *Journal of Basic Writing* 28 (2): 50–69.

Adams v. Califano. 430 F.Supp 118 (D.D.C. 1977).

Adams v. Richardson. 356 F.Supp 92 (D.D.C. 1973).

"Administration to End Appeal of Race Ruling." 1983. *Washington Post,* June 19, C11.

Ahmed, Sara. 2012. *On Being Included: Racism and Diversity in Institutional Life.* Durham, NC: Duke University Press.

Alabama State Teachers Association v. Alabama Public School and College Authority. 289 F. Supp. 784 (M.D. Alabama 1968).

Alabama State Teachers Association v. Alabama Public School and College Authority. 393 US 400 (S. Ct. 1969).

Al-Amin, Karima. 1982. Letter to Howard Jordan, May 26. RCB 55408, C14649. Georgia Archives, Morrow.

An Alternative Plan for the Desegregation of the University System of Georgia. 1977. Atlanta, GA: University System, Board of Regents. Asa H. Gordon Library Special Collections, Savannah State University, Savannah, GA. https://archive.org/details/alterna tiveplanf00anon.

Ampadu, Lena. 2007. "Modeling Orality: African American Rhetorical Practices and the Teaching of Writing." In *African American Rhetoric(s): Interdisciplinary Perspectives,* edited by Elaine B. Richardson and Ronald L. Jackson II. Carbondale: Southern Illinois University Press, 136–154.

Anderson, Carol. 2016. *White Rage: The Unspoken Truth of Our Racial Divide.* New York: Bloomsbury.

Anderson, Elijah. 2012. "The Iconic Ghetto." *Annals of the American Academy of Political and Social Science* 642 (1): 8–24.

Andersson, Kelsey Kaylene. 2006. "Savannah, Georgia: Local Compliance to *Brown v. Board of Education.*" MA thesis, Armstrong Atlantic State University, Savannah.

Annamma, Subini Ancy, Darrell D. Jackson, and Deb Morrison. 2016. "Conceptualizing Color-Evasiveness: Using Dis/Ability Critical Race Theory to Expand a Color-Blind Racial Ideology in Education and Society." *Race Ethnicity and Education* 20 (2): 147–162.

Anson, Chris M. 2012. "Black Holes: Writing across the Curriculum, Assessment, and the Gravitational Invisibility of Race." In *Race and Writing Assessment,* edited by Asao B. Inoue and Mya Poe. New York: Peter Lang, 15–28.

Applebee, Arthur N., Judith A. Langer, and Ina V.S. Mullis. 1985. *Writing Trends across the Decade, 1974–84.* Princeton, NJ: National Assessment of Educational Progress at Educational Testing Service.

Armstrong College. 1960. *Bulletin of Armstrong College of Savannah, 1960–1961.* Lane Library Special Collections at Georgia Southern University, Savannah. https://archive.org/de tails/bulletin5664arms/page/n371/mode/2up.

https://doi.org/10.7330/9781646422036.c006

Armstrong State College. 1972. *Armstrong State College Catalogue: 1972–1973*. Lane Library Special Collections at Georgia Southern University, Savannah. https://archive.org/details/bulletin7273arms/.

Armstrong State College. 1974. *Catalogue and General Bulletin: Armstrong State College Catalogue: 1974–1975*. Lane Library Special Collections at Georgia Southern University, Savannah. https://archive.org/details/armstrong7475arms.

Armstrong State College. 1976. *Armstrong State College Bulletin 1976–1977*. Lane Library Special Collections at Georgia Southern University, Savannah. https://archive.org/details/armstrong7677arms.

Armstrong State College. 1977. *Armstrong State College Bulletin 1977–1978*. Lane Library Special Collections at Georgia Southern University, Savannah. https://archive.org/details/armstrong7778arms.

"ASC Submits Desegregation Plan to HEW." 1974. *The Inkwell* (February 14) 38 (16): 1.

Ashmore, Henry. 1969a. Letter to George L. Simpson, January 9. Box 29, Folder 2. Lane Library Special Collections at Georgia Southern University, Savannah.

Ashmore, Henry. 1969b. Letter to George L. Simpson, February 3. Box 29, Folder 2. Lane Library Special Collections at Georgia Southern University, Savannah.

Ashmore, Henry. 1972. Letter to George L. Simpson, June 26. Box 18A, Folder 15. Lane Library Special Collections at Georgia Southern University, Savannah.

Ashmore, Henry L. 1979. Letter to Edward Brantley, March 19. Box 18A, Folder 15. Lane Library Special Collections at Georgia Southern University, Savannah.

Ashmore, Henry L. 1980. Letter to Vernon Crawford, February 27. Box 50.2, Folder 16B. Lane Library Special Collections at Georgia Southern University, Savannah.

Ashmore, Henry. 1982. *Armstrong State College Annual Report for July 1, 1981–June 30, 1982*. Minis Reading Room. Lane Library Special Collections at Georgia Southern University, Savannah.

Ayers v. Allain. 674 F.Supp. 1523 (N.D. Miss. 1987).

Ayers v. Fordice. 879 F.Supp. 1419 (N.D. Miss. 1995).

Ayers v. Fordice. 111 F.3d 1183 (5th Cir. Miss. 1997).

Back, Christine J., and JD S. Hsin. 2019. "'Affirmative Action' and Equal Protection in Higher Education." *Congressional Research Service*, January 31. https://crsreports.congress.gov.

Baddour, Elizabeth. 2020. "Juanita Williamson and the HBCU Influence in Writing Instruction." *Spark: A 4C4Equality Journal* 2. https://sparkactivism.com/volume-2-call/vol-2-intro/juanita-williamson-hbcu-influence/.

Baker, Scott. 1995. "Testing Equality: The National Teacher Examination and the NAACP's Legal Campaign to Equalize Teachers' Salaries in the South, 1936–63." *History of Education Quarterly* 35 (1): 49–64.

Baker-Bell, April. 2020. *Linguistic Justice: Black Language, Literacy, Identity, and Pedagogy*. New York: Routledge.

Balester, Valerie. 2012. "How Writing Rubrics Fail: Toward a Multicultural Model." In *Race and Writing Assessment*, edited by Asao B. Inoue and Mya Poe. New York: Peter Lang, 63–78.

Ball, Arnetha F. 1993. "Incorporating Ethnographic-Based Techniques to Enhance Assessments of Culturally Diverse Students' Written Exposition." *Educational Assessment* 1 (3): 255–281.

Ball, Arnetha F. 1997. "Expanding the Dialogue on Culture as a Critical Component When Assessing Writing." *Assessing Writing* 4 (2): 169–202.

Ball, Arnetha F., and Ted Lardner. 2005. *African American Literacies Unleashed*. Carbondale: Southern Illinois University Press.

Banks, Adam J. 2006. *Race, Rhetoric, and Technology: Searching for Higher Ground*. Mahwah, NJ: Lawrence Erlbaum Associates, Inc.

Bauder, David. 2020. "AP Says It Will Capitalize Black But Not White." *AP News*, July 20. https://apnews.com/7e36c00c5af0436abc09e051261ffff1f.

Bazerman, Charles, Joseph Little, Lisa Bethel, Teri Chavkin, Danielle Fouquette, and Janet Garufis. 2005. *Reference Guide to Writing across the Curriculum.* West Lafayette, IN: Parlor.

Bell, Derrick A., Jr. 2005. "The Unintended Lessons in *Brown v. Board of Education.*" *New York Law School Law Review* 49: 1053–1067.

Bell, Jim. 1989. "What Are We Talking About: A Content Analysis of the Writing Lab Newsletter, April 1985 to October 1988." *Writing Lab Newsletter* 13 (7): 1–5.

Bell-Scott, Patricia, Beverly Guy-Sheftall, and Jacqueline Jones Royster. 1991. "The Promise and Challenge of Black Women's Studies: A Report from the Spelman Conference, May 25–26, 1990." *National Women's Studies Association Journal* 3 (2): 281–288.

Benjamin, Ludy T., Jr., and Ellen M. Crouse. 2002. "The American Psychological Association's Response to *Brown v. Board of Education*: The Case of Kenneth B. Clark." *American Psychologist* 57 (1): 38–50.

"Black Students Stage Walkout of Lecture." 1973. *The Inkwell* (November 15) 38 (9): 1.

"Blacks Express Grievances." 1974. *The Inkwell* (November 27) 39 (11): 1.

Board of Regents of the University System of Georgia. 1973. Minutes of the Special Meeting of the Board of Regents of the University System of Georgia Held in the Office of the Board of Regents, June 6. Box 21E, Folder 7. Lane Library Special Collections at Georgia Southern University, Savannah.

Bombardieri, Marcella. 2019. "How to Fix Education's Racial Inequities, One Tweak at a Time." *Politico.* https://www.politico.com/agenda/story/2019/09/25/higher-education-racial-inequities-000978.

Bonilla-Silva, Edward. 2006. *Racism without Racists: Color-Blind Racism and the Persistence of Racial Inequality in the United States,* 2nd ed. Lanham, MD: Rowman and Littlefield.

Bosmajian, Haig A. 1969. "The Language of White Racism." *College English* 31 (3): 263–272.

Botan, Carl, and Geneva Smitherman. 1991. "Black English in the Integrated Workplace." *Journal of Black Studies* 22 (2): 168–185.

Bouquet, Elizabeth. 1999. " 'Our Little Secret': A History of Writing Centers, Pre- to Post-Open Admissions." *College Composition and Communication* 50 (3): 463–482.

Boyd, William M., II. 1974. *Desegregating America's Colleges: A Nationwide Survey of Black Students, 1972–73.* New York: Praeger.

Braddock, Richard, Richard Lloyd-Jones, and Lowell Schoer. 1963. *Research in Written Composition.* Champaign, IL: National Council of Teachers of English.

Brandt, Deborah. 2001. *Literacy in American Lives.* Cambridge: Cambridge University Press.

Braswell, Brian. 1983. "Deseg Plan on Hold as Officials Argue over It." *Red and Black,* September 22, n.p. RCB 1393, C32221. Georgia Archives, Morrow.

Bridges, Jean Bolen. 1977. "How Do You Grab a Tiger By the Tail?" *Teaching English in the Two-Year College* 3 (1): 25–27.

Brooks, F. Erik. 2014. *Tigers in the Tempest: Savannah State University and the Struggle for Civil Rights.* Macon, GA: Mercer University Press.

Brown, Earl F. 1979. Letter to Joseph Califano, January 10. C 14647. Georgia Archives, Morrow.

Brown, Hugh. 1968. "Remedial English Class Report." Box 29, Folder 1. Lane Library Special Collections at Georgia Southern University, Savannah.

Brown, Laura Clark, and Nancy Kaiser. 2012. "Opening Archives on the Recent American Past: Reconciling the Ethics of Access and the Ethics of Privacy." In *Doing Recent History: On Privacy, Copyright, Video Games, Institutional Review Boards, Activist Scholarship, and History That Talks Back,* edited by Renee Christine Romano. Athens: University of Georgia Press, 59–82.

Brown, M. Christopher. 1999. *The Quest to Define Collegiate Desegregation: Black Colleges, Title VI Compliance, and Post-Adams Litigation.* Westport, CT: Bergin and Garvey.

Brown, M. Christopher. 2004. "Collegiate Desegregation as Progenitor and Progeny of *Brown v. Board of Education*: The Forgotten Role of Postsecondary Litigation, 1908–1990." *Journal of Negro Education* 73 (3): 341–349.

Brown, Rexford. 1978. "What We Know Now and How We Could Know More about Writing Ability in America." *Journal of Basic Writing* 1 (4): 1–6.

Brown, Roscoe C., Jr. 1986. "Testing Black Student Writers." In *Writing Assessment: Issues and Strategies*, edited by Karen Greenberg, Harvey Wiener, and Richard A. Donovan. New York: Longman, 98–106.

Brown v. Board of Education of Topeka. 347 US 483 (S. Ct. 1954).

Brown v. Board of Education of Topeka. 349 US 294 (S. Ct. 1955).

Bruch, Patrick, and Richard Marback. 2005. "Critical Hope, 'Students' Right,' and the Work of Composition Studies." In *The Hope and the Legacy: The Past, Present, and Future of Students' Right to Their Own Language*, edited by Patrick Bruch and Richard Marback. New York: Hampton, vii–xvii.

Bruning, W. H. 1984. "Georgia Press Conference," May 31. RCB 1393, C32221. Georgia Archives, Morrow.

Burnett, Robert A. 1983. *Armstrong State College Annual Report for July 1, 1982–June 30, 1983*. Minis Reading Room. Lane Library Special Collections at Georgia Southern University, Savannah.

Burnett, Robert A. 1984. *Armstrong State College Annual Report for July 1, 1983–June 30, 1984*. Minis Reading Room. Lane Library Special Collections at Georgia Southern University, Savannah.

Burnett, Robert A. 1986. *Armstrong State College Annual Report for July 1, 1985–June 30, 1986*. Minis Reading Room. Lane Library Special Collections at Georgia Southern University, Savannah.

Burrows, Cedric D. 2016. "Writing While Black: The Black Tax on African-American Graduate Writers." *Praxis* 14 (1). http://www.praxisuwc.com/burrows-141.

Califano, Joseph A., Jr. 1977. Telegram to George Busbee, July 5. RCB 16563. Georgia Archives, Morrow.

Califano, Joseph A., Jr. 1981. *Governing America: An Insider's Report from the White House and the Cabinet*. New York: Simon and Schuster.

Carnevale, Anthony P., and Jeff Strohl. 2013. *Separate and Unequal: How Higher Education Reinforces the Intergenerational Reproduction of White Privilege*. Washington, DC: Georgetown University Public Policy Institute.

Carnevale, Anthony P., Martin Van Der Werf, Michael C. Quinn, Jeff Strohl, and Dmitri Repnikov. 2018. *Our Separate and Unequal Public Colleges: How Public Colleges Reinforce White Racial Privilege and Marginalize Black and Latino Students*. Washington, DC: Georgetown University Public Policy Institute.

Carroll, Archie B. 1983. "Corporate Social Responsibility: Will Industry Respond to Cutbacks in Social Program Funding?" *Vital Speeches of the Day* 49 (19): 604–608.

Cheek, Wanda K. 1981. Letter to Gary Barnes, January 14. RCB 55407, C14647. Georgia Archives, Morrow.

Cheramie, Deany M. 2004. "Sifting through Fifty Years of Change: Writing Program Administration at an Historically Black University." In *Historical Studies of Writing Program Administration: Individuals, Communities, and the Formation of a Discipline*, edited by Barbara L'Eplattenier and Lisa Mastrangelo. West Lafayette, IN: Parlor, 146–166.

Chiteman, Michael D. 1987. "The Writing Center and Institutional Politics: Making Connections with Administration and Faculty." *Writing Lab Newsletter* 11 (8): 1–4.

Chun, Edna B., and Joe R. Feagin. 2022. "Introduction." In *Who Killed Higher Education? Maintaining White Dominance in a Desegregating Era*, edited by Edna B. Chun and Joe R. Feagin. New York: Routledge, 1–16.

Clark, Kenneth B., Martin Deutsch, Alan Gartner, Francis Keppel, Hylan Lewis, Thomas Pettigrew, Lawrence Plotkin, and Frank Riessman. 1972. *The Educationally Deprived: The Potential for Change*. New York: Metropolitan Applied Research Center, Inc.

Clary-Lemon, Jennifer. 2009. "The Racialization of Composition Studies: Scholarly Rhetoric of Race since 1990." *College Composition and Communication* 61 (2): W1–W17.

Cleary, Annie T., and Thomas L. Hilton. 1966. *An Investigation of Item Bias*. Research Development Reports, vol. 12. Princeton, NJ: College Entrance Examination Board.

Cole, Marlene. 1982. "A Dual Purpose Writing Lab." *Writing Lab Newsletter* 6 (6): 4.

College Board. 2018. *Accuplacer: WritePlacer Guide with Sample Essays*. https://accuplacer.collegeboard.org/accuplacer/pdf/accuplacer-writeplacer-sample-essays.pdf.

College Language Association. 2020. "The College Language Association History." https://www.clascholars.org/history.

Comfort, Juanita Rodgers. 2000. "Becoming a Writerly Self: College Writers Engaging Black Feminist Essays." *College Composition and Communication* 51 (4): 540–559.

Comfort, Juanita Rodgers, Karen Fitts, William B. Lalicker, Chris Teutsch, and Victoria Tischio. 2003. "Beyond First-Year Composition: Not Your Grandmother's General Education Composition Program." *WPA: Writing Program Administration* 26 (3): 67–86.

Complete College America. 2017. *Alliance Compact Scaling Standards*. https://completecollege.org/wp-content/uploads/2017/09/Alliance-Compact-and-Scaling-Standards-FINAL-WEB-3.15.18.pdf.

Complete College Georgia. 2019. "About Complete College Georgia." https://completega.org/content/about-complete-college-georgia.

"Composition Courses for the Underprepared Freshman." 1969. *College Composition and Communication* 20 (3): 248–249.

Condon, Frankie, and Vershawn Ashanti Young. 2017. "Introduction." In *Performing Antiracist Pedagogy in Rhetoric, Writing, and Communication*, edited by Vershawn Ashanti Young and Frankie Condon. Fort Collins, CO: WAC Clearinghouse, 3–18. https://wac.colostate.edu/books/atd/antiracist/.

Connell, Christopher. 1981a. "Bell Wants to Reopen Desegregation Talks with Eight States." *Associated Press*, March 4.

Connell, Christopher. 1981b. "Education Department May Be Headed for Reagan Reincarnation." *Associated Press*, January 16.

Constantine v. Southwestern Louisiana Institute. 120 F.Supp 417 (W.D. La 1954).

Control Data Corp. 1984. Press Release. "Plato Terminals for Georgia State University System." May 31. RCB 1393, C32221. Georgia Archives, Morrow.

Cook, Eugene. 1955. Letter from the Attorney General, September 16. RCB 10596. Georgia Archives, Morrow.

Cooper, Charles R. 1981. *The Nature and Measurement of Competency Testing in English*. Urbana, IL: National Council of Teachers of English.

Cooper, Charles R., and Lee Odell, editors. 1977. *Evaluating Writing: Describing, Measuring, Judging*. Urbana, IL: National Council of Teachers of English.

Corbett, Edward P.J. 1969. "The Rhetoric of the Open Hand and the Rhetoric of the Closed Fist." *College Composition and Communication* 20 (5): 288–296.

Coupet, Jason. 2017. "Strings Attached? Linking Historically Black Colleges and Universities' Public Revenue Sources with Efficiency." *Journal of Higher Education Policy and Management* 39 (1): 40–57.

Cousins, Robert. 1954. Letter to W. E. Turner. RCB 10596. Georgia Archives, Morrow.

Craig, Collin Lamont, and Staci M. Perryman-Clark. 2011. "Troubling the Boundaries: (De)Constructing WPA Identities at the Intersections of Race and Gender." *WPA: Writing Program Administration* 34 (2): 37–58.

Craig, Sherri. 2016. "A Story-less Generation: Emergent WPAs of Color and the Loss of Identity through Absent Narratives." *WPA: Writing Program Administrators* 39 (2): 16–20.

Crain, Brad. 1982. "Proposal for an ASC Writing Center." Memo to Henry L. Ashmore, February 3. Box 23B, Folder 2. Lane Library Special Collections at Georgia Southern University, Savannah.

Crenshaw, Kimberlé Williams. 1988. "Race, Reform, and Retrenchment: Transformation and Legitimation in Antidiscrimination Law." *Harvard Law Review* 101 (7): 1331–1387.

Crenshaw, Kimberlé Williams. 2017. "Race Liberalism and the Deradicalization of Racial Reform." *Harvard Law Review* 130 (2298): 2298–2319.

Crew, Louie. 1977. "The New Alchemy." *College English* 38 (7): 707–711.

Crowley, Sharon. 1998. *Composition in the University: Historical and Polemical Essays.* Pittsburgh, PA: University of Pittsburgh Press.

"Culturally Disadvantaged." 1966. *College Composition and Communication* 17 (3): 184–185.

Dandy, Evelyn Baker. 1991. *Black Communications: Breaking down the Barriers.* Chicago: African American Images.

Dandy, Evelyn Baker. 2017. Personal Interview. October 11, Savannah, GA.

Dasher, Thomas E. 1986–1987. "From 'No' to 'Maybe': One Instructor's Experience with the Regents' Test in Georgia." *CEA Forum* 16 (4) and 17 (1): 12–14.

Davido, John F., and Samuel L. Gaertner. 2004. "Aversive Racism." *Advances in Experimental Social Psychology* 36: 1–52.

Davila, Bethany. 2012. "Indexicality and 'Standard' Edited American English: Examining the Link between Conceptions of Standardness and Perceived Authorial Identity." *Written Communication* 29 (2): 180–207.

Davila, Bethany. 2016. "The Inevitability of 'Standard' English: Discursive Constructions of Standard Language Ideologies." *Written Communication* 33 (2): 127–148.

Davila, Bethany. 2017. "Standard English and Colorblindness in Composition Studies: Rhetorical Constructions of Racial and Linguistic Neutrality." *WPA: Writing Program Administration* 40 (2): 154–173.

Davis, Marianna White. 1994. *History of the Black Caucus.* Urbana, IL: National Council of Teachers of English.

Defunis v. Odegaard. 416 US 312 (S. Ct. 1974).

Denley, Tristan. 2017. "Corequesite Academy: English." University System of Georgia. http://www.completegeorgia.org/sites/default/files/resources/Denley_CoRequisite_Academy_English.pdf.

Dennard, Charles. 1974. "Pendexter, Strozier, Clarke." *The Inkwell* (July 31) 39 (3): 3–4, 7.

Division of Humanities. 1970. "Departmental Self-Study Reports." Report to the Commission on Colleges, Southern Association of Colleges and Schools, December. Record E11. Asa H. Gordon Library, Savannah State University, Savannah, GA.

Dodds, Dewey E. 1969a. Letter to Henry L. Ashmore, May 21. Box 41, Folder 2. Lane Library Special Collections at Georgia Southern University, Savannah.

Dodds, Dewey E. 1969b. Letter to Henry L. Ashmore, July 17. Box 41.2, Folder 11. Lane Library Special Collections at Georgia Southern University, Savannah.

Donlon Henry S., and William H. Angoff. 1971. "The Scholastic Aptitude Test." In *The College Board Admissions Testing Program: A Technical Report on Research and Development Activities Relating to the Scholastic Aptitude Test and Achievement Tests,* edited by William H. Angoff. Princeton, NJ: College Entrance Examination Board, 15–48.

Douglas, Michael A. 1993. "A Successful Individualized Writing Lab Module." *Journal of Developmental Education* 16 (3): 24–27.

Douglas-Gabriel, Danielle. 2017. "Courts Side with Maryland HBCUs in Long-Standing Case over Disparities in State Higher Education." *Washington Post,* November 9.

Educational Testing Service. 1975. *The Test of Standard Written English: A Preliminary Report.* Princeton, NJ: College Entrance Examination Board.

Educational Testing Service. 1977. *Using and Interpreting Scores on the CGP Self-Scoring Placement Tests in English and Mathematics.* Princeton, NJ: College Entrance Examination Board.

Egan, Paul J., and Victor A. Ferre. 1989. "Predicting Performance on the National Teacher Examinations Core Battery." *Journal of Educational Research* 82 (4): 227–230.

Emig, Janet. 1971. *The Composing Process of Twelfth Graders.* Urbana, IL: National Council of Teachers of English.

Epps-Robertson, Candace. 2018. *Resisting Brown: Race, Literacy, and Citizenship in the Heart of Virginia.* Pittsburgh, PA: University of Pittsburg Press.

Espinosa, Lorelle L., Jonathan M. Turk, Morgan Taylor, and Hollie M. Chessman. 2019. *Race and Ethnicity in Higher Education: A Status Report.* Washington, DC: American Council on Education.

Evans, Stephanie Y. 2007. "Women of Color in American Higher Education." *Thought and Action* 23: 131–138.

"The Faculty Workload and Rewards Project." 2019. University of Maryland. https://facultyworkloadandrewardsproject.umd.edu.

Faigley, Lester. 1992. *Fragments of Rationality: Postmodernity and the Subject of Composition.* Pittsburgh, PA: University of Pittsburgh Press.

Farmer, Ashley. 2018. "Archiving While Black." *Chronicle of Higher Education,* July 22. https://www.chronicle.com/article/archiving-while-black/.

Fester, Rachel, Marybeth Gasman, and Thai-Huy Nguyen. 2012. "We Know Very Little: Accreditation and Historically Black Colleges and Universities." *Journal of Black Studies* 43 (7): 806–819.

Field, Linda. 1979. "Armstrong, Savannah State Exchange Going Smoothly." *Atlanta Constitution,* December 26, 1A, 9A.

Fincher, Cameron. 1982. "Who Studies Developmental Studies?" *Banner-Herald/Daily News,* October 3, 3C. Box 612B, Folder 16. Lane Library Special Collections at Georgia Southern University, Savannah.

Fincher, Cameron. 2003. *Historical Development of the University System of Georgia: 1923–2002,* 2nd ed. Athens, GA: Institute of Higher Education.

Finkelstein, Martin J., Valerie Martin Conley, and Jack H. Schuster. 2016. *Taking the Measure of Faculty Diversity.* New York: TIAA Institute. https://www.tiaainstitute.org/publication/taking-measure-faculty-diversity.

Fiske, Edward B. 1982. "Fewer Blacks Enter Universities; Recession and Aid Cuts Are Cited." *New York Times,* November 28, A1.

"Five Demands." 1969. *CUNY Digital History Archive.* American Social History Productions, Inc. https://cdha.cuny.edu/items/show/6952.

Flaugher, Ronald L. 1970. *Testing Practices, Minority Groups, and Higher Education: A Review and Discussion of the Research.* Princeton, NJ: Educational Testing Service.

Ford, Dwedor Morais. 2016. "HBCU Writing Centers Claiming an Identity in the Academy." In *Setting a New Agenda for Student Engagement and Retention in Historically Black Colleges and Universities,* edited by Charles B.W. Prince and Rochelle L. Ford. Hershey, PA: IGI Global, 37–48.

Ford, Nick Aaron. 1967. "Improving Reading and Writing Skills of Disadvantaged College Freshmen." *College Composition and Communication* 18 (2): 99–105.

"Fourth Segment of *A Plan for the Further Desegregation of the University System of Georgia.*" 1978. Box 41, Folder 21. Lane Library Special Collections at Georgia Southern University, Savannah.

Fowler, Judy, and Robert Ochsner. 2012. "Evaluating Essays across Institutional Boundaries: Teacher Attitudes toward Dialect, Race, and Writing." In *Race and Writing Assessment,* edited by Asao B. Inoue and Mya Poe. New York: Peter Lang, 111–126.

Fox, Tom. 1999. *Defending Access: A Critique of Standards in Higher Education.* Portsmouth, NH: Boynton/Cook.

"Freshman English in the New Urban University." 1969. *College Composition and Communication* 20 (3): 249–250.

Fulford, Collie. 2019. "Subverting Austerity: Advancing Writing at a Historically Black University." *Pedagogy: Critical Approaches to Teaching Literature, Language, Composition, and Culture* 19 (2): 225–241.

Fulwiler, Toby, Michael E. Gorman, and Margaret E. Gorman. 1986. "Changing Faculty Attitudes toward Writing." In *Writing across the Disciplines: Research into Practice*, edited by Art Young and Toby Fulwiler. Portsmouth, NH: Boynton/Cook, 53–67.

Gafford Muhammed, Crystal. 2009. "Mississippi Higher Education Desegregation and the Interest Convergence Principle: A CRT Analysis of the 'Ayers Settlement.'" *Race, Ethnicity and Education* 12 (3): 319–336.

Garcia, Gina Ann. 2019. *Becoming Hispanic Serving Institutions*. Baltimore: Johns Hopkins University Press.

García de Müeller, Genevieve, and Iris Ruiz. 2017. "Race, Silence, and Writing Program Administration: A Qualitative Study of US College Writing Programs." *WPA: Writing Program Administration* 40 (1): 19–39.

Gardner, Eileen M. 1990. "Back to Basics for Black Education." In *Critical Issues: A Conservative Agenda for Black Americans*, 2nd ed., edited by Joseph Perkins. Washington, DC: Heritage Foundation, 39–51.

Gardner, David Pierpont. 1983. *A Nation at Risk: The Imperative for Educational Reform*. Washington, DC: National Commission on Excellence in Education, US Department of Education.

Gardner Institute. 2018. "Our Mission, Vision, and History." https://www.jngi.org/mission -vision-history.

Geier v. Alexander. 593 F. Su 1263 (M.D. Tenn. 1984).

Geier v. University of Tennessee. 597 F.2d 1056 (6th Cir 1979).

General Assembly. 1959. *Acts and Resolutions of the General Assembly of the State of Georgia*, vol. 1. Atlanta: Longino and Porter, Inc. https://heinonline.org/HOL/P?h=hein.ssl /ssga0115&i=1.

Georgia State College. 1949. *Georgia State College: Catalogue Issue. Bulletin 1948–1949 with Announcements for 1949–1950.* Asa H. Gordon Library, Savannah State University, Savannah, GA. https://archive.org/details/georgiastatecol251949geor.

Gilyard, Keith. 1991. *Voices of the Self: A Study of Language Competence*. Detroit: Wayne State University Press.

Gilyard, Keith, and Adam J. Banks. 2018. *On African-American Rhetoric*. New York: Routledge.

Glenn, Cheryl, and Jessica Enoch. 2010. "Invigorating Historiographic Practices in Rhetoric and Composition Studies." In *Working in the Archives: Practical Research Methods for Rhetoric and Composition*, edited by Alexis E. Ramsey, Wendy B. Sharer, Barbara L'Eplattenier, and Lisa Mastrangelo. Carbondale: Southern Illinois University Press, 11–27.

Glover, Nathlyn. 1977. "Opinion Poll." *Tiger's Roar*, February, 3. Asa H. Gordon Library, Savannah State University, Savannah, GA.

Gold, David. 2008. *Rhetoric at the Margins: Revising the History of Writing Instruction in American Colleges, 1873–1947*. Carbondale: Southern Illinois University Press.

Goldstein, Michael B., and Blain B. Butner. 1987. "Dismissal of *Adams* Desegregation Cases." Memo to *Adams* States SHEEOs, December 17. RCB 55407, C14647. Georgia Archives, Morrow.

González, Carlos. 2017. "A Long Journey to Justice: The Story of the 'Geier' Case and the Desegregation of Tennessee Higher Education." *TBA Law Blog* 53 (12). https://www .tba.org/index.cfm?pg=LawBlog&blAction=showEntry&blogEntry=29526.

"Governor's Press Conference." 1983. July 6. RCB 1682, C123153. Georgia Archives, Morrow.

Graff, Harvey J. 1991. *The Literacy Myth: Cultural Integration and Social Structure in the Nineteenth Century*, 2nd ed. New Brunswick, NJ: Transaction.

Green, David F., Jr. 2016. "Expanding the Dialogue on Writing Assessment at HBCUs: Foundational Assessment Concepts and Legacies of Historically Black Colleges and Universities." *College English* 79 (2): 152–173.

Green, David F., Jr. 2019. "A Seat at the Table: Reflections on Writing Studies and HBCU Writing Programs." In *Black Perspectives in Writing Program Administration: From the Margins to the Center*, edited by Staci M. Perryman-Clark and Collin Lamont Craig. N.p.: Conference on College Composition and Communication of the National Council of Teachers of English, 51–73.

Green v. County School Board of New Kent County, Virginia. 391 US 430 (S. Ct. 1968).

Greene, Nicole Pepinster. 2008. "Basic Writing, Desegregation, and Open Admissions in Southwest Louisiana." In *Basic Writing in America: The History of Nine College Programs*, edited by Nicole Pepinster Greene and Patricia J. McAlexander. New York: Hampton, 71–99.

Grego, Rhonda C., and Nancy S. Thompson. 2007. *Teaching/Writing in Thirdspaces: The Studio Approach.* Carbondale: Southern Illinois University Press.

Guinn, Dorothy Margaret. 1976. "Freshman Composition: The Right Texts But the Wrong Students Walk in the Door." *College Composition and Communication* 27 (4): 344–349.

Gusa, Diane Lynn. 2010. "White Institutional Presence: The Impact of Whiteness on Campus Climate." *Harvard Educational Review* 80 (4): 464–489.

Hake, Rosemary. 1978. "With No Apology: Teaching to the Test." *Journal of Basic Writing* 1 (4): 39–62.

Hall, Clyde W. 1991. *One Hundred Years of Educating at Savannah State College, 1890–1990.* East Peoria, IL: Versa.

Halstead, Kent D. 1974. *Statewide Planning in Higher Education.* Washington, DC: US Department of Health, Education, and Welfare.

Hammond, J. W. 2018. "Toward a Social Justice Historiography for Writing Assessment." In *Writing Assessment, Social Justice, and the Advancement of Opportunity*, edited by Mya Poe, Asao B. Inoue, and Norbert Elliot. Boulder: WAC Clearinghouse, 41–70. https://wac.colostate.edu/books/perspectives/assessment/.

Hansen, Jane O. 1983. "Is Regents Test Racially Biased?" *Atlanta Constitution*, July 13, 1A, 4A.

Hansen, John, and Tom McCracken. 1975. "Request to the Department of Health, Education, and Welfare for Money for Instruction," December 18. Box 40, Folder 9. Lane Library Special Collections at Georgia Southern University, Savannah.

Harbour, Clifford P. 2020. "Dominant and Shadow Narratives Regarding the Desegregation of North Carolina Public Higher Education." *Community College Review* 48 (2): 156–172.

Harper, Shaun R., Lori D. Patton, and Ontario S. Wooden. 2009. "Access and Equity for African American Students in Higher Education: A Critical Race Historical Analysis of Policy Efforts." *Journal of Higher Education* 80 (4): 389–414.

Harris, Adam. 2018. "They Wanted Desegregation, They Settled for Money, and It's about to Run Out." *Chronicle of Higher Education*, March 26. https://www.chronicle.com/article/they-wanted-desegregation-they-settled-for-money-and-its-about-to-run-out/.

Harris, Jeanette. 1982. "Redefining the Role of the Writing Center." *Writing Lab Newsletter* 7 (3): 1–2.

Harris, Joseph. 1997. *A Teaching Subject: Composition since 1966.* Upper Saddle River, NJ: Prentice Hall, Inc.

Harris, Muriel. 1982. "Editor's Introduction." *Writing Lab Newsletter* 7 (3): 1.

Harris, Muriel, and Kathleen Blake Yancey. 1980. "Beyond Freshman Comp: Expanded Uses of the Writing Lab." *Writing Center Journal* 1 (1): 41–49.

Hart, David M. 2005. "From 'Ward of the State' to 'Revolutionary without a Movement': The Political Development of William C. Norris and Control Data Corporation, 1957–1986." *Enterprise and Society: The International Journal of Business History* 6 (2): 197–223.

Hasson, Judi. 1980. "Conservative Group Urges Changes in Affirmative Action Policies." *United Press International,* November 13.

Haswell, Richard, and Norbert Elliot. 2019. *Early Holistic Scoring of Writing: A Theory, a History, a Reflection.* Logan: Utah State University Press.

Haviland, Carol Peterson. 1985. "Writing Centers and Writing-across-the-Curriculum: An Important Connection." *Writing Center Journal* 5.6 (2–1): 25–30.

Haygood, Twila. 1973. "Mrs. Madie Dixon." Lane Library Special Collections at Georgia Southern University, Savannah. https://digitalcommons.georgiasouthern.edu/happiness-lane/8/.

Haynes, Leonard L., III, editor. 1978. *A Critical Examination of the Adams Case: A Source Book.* Washington, DC: Institute for Services to Education.

Healy, Patrick. 1996. "Mississippi Colleges Await Results of Tougher Admissions Standards." *Chronicle of Higher Education* (July 12) 42 (44): A30–A31.

Henderson, Harold P., and Gary L. Roberts. 1988. *Georgia Governors in an Age of Change: From Ellis Arnall to George Busbee.* Athens: University of Georgia Press.

Herbold, Hilary. 1994–1995. "Never a Level Playing Field: Blacks and the GI Bill." *Journal of Blacks in Higher Education* 6 (Winter): 104–108.

Hill, Renee Franklin. 2012. "Still Digitally Divided? An Assessment of Historically Black College and University Library Web Sites." *Journal of Academic Librarianship* 38 (1): 6–12.

Hill, Susan T. 1985. *The Traditionally Black Institutions of Higher Education: 1860–1982.* Washington, DC: National Center for Education Statistics. https://nces.ed.gov/pubsearch/pubsinfo.asp?pubid=84308.

Hoffer, Peter Charles, Williamjames Hull Hoffer, and N.E.H. Hull. 2007. *The Supreme Court: An Essential History.* Lawrence: University Press of Kansas.

Hooper, John W. 1979. "Special Studies Quarterly Report." Memo to Presidents, University System of Georgia Institutions, January 17. Box 29, Folder 8. Lane Library Special Collections at Georgia Southern University, Savannah.

Horner, Bruce, and Min-Zhan Lu. 1999. *Representing the "Other": Basic Writers and the Teaching of Basic Writing.* Urbana, IL: National Council of Teachers of English.

Hunt v. Arnold. 172 F.Supp 847 (N.D. Georgia 1959).

Hurtado, Sylvia, Jeffrey F. Milem, Alma R. Clayton-Pedersen, and Walter R. Allen. 1998. "Enhancing Campus Climates for Racial/Ethnic Diversity: Educational Policy and Practice." *Review of Higher Education* 21 (3): 279–302.

Inman, Joyce Olewski. 2013. "'Standard' Issue: Public Discourse, *Ayers v. Fordice,* and the Dilemma of the Basic Writer." *College English* 75 (3): 298–318.

Inoue, Asao B. 2009. "The Technology of Writing Assessment and Racial Validity." In *Handbook of Research on Assessment Technologies, Methods, and Applications in Higher Education,* edited by Christopher S. Schreiner. Hershey, PA: IGI Global, 97–120.

Inoue, Asao B. 2015. *Antiracist Writing Assessment Ecologies.* Fort Collins, CO: WAC Clearinghouse. https://wac.colostate.edu/books/perspectives/inoue/.

Inoue, Asao B., and Mya Poe, editors. 2012. *Race and Writing Assessment.* New York: Peter Lang.

Isaacs, Emily. 2018. *Writing at the State U: Instruction and Administration at 106 Comprehensive Universities.* Logan: Utah State University Press.

Jackson, Hope, and Karen Keaton Jackson. 2016. "Where We Are: Historically Black Colleges and Universities and Writing Programs." *Composition Studies* 44 (2): 153–157.

Jackson, Karen Keaton. 2009. "A Tale of Two Schools: A Collaborative Workshop." *Southern Discourse* 12 (2): 3–11.

Jackson, Karen Keaton, Hope Jackson, and Dawn N. Hicks Tafari. 2019. "We Belong in the Discussion: Including HBCUs in Conversations about Race and Writing." *College Composition and Communication* 71 (2): 184–214.

Jaffe, A. J., Walter Adams, and Sandra G. Meyers. 1968. *Negro Higher Education in the 1960's.* New York: Praeger.

Jarratt, Susan C. 2009. "Classics and Counterpublics in Nineteenth Century Historically Black Colleges." *College English* 72 (2): 134–159.

Jensen, George H. 1988. "Bureaucracy and Basic Writing Programs; or, Fallout from the Jan Kemp Trial." *Journal of Basic Writing* 7 (1): 30–37.

Johnson, David, and Lewis VanBrackle. 2012. "Linguistic Discrimination in Writing Assessment: How Raters React to African American 'Errors', ESL Errors, and Standard English Errors on a State-Mandated Writing Exam." *Assessing Writing* 17: 35–54.

Johnson, Harold T., and Morrill M. Hall, editors. 1968. "School Desegregation, Educational Change, and Georgia." Georgia Association for Supervision and Curriculum, Development, and School Desegregation Educational Center, University of Georgia. RCB 25505, C557372. Georgia Archives, Morrow.

Johnson, Otis S. 2016. *From 'N Word to Mr. Mayor: Experiencing the American Dream.* Brookfield, MO: Donning Company.

Jolly, Peggy. 1980. "Three Approaches to Teaching: The Laboratory Alternative." *Writing Lab Newsletter* 5 (2): 3–4.

Jones, Tiffany. 2017. "Can Equity Be Bought? A Look at Outcomes-Based Funding in Higher Ed." The Education Trust. https://edtrust.org/the-equity-line/can-equity-bought -outcomes-based-funding/.

Jones, William. 1993. "Basic Writing: Pushing against Racism." *Journal of Basic Writing* 12 (1): 72–80.

Jordan, June. 1981. "White English/Black English: The Politics of Translation (1972)." In *Civil Wars.* Boston: Beacon, 59–73.

Kaplan, Robert B. 1969. "On a Note of Protest (in a Minor Key): Bidialectism vs. Bidialectism." *College English* 30 (5): 386–389.

Karabel, Jerome. 2006. *The Chosen: The Hidden History of Admission and Exclusion at Harvard, Yale, and Princeton*, 2nd ed. Boston: Mariner Books.

Kelly, Ernece B. 1968. "Murder of the American Dream." *College Composition and Communication* 19 (2): 106–108.

Kelly, Lou. 1980. "One-on-One, Iowa City Style: Fifty Years of Individualized Writing Instruction." *Writing Center Journal* 1 (1): 4–19.

"Key Events in Black Higher Education: JBHE Chronology of Major Landmarks in the Progress of African Americans in Higher Education." 2020. *Journal of Blacks in Higher Education.* https://www.jbhe.com/chronology/.

Keyes v. School District no. 1, Denver. 413 US 189 (S. Ct. 1973).

Kiehle, Fred E., III. 1983. "Draft of Participation in Postsecondary Education: Factors and Options for Georgia," October. Governor's Committee on Postsecondary Education. RCB 15291. Georgia Archives, Morrow.

Kinlock, Valerie Felita. 2005. "Revisiting the Promise of *Students' Right to Their Own Language*: Pedagogical Strategies." *College Composition and Communication* 57 (1): 83–113.

Kirklighter, Cristina, Diana Cárdenas, and Susan Wolff Murphy, editors. 2007. *Teaching Writing with Latino/a Students: Lessons Learned at Hispanic Serving Institutions.* Albany: State University of New York Press.

Knight v. Alabama. 933 F.2D (N.D. Alabama 1991).

Knight v. Alabama. 476 F.3d 1219 (US Court of Appeals Eleventh Circuit 2007).

Kobrin, Jennifer L., Hui Deng, and Emily J. Shaw. 2011. "The Association between SAT Prompt Characteristics, Response Features, and Essay Scores." *Assessing Writing* 16 (3): 154–169.

Kruse, Kevin M. 2007. *White Flight: Atlanta and the Making of Modern Conservatism.* Princeton, NJ: Princeton University Press.

Kynard, Carmen. 2008. "Writing While Black: The Colour Line, Black Discourses, and Assessment in the Institutionalization of Writing Instruction." *English Teaching: Practice and Critique* 7 (2): 4–34.

Kynard, Carmen. 2013. *Vernacular Insurrections: Race, Black Protest, and the New Century in Composition-Literacies Studies.* Albany: State University of New York Press.

Kynard, Carmen, and Robert Eddy. 2009. "Toward a New Critical Framework: Color-Conscious Political Morality and Pedagogy at Historically Black and Historically White Colleges and Universities." *College Composition and Communication* 61 (1): W24–W44.

Labov, William. 1972. "Academic Ignorance and Black Intelligence." *The Atlantic*, June. https://www.theatlantic.com/past/docs/issues/95sep/ets/labo.htm.

Ladson-Billings, Gloria, and William F. Tate IV. 1995. "Toward a Critical Race Theory of Education." *Teachers College Record* 97 (1): 47–68.

Lamos, Steve. 2009. "What's in a Name: Institutional Critique, Writing Program Archives, and the Problem of Administrator Identity." *College English* 71 (4): 389–414.

Lamos, Steve. 2011. *Interests and Opportunities: Race, Racism, and University Writing Instruction in the Post-Civil Rights Era.* Pittsburgh, PA: University of Pittsburgh Press.

Lamos, Steve. 2012a. "Institutional Critique in Composition Studies: Methodological and Ethical Considerations for Researchers." In *Writing Studies Research in Practice*, edited by Lee Nickoson and Mary P. Sheridan. Carbondale: Southern Illinois University Press, 158–170.

Lamos, Steve. 2012b. "Minority-Serving Institutions, Race-Conscious 'Dwelling,' and Possible Futures for Basic Writing at Predominantly White Institutions." *Journal of Basic Writing* 31 (1): 4–35.

Languages, Literature, and Dramatic Arts. 1982. Minutes of the Department Meeting, June 3. Box 23B, Folder 2. Lane Library Special Collections at Georgia Southern University, Savannah.

Languages, Literature, and Dramatic Arts. 1984. Minutes of the Department Meeting, February 20. Box 17, Folder 29. Lane Library Special Collections at Georgia Southern University, Savannah.

Lathan, Rhea Estelle. 2015. *African American Civil Rights Literacy Activism, 1955–1967.* Studies in Writing and Rhetoric, Urbana, IL: National Council of Teachers of English.

Lavoie, John. 1979. Untitled Photograph. "Savannah State College: 1960s–1980s." *Savannah Morning News.* https://www.savannahnow.com/photogallery/GA/20120307/PHOTOGALLERY/303079653/PH/1.

Lawrence, Jill. 1987. "No Sanctions against Colleges with Failing Desegregation Plans." *Associated Press*, October 3.

Lemann, Nicholas. 2000. *The Big Test: The Secret History of American Meritocracy.* New York: Farrar, Straus and Giroux.

Lerner, Neal. 2009. *The Idea of a Writing Laboratory.* Carbondale: Southern Illinois University Press.

Letukas, Lynn. 2015. "Nine Facts about the SAT That Might Surprise You." New York: College Board. https://files.eric.ed.gov/fulltext/ED562751.pdf.

Lewis, Nancy. 1974. "Colleges' Problem Is Black and White." *Atlanta Constitution*, April 21, 6c.

Lindsey, Peggy, and Deborah J. Crusan. 2011. "How Faculty Attitudes and Expectations toward Student Nationality Affect Writing Assessment." *Across the Disciplines: A Journal of Language, Learning, and Academic Writing* 8. https://corescholar.libraries.wright.edu/english/247.

Lippi-Green, Rosina. 2011. *English with an Accent: Language, Ideology, and Discrimination in the United States*, 2nd ed. New York: Routledge.

Litolff, Edwin H., III. 2007. "Higher Education Desegregation: An Analysis of State Efforts in Systems Formerly Operating Segregated Systems of Higher Education." *LSU Doctoral Dissertations.* https://digitalcommons.lsu.edu/gradschool_dissertations/3134.

Lockett, Alexandria. 2019. "Why I Call It the Academic Ghetto." *Praxis* 16 (2). http://www.praxisuwc.com/162-lockett.

Lockett, Alexandria, and Sarah RudeWalker. 2016. "Creative Disruption and the Potential of Writing at HBCUs." *Composition Studies* 44 (2): 172–178.

Lockett, Alexandria, Shawanda Stewart, Brian J. Stone, Adrienne Redding, Jonathan Bush, Jeanne LaHaie, Staci M. Perryman-Clark, and Collin Lamont Craig. 2019. "Reflective Moments: Showcasing University Writing Program Models for Black Student Success." In *Black Perspectives in Writing Program Administration: From the Margins to the Center*, edited by Staci M. Perryman-Clark and Collin Lamont Craig. Urbana, IL: Conference on College Composition and Communication of the National Council of Teachers of English, 115–140.

Lovelace, Alice. 1979. "The Georgia Desegregation Plan." *Southern Changes: The Journal of the Southern Regional Council* 1 (8): 12–13.

Lucas, Brad, and Margaret M. Strain. 2010. "Keeping the Conversation Going: The Archives and Oral History." In *Working in the Archives: Practical Research Methods for Rhetoric and Composition*, edited by Alexis E. Ramsey, Wendy B. Sharer, Barbara L'Eplattenier, and Lisa Mastrangelo. Carbondale: Southern Illinois University Press, 259–277.

Lueck, Amy. 2020. *A Shared History: Writing in the High School, College, and University, 1856–1886*. Carbondale: Southern Illinois University Press.

Lunsford, Andrea A., Helene Moglen, and James Slevin. 1990. *The Right to Literacy*. New York: Modern Language Association of America.

Maeroff, Gene I. 1983. "Black Colleges' Failure to Draw Whites in South Is Focus of Desegregation Suit." *New York Times*, July 17, A11.

Maher, Jane. 1997. *Mina P. Shaughnessy: Her Life and Work*. Urbana, IL: National Council of Teachers of English.

Maltz, Earl M. 2016. *The Coming of the Nixon Court: The 1972 Term and the Transformation of Constitutional Law*. Lawrence: University Press of Kansas.

Maples, Rebeka L. 2014. *The Legacy of Desegregation: The Struggle for Equality in Higher Education*. New York: Palgrave Macmillan.

Marinara, Martha, and Mark McBeth. 2011. "Queer Caucus, Renaming Curiosity/ Resisting Ignorance: Interviewing Queerness." In *Listening to Our Elders: Working and Writing for Change*, edited by Samantha Blackmon, Cristina Kirklighter, and Steve Parks. Logan: Utah State University Press, 155–174.

Marks, Joseph L. 1983. *Georgia Postsecondary Education: FactFinder 1983*. Atlanta: Governor's Committee on Postsecondary Education. RCB 15291, Folder "Governor's Committee on Postsecondary Education." Georgia Archives, Morrow.

Martin Luther King Junior Elementary School Children v. Ann Arbor School District Board. 473 F.Supp. 1371 (E.D. Mich. 1979).

Masters, Thomas. 2010. "Reading the Archive of Freshman English." In *Working in the Archives: Practical Research Methods for Rhetoric and Composition*, edited by Alexis E. Ramsey, Barbara L'Eplattenier, Lisa Mastrangelo, and Wendy B. Sharer. Carbondale: Southern Illinois University Press, 157–168.

Matlin, Daniel. 2012. "Who Speaks for Harlem? Kenneth B. Clark, Albert Murray, and the Controversies of Black Urban Life." *Journal of American Studies* 46 (4): 875–894.

Maynor, Joan D.S. n.d. "Developmental Studies: A Twenty-Year Chronicle of a Mission 'In Progress.'" Record E12. Special Collections at Asa H. Gordon Library, Savannah State University, Savannah, GA.

McDavid, Raven I., Jr. 1965. "American Social Dialects." *College English* 26 (4): 254–260.

McFarland, Kathi. 1983. "Leaders Promise SSC Fight." *Savannah Morning News*, July 25.

McIver, Isaiah. 1972. "The Testing Movement and Blacks." *Faculty Research Edition of the Savannah State College Bulletin* 26 (2). http://hdl.handle.net/11286/612352.

Mellon, John C. 1975. *National Assessment and the Teaching of English: Results of the First National Assessment of Educational Progress in Writing, Reading, and Literature—Implications for Teaching and Measurement in the English Language Arts*. Washington, DC: National Institute of Education.

Mendelsohn, Sue. 2017. "Raising Hell: Literacy Instruction in Jim Crow America." *College English* 80 (1): 35–62.

Mendenhall, Annie S. 2014. "The Composition Specialist as Flexible Expert: Identity and Labor in the History of Composition." *College English* 77 (1): 11–31.

Mendenhall, Annie S. 2016. "'At a Hinge of History' in 1963: Rereading Disciplinary Origins in Composition." In *Microhistories of Composition*, edited by Bruce McComisky. Logan: Utah State University Press, 39–57.

Meyer, Ann. 2019. "Savannah State Enrollment Drops, State Regents Name New Chair." *Savannah Morning News*, November 12.

Michael, Deanna L. 2008. *Jimmy Carter as Educational Policymaker: Equal Opportunity and Efficiency*. Albany: State University of New York Press.

Milliken v. Bradley. 418 US 717 (S. Ct. 1974).

Mills, Charles W. 1997. *The Racial Contract*. Ithaca, NY: Cornell University Press.

Millward, Jody, Sandra Starkey, and David Starkey. 2007. "Teaching English in a California Two-Year Hispanic-Serving Institution: Complexities, Challenges, Programs, and Practices." In *Teaching Writing with Latino/a Students: Lessons Learned at Hispanic Serving Institutions*, edited by Cristina Kirklighter, Diana Cárdenas, and Susan Wolff Murphy. Albany: State University of New York Press, 37–59.

Minchin, Timothy J., and John A. Salmond. 2011. *After the Dream: Black and White Southerners since 1965*. Lexington: University Press of Kentucky.

Minkoff, Harvey, and Evelyn B. Melamed. 1975. "Response to Lawrence D. Freeman, 'The Students' Right to Their Own Language: Its Legal Bases.'" *College Composition and Communication* 26 (3): 311–312.

Minor, James T. 2008. "Segregation Residual in Higher Education: A Tale of Two States." *American Educational Research Journal* 45 (4): 861–885.

Mitgang, Lee. 1985. "Declining Black College Pool Makes Desegregation Tougher." *Associated Press*, August 8.

Moore, Don, K. Terry Schurr, and L. W. Henriksen. 1991. "Correlations of National Teacher Examination Core Battery Scores and College Grade Point Average with Teaching Effectiveness of First-Year Teachers." *Educational and Psychological Measurement* 51 (4): 1023–1028.

"More Blacks in Colleges: New Order's Wide Impact." 1977. *U.S. News and World Report*, July 18, 69.

Morris, Aldon, Walter Allen, David Maurrasse, and Derrick Gilbert. 1994. "White Supremacy and Higher Education: The Alabama Higher Education Desegregation Case." *National Black Law Journal* 14 (1): 59–91.

Moss, Beverly J. 2003. *A Community Text Arises: A Literate Text and a Literacy Tradition in African-American Churches*. New York: Hampton.

Mullican, James S. 1971. "'A Short Vision': Stimulus for Writing." *College Composition and Communication* 22 (3): 260–261.

Murphy, Richard T., and Lola Rhea Appel. 1977. *Evaluation of the PLATO IV Computer-Based Education System in the Community College*. Princeton, NJ: Educational Testing Service, June.

Musgrave, Marian E. 1971. "Failing Minority Students: Class, Caste, and Racial Bias in American Colleges." *College Composition and Communication* 22 (1): 24–29.

n.a. 1955. August 26. RCB 10596. Georgia Archives, Morrow.

n.a. n.d. Unmarked notes on the Regents' Test. RCB 1682, C123153. Georgia Archives, Morrow.

NAACP. 1976. *NAACP Report on Minority Testing*. Washington, DC: US Department of Health, Education, and Welfare.

Nash, Charles R. 1978. Letter to George L. Simpson Jr., January 4. Box 29, Folder 8. Lane Library Special Collections at Georgia Southern University, Savannah.

National Advisory Commission on Civil Disorders. 1968. *Report of the National Advisory Commission on Civil Disorders*. Princeton, NJ: Princeton University Press. https://heinonline.org/HOL/P?h=hein.prescomm/renadvccids0001&i=1.

National Center for Education Statistics. 2011. *The Nation's Report Card: Writing 2011.* NCES 2012-470. Washington, DC: Institute of Educational Sciences. https://nces.ed.gov /nationsreportcard/pubs/main2011/2012470.aspx#section2.

Nembhard, Judith P. 1983. "A Perspective on Teaching Black Dialect Students to Write Standard English." *Journal of Negro Education* 52 (1): 75–82.

Newman, Beatrice Méndez. 2007. "Teaching Writing at Hispanic Serving Institutions." In *Teaching Writing with Latino/a Students: Lessons Learned at Hispanic Serving Institutions,* edited by Cristina Kirklighter, Diana Cárdenas, and Susan Wolff Murphy. Albany: State University of New York Press, 17–36.

Newman, Frank. 1973. *The Second Newman Report: National Policy and Higher Education.* Cambridge: MIT Press.

"1979–80 (Five Year Plan)." 1979. Box 40, Folder 16. Lane Library Special Collections at Georgia Southern University, Savannah.

Nixon, Richard. 1970. *School Desegregation, "A Free and Open Society": A Policy Statement.* March 24. Washington, DC: Superintendent of Documents, US Government Printing Office. https://hdl.handle.net/2027/purl.32754050019078.

Nordquist, Dick. 1982. "The Writing Center." Memo to Brad Crain, January 30. Box 23b, Folder 2. Lane Library Special Collections at Georgia Southern University, Savannah.

North, Stephen M. 1984. "The Idea of a Writing Center." *College English* 46 (5): 433–446.

Office of the Chancellor. 1990. "Minority Educators in the Public Schools." Report. RCB 55407, C14645. Georgia Archives, Morrow.

Olivas, Michael A. 2013. *Suing Alma Mater: Higher Education and the Courts.* Baltimore: Johns Hopkins University Press.

Omi, Michael, and Howard Winant. 2015. *Racial Formation in the United States,* 3rd ed. New York: Routledge.

O'Neil, Wayne. 1972. "The Politics of Bidialectism." *College English* 33 (4): 433–438.

Otte, George, and Rebecca Williams Mlynarczyk. 2010. *Basic Writing.* West Lafayette, IN: Parlor. https://wac.colostate.edu/books/referenceguides/basicwriting/.

"Overseeing the University System of Georgia." 2021. University System of Georgia. https://www.usg.edu/regents/.

Owings, Huey Allen. 1974. "Accountability and the Composition Program: Implications of the Regents Testing Program of the University System of Georgia." Paper presented at the Annual Meeting of the Conference on College Composition and Communication, April, Anaheim, CA.

Oxford, C. T., George Busbee, and the University System of Georgia Board of Regents. 1977. *Plan for the Further Desegregation of the University System of Georgia.* Asa H. Gordon Library Special Collections, Savannah State University, Savannah, GA. https://archive .org/details/planforfurtherde00oxfo.

Palmquist, Mike, Pam Childers, Elaine Maimon, Joan Mullin, Rich Rice, Alisa Russell, and David R. Russell. 2020. "Fifty Years of WAC: Where Have We Been? Where Are We Going?" *Across the Disciplines* 17 (3–4). https://wac.colostate.edu/atd/archives/vol ume17/wac50/.

Panetta, Leon. 1969. "'Sample Copy' of the 1970 Compliance Report of Institutions of Higher Education under Title VI of the Civil Rights Act of 1964." Memorandum for Presidents of Institutions of Higher Education Participating in Federal Assistance Programs, December 22. Box 41, Folder 2. Lane Library Special Collections at Georgia Southern University, Savannah.

Pashia, Angela. 2017. "Examining Structural Oppression as a Component of Information Literacy: A Call for Librarians to Support #BlackLivesMatter through Our Teaching." *Journal of Information Literacy* 11 (2): 86–104.

Payne, Charles M. 2004. "'The Whole United States Is Southern!' *Brown v. Board* and the Mystification of Race." *Journal of American History* 91 (1): 83–91.

Pazant, Rosalie F. 1984. "Say What?" *Stylus: Developmental Studies, a Quarterly Bulletin for Faculty, Staff, and Students*, March, 1–2. Record E36. Asa H. Gordon Library Special Collections, Savannah State University, Savannah, GA.

Pendexter, Hugh. 1974. "Supplementary Statistics on Remedial English." Memo to H. Dean Propst, September 3. Box 60.1, Folder 8. Lane Library Special Collections at Georgia Southern University, Savannah.

Perna, Laura W., Jeffrey Milem, Danette Gerald, Evan Baum, Heather Rowan, and Neal Hutchens. 2006. "The Status of Equity for Black Undergraduates in Public Higher Education in the South: Still Separate and Unequal." *Research in Higher Education* 47 (2): 197–228.

Perryman-Clark, Staci M. 2013. *Afrocentric Teacher-Research: Rethinking Appropriateness and Inclusion*. New York: Peter Lang.

Perryman-Clark, Staci M. 2016. "Who We Are(n't) Assessing: Racializing Language and Writing Assessment in Writing Program Administration." *College English* 79 (2): 206–211.

Perryman-Clark, Staci M., and Collin Lamont Craig. 2019a. "Black Student Success Models: Institutional Profiles of Writing Programs." In *Black Perspectives in Writing Program Administration: From the Margins to the Center*, edited by Staci M. Perryman-Clark and Collin Lamont Craig. Urbana, IL: Conference on College Composition and Communication of the National Council of Teachers of English, 101–114.

Perryman-Clark, Staci M., and Collin Lamont Craig. 2019b. "Introduction: Black Matters: Writing Program Administration in Twenty-First-Century Higher Education." In *Black Perspectives in Writing Program Administration: From the Margins to the Center*, edited by Staci M. Perryman-Clark and Collin Lamont Craig. Urbana, IL: Conference on College Composition and Communication of the National Council of Teachers of English, 1–27.

Phillips, Layli. 2000. "Recontextualizing Kenneth B. Clark: An Afrocentric Perspective on the Paradoxical Legacy of a Model Psychologist-Activist." *History of Psychology* 3 (2): 142–167.

Piché, Gene L., Donald L. Rubin, Lona J. Turner, and Michael L. Michlin. 1978. "Teachers' Subjective Evaluations of Standard and Black Nonstandard English Compositions: A Study of Written Language and Attitudes." *Research in the Teaching of English* 12 (2): 107–118.

Pimentel, Octavio, Charise Pimentel, and John Dean. 2017. "The Myth of the Colorblind Writing Classroom: White Instructors Confront White Privilege in Their Classrooms." In *Performing Anti-Racist Pedagogy in Rhetoric, Writing, and Communication*, edited by Frankie Condon and Vershawn Ashanti Young. Fort Collins, CO: WAC Clearinghouse, 109–122.

Pixton, William H. 1974. "A Contemporary Dilemma: The Question of Standard English." *College Composition and Communication* 25 (4): 247–253.

"A Plan for the Further Integration of the University System of Georgia." 1973, June 11. Box 41, Folder 5. Lane Library Special Collections at Georgia Southern University, Savannah.

Poe, Mya. 2013. "Re-framing Race in Teaching Writing across the Curriculum." *Across the Disciplines* 10 (3). https://wac.colostate.edu/docs/atd/race/poe.pdf.

Poe, Mya, and John Aloysius Cogan Jr. 2016. "Civil Rights and Writing Assessment: Using the Disparate Impact Approach as a Fairness Methodology to Evaluate Social Impact." *Journal of Writing Assessment* 9 (1). http://journalofwritingassessment.org/article.php?article=97.

Poe, Mya, Norbert Elliot, John Aloysius Cogan Jr., and Tito G. Nurudeen Jr. 2014. "The Legal and the Local: Using Disparate Impact Analysis to Understand the Consequences of Writing Assessment." *College Composition and Communication* 65 (4): 588–611.

Poe, Mya, Asao B. Inoue, and Norbert Elliot. 2018. "Introduction: The End of Isolation." In *Writing Assessment, Social Justice, and the Advancement of Opportunity*, edited by Mya Poe, Asao B. Inoue, and Norbert Elliot. Fort Collins, CO: WAC Clearinghouse, 3–38. https://wac.colostate.edu/books/perspectives/assessment/.

Pounds, Haskin. 1983. "1983 Annual Progress Report to the Office of Civil Rights." Memo to Howard Jordan, October 3. RCB 55407, C14647. Georgia Archives, Morrow.

Powe, Lucas A., Jr. 2000. *The Warren Court and American Politics.* Cambridge, MA: Harvard University Press.

Powell, Bertie Jeffress. 1984. "A Comparison of Students' Attitudes and Success in Writing." *Journal of Negro Education* 53 (2): 114–123.

Powell, Katrina M., and Pamela Takayoshi. 2003. "Accepting the Roles Created for Us: The Ethics of Reciprocity." *College Composition and Communication* 54 (3): 394–422.

Pratt, Robert A. 2002. *We Shall Not Be Moved: The Desegregation of the University of Georgia.* Athens: University of Georgia Press.

Prendergast, Catherine. 1998. "Race: The Absent Presence in Composition Studies." *College Composition and Communication* 50 (1): 36–53.

Prendergast, Catherine. 2003. *Literacy and Racial Justice: The Politics of Learning after* Brown v. Board of Education. Carbondale: Southern Illinois University Press.

Presley, John W., and William M. Dodd. 2008. "The Political History of Developmental Studies in the University System of Georgia." *Community College Enterprise* 14 (2): 37–55.

Pritchard, Eric Darnell. 2017. *Fashioning Lives: Black Queers and the Politics of Literacy.* Carbondale: Southern Illinois University Press.

"The Process of Composing: Invention or Pre-Writing?" 1970. *College Composition and Communication* 21 (3): 285–286.

Propst, H. Dean. 1984. Letter to Harry M. Singleton. RCB 1393, C 32221. Georgia Archives, Morrow.

Propst, H. Dean. 1988. "Consolidation Study: Darton College/Albany State College and Armstrong State College/Savannah State College Final Report." May 11. C14658. Georgia Archives, Morrow.

"Questions and Answers on the School Segregation Proposal." 1954. *Georgia State*, October 21, 4. RCB 10596. Georgia Archives, Morrow.

Quirk, Thomas J., Barbara J. Witten, and Susan F. Weinberg. 1973. "Review of Studies of the Concurrent and Predictive Validity of the National Teacher Examinations." *Review of Educational Research* 43 (1): 89–113.

Rankin, Joy. 2015. "From Mainframes to the Masses: A Participatory Computing Movement in Minnesota Education." *Information and Culture* 52 (2): 197–216.

Ravan, Andee, Tom Milam, and Bill D. Fettner. 1978. "An External Evaluation of the Title III (BIDP) Program." Box 18A, Folder 15. Lane Library Special Collections at Georgia Southern University, Savannah.

Rayburn, Wendell Gilbert, and Luetta Colvin Millege. 1981. "Savannah State College Self-Study Report of the School of Humanities and Social Sciences." Record E32. Asa H. Gordon Library, Savannah State University, Savannah, GA.

Raz, Mical. 2013. *What's Wrong with the Poor? Psychiatry, Race, and the War on Poverty.* Chapel Hill: University of North Carolina Press.

Redd, Teresa M. 1992. "Untapped Resources: 'Styling' in Black Students' Writing for Black Audiences." Paper presented at the Annual Meeting of the American Educational Research Association, April 20–24, San Francisco, CA.

Redd, Teresa M. 1993. "An Afrocentric Curriculum in a Composition Classroom: Motivating Students to Read, Write, and Think." Paper presented at the Conference on College Composition and Communication, March 31–April 3, San Diego, CA.

Redd, Teresa M. 2012. "An HBCU Perspective on Academically Adrift." *College Composition and Communication* 83 (3): 499–506.

Redd, Teresa M., and Karen Schuster Webb. 2005. *A Teacher's Introduction to African American English: What a Writing Teacher Should Know.* Urbana, IL: National Council of Teachers of English.

Reeves, Alexis Scott. 1978. "Officials Blamed for School Plan Flop." *Atlanta Constitution,* February 3, 16A.

Regents of the University of California v. Bakke. 438 US 265 (S. Ct. 1978).

Regents of the University System of Georgia. 1974. *A Plan for the Further Desegregation of the University System of Georgia.* Submitted to the Office of Civil Rights, Department of Health, Education, and Welfare, Washington, DC. Special Collections LC 212.72 G1, G46. Lane Library Special Collections at Georgia Southern University, Savannah.

"Remedial English at ASC." 1973. Box 29, Folder 4. Lane Library Special Collections at Georgia Southern University, Savannah.

Rentz, Robert R. 1979. "Testing and the College Degree." In *Measurement and Educational Policy,* edited by William B. Schrader. Educational Testing Service, San Francisco: Jossey-Bass, Inc., 71–78.

Rice, Bradley R. 1988. "Lester Maddox and the Politics of Populism." In *Georgia Governors in an Age of Change: From Ellis Arnall to George Busbee,* edited by Harold P. Henderson and Gary L. Roberts. Athens: University of Georgia Press, 193–210.

Rich, Spencer. 1978. "Califano Hit on Desegregation Plan." *Washington Post,* May 26, A4.

Richards, Bill. 1979. "Hot Potato Waits on Back Burner for New Cabinet Member." *Washington Post,* December 18.

Richardson, Elaine. 2003. *African American Literacies.* New York: Routledge.

Richardson, Elaine. 2004. "Coming from the Heart: African American Students, Literacy Stories, and Rhetorical Education." In *African American Rhetoric(s): Interdisciplinary Perspectives,* edited by Elaine B. Richardson and Ronald L. Jackson II. Carbondale: Southern Illinois University Press, 155–169.

Richardson, Elaine, and Keith Gilyard. 2001. "Students' Right to Possibility: Basic Writing and African American Rhetoric." In *Insurrections: Approaches to Resistance in Composition Studies,* edited by Andrea Greenbaum. Albany: State University of New York Press, 37–51.

Richburg, Keith B. 1985a. "Fewer Blacks Finding Way to College; Past Gains Have Given Way to Declining Enrollment." *Washington Post,* July 6, A1.

Richburg, Keith B. 1985b. "Minorities' College Rate Seen Falling; Lag in Financial Aid Viewed as Factor." *Washington Post,* March 24, A15.

Ritter, Kelly. 2009. *Before Shaughnessy: Basic Writing at Yale and Harvard, 1920–1960.* Carbondale: Southern Illinois University Press.

Rogers, Ibram H. 2012. *The Black Campus Movement: Black Students and the Racial Reconstitution of Higher Education, 1965–1972.* New York: Palgrave Macmillan.

Rooks, Noliwe M. 2006. *White Money/Black Power: The Surprising History of African American Studies and the Crisis of Race and Higher Education.* Boston: Beacon.

Rose, Shirley K. 1999. "Two Disciplinary Narratives for Non-Standard English in the Classroom: Citation Histories of Shaughnessy's *Errors and Expectations* and Smitherman's *Talkin' and Testifyin'*." In *History, Reflection, and Narrative: The Professionalization of Composition, 1963–1983,* edited by Mary Rosner, Beth Boehm, and Debra Journet. Stamford, CT: Apex, 187–204.

Rosenthal, Jack. 1970. "Nixon Contests Scranton Report on Healing Rifts." *New York Times,* December 13, 1.

Rothstein, Richard. 2017. *The Color of Law: A Forgotten History of How Our Government Segregated America.* New York: W. W. Norton.

Royster, Jacqueline Jones. 2000. *Traces of a Stream: Literacy and Social Change among African American Women.* Pittsburgh: University of Pittsburgh Press.

Royster, Jacqueline Jones, and Gesa E. Kirsch. 2012. *Feminist Rhetorical Practices: New Horizons for Rhetoric, Composition, and Literacy Studies.* Carbondale: Southern Illinois University Press.

Royster, Jacqueline Jones, and Jean C. Williams. 1999. "History in the Spaces Left: African American Presence and Narratives of Composition Studies." *College Composition and Communication* 50 (4): 563–584.

Ruecker, Todd, Dawn Shephard, Heidi Estrem, and Beth Brunk-Chavez. 2017. "Retention, Persistence, and Writing: Expanding the Conversation." In *Retention, Persistence, and Writing Programs*, edited by Todd Ruecker, Dawn Shephard, Heidi Estrem, and Beth Brunk-Chavez. Logan: Utah State University Press, 3–18.

Ruiz, Iris D. 2016. *Reclaiming Composition for Chicano/as and Other Ethnic Minorities: A Critical History and Pedagogy*. New York: Palgrave Macmillan.

Russell, David R. 2002. *Writing in the Academic Disciplines: A Curricular History*, 2nd ed. Carbondale: Southern Illinois University Press.

Sack, Kevin, 1984a. "Regents, Feds End Dispute over Test." *Atlanta Journal*, June 1, 1D, 6D.

Sack, Kevin. 1984b. "Rights Aid Praises Regents Test Accord." *Atlanta Constitution*, June 3, 48A.

Sack, Kevin. 1984c. "State Regents Test Dispute Near Settlement." *Atlanta Journal*, May 16, 1A, 11A.

Samuels, Albert L. 2004. *Is Separate Unequal? Black Colleges and the Challenge to Desegregation*. Lawrence: University Press of Kansas.

Savannah Community Liaison Committee. 1978. *Final Report from Savannah Community Liaison Committee to the Board of Regents on the Desegregation of Armstrong State College and Savannah State College*. July 5. Box 43, Folders 29A–D. Lane Library Special Collections at Georgia Southern University, Savannah.

Savannah State College. 1968. *Savannah State College Bulletin: General Catalog Issue, April 1968: Announcements for 1968–1969*. Asa H. Gordon Library, Savannah State University, Savannah, GA. https://archive.org/details/savannahstatebul51968sava.

Savannah State College. 1970. *Savannah State College Bulletin: General Catalog Issue, April 1970: Announcements for 1970–1971*. Asa H. Gordon Library, Savannah State University, Savannah, GA. https://archive.org/details/savannahstatebul51970sava.

Savannah State College. 1972. *Savannah State College Bulletin: General Catalog Issue, 1972–1974*. Asa H. Gordon Library, Savannah State University, Savannah, GA. https://archive.org/details/savannahstatebul72sava.

Savannah State College. 1974. *Savannah State College Bulletin: General Catalog Issue, 1974–1975*. Asa H. Gordon Library, Savannah State University, Savannah, GA. https://archive.org/details/savannahstatebul74sava.

Savannah State College. 1977. *Savannah State College Bulletin: General Catalog Issue, 1976–1978, Supplemental Issue 1977–1978*. Asa H. Gordon Library, Savannah State University, Savannah, GA. https://archive.org/details/savannahstatecol77sava.

Savannah State College. 1989. *Savannah State College Bulletin: General Catalog Issue, 1989–1990*. Asa H. Gordon Library, Savannah State University, Savannah, GA. https://archive.org/details/savannahstatecol89sava.

Savannah State University. 1998. *Savannah State University Bulletin: General Catalog Issue, 1998–2000*. Asa H. Gordon Library, Savannah State University, Savannah, GA. https://archive.org/details/savannahstate19982000sava.

Schmidt, William E. 1984. "U.S. to Drop Exam Bias Charges against Georgia." *New York Times*, June 3, A31.

Schrader, W. B. 1971. "The Predictive Validity of College Board Admissions Tests." In *The College Board Admissions Testing Program: A Technical Report on Research and Development Activities Relating to the Scholastic Aptitude Test and Achievement Tests*, edited by William H. Angoff. Princeton, NJ: College Entrance Examination Board, 117–181.

Scranton, William W., James F. Ahern, Erwin D. Canham, James E. Cheek, Benjamin O. Davis, Martha A. Derthick, Bayless Manning, Revius O. Ortique Jr., and Joseph Rhodes Jr. 1970. *The Report of the President's Commission on Campus Unrest*. Washington, DC: President's Commission on Campus Unrest.

"Secretary's Reports." 1977. *College Composition and Communication* 28 (3): 286–291.

Sellers Diamond, Alfreda A. 2008. "Black, White, Brown, Green, and *Fordice*: The Flavor of Higher Education in Louisiana and Mississippi." *Hastings Race and Poverty Law Journal* 5 (1): 57–128.

Semas, Philip W. 1974. "80,000 High-School Graduates Studied: Minorities' Academic Preparation Better than Generally Believed." *Chronicle of Higher Education*, May 28, 7.

"7 of 8 Negro Applicants Rejected Again by Tech." 1961. *Atlanta Constitution*, August 4, 9.

Shaughnessy, Mina P. 1977. *Errors and Expectations: A Guide for the Teacher of Basic Writing.* New York: Oxford University Press.

Sheils, Merrill. 1975. "Why Johnny Can't Write." *Newsweek* 92 (December 8), 58–63.

Simpson, George L., Jr. 1977. Letter to David S. Tatel, December 15. RCB 28660, "Desegregation Response." Georgia Archives, Morrow.

Simpson, George L., Jr., and Charles T. Oxford. 1978. Letter to David S. Tatel, March 8. Box 41, Folder 20. Lane Library Special Collections at Georgia Southern University, Savannah.

Skinnell, Ryan. 2016. *Conceding Composition: A Crooked History of Composition's Institutional Fortunes.* Logan: Utah State University Press.

Sledd, James. 1969. "Bi-Dialectism: The Linguistics of White Supremacy." *The English Journal* 58 (9): 1307–1315, 1329.

Smith, Christi Michelle. 2016. *Reparation and Reconciliation: The Rise and Fall of Integrated Higher Education.* Chapel Hill: University of North Carolina Press.

Smitherman, Geneva. 1971. "Black Idiom." *Negro American Literature Forum* 5 (3): 88–91.

Smitherman, Geneva. 1977. *Talkin and Testifyin: The Language of Black America.* Boston: Houghton Mifflin.

Smitherman, Geneva, editor. 1981. *Black English and the Education of Black Children and Youth: Proceedings of the National Invitational Symposium on the* King *Decision.* Detroit: Wayne State University Press.

Smitherman, Geneva. 1993. "'The Blacker the Berry, the Sweeter the Juice': African American Student Writers and the National Assessment of Educational Progress." Paper presented at the Annual Meeting of the National Council of Teachers of English, November 17–22, Pittsburgh, PA.

Smitherman-Donaldson, Geneva. 1987. "Toward a National Public Policy on Language." *College English* 49 (1): 29–36.

Snyder, Thomas D., Cristobal de Bray, and Sally A. Dillow. 2016. "Digest of Educational Statistics." National Center for Education Statistics. https://nces.ed.gov/pubsearch/pubs info.asp?pubid=2017094.

Soliday, Mary. 2002. *The Politics of Remediation: Institutional and Student Needs in Higher Education.* Pittsburgh, PA: University of Pittsburgh Press.

"Special Studies Program, Winter Quarter Report." 1975. March 31. Box 29, Folder 4. Lane Library Special Collections at Georgia Southern University, Savannah.

Spencer-Maor, Faye, and Robert E. Randolph Jr. 2016. "Shifting the Talk: Writing Studies, Rhetoric, and Feminism at HBCUs." *Composition Studies* 44 (2): 179–182.

Spikes, W. Curtis, and Lerah A. Spikes. 1983. "Development of a College Curriculum to Enhance Essay Writing Skills at a Predominantly Black College." *Journal of Negro Education* 52 (2): 110–117.

Stanley, Jane. 2010. *The Rhetoric of Remediation: Negotiating Entitlement and Access to Higher Education.* Pittsburgh, PA: University of Pittsburgh Press.

Staples, Brent. 1986. "The Dwindling Black Presence on Campus." *New York Times*, April 27, 46.

"A Statement Given in Behalf of a Resolution about Writing Lab Professionals." 1981. *Writing Lab Newsletter* 5 (10): 4.

"The Status of Freshman Composition." 1968. *College Composition and Communication* 19 (1): 81–85.

Stocker, Erich Franz. 1977. "Preliminary Conclusions Special Studies Research." Memo to Henry Ashmore, November 23. Box 42, Folder 27. Lane Library Special Collections at Georgia Southern University, Savannah.

Stocker, Erich Franz. 1978. "Regents' Examination Failure Rate." Memo to Henry Ashmore, April 25. Box 42, Folder 27. Lane Library Special Collections at Georgia Southern University, Savannah.

Stone, Brian J., and Shawanda Stewart. 2016. "HBCUs and Writing Programs: Critical Hip Hop Language Pedagogy and First-Year Student Success." *Composition Studies* 44 (2): 183–186.

Stone, Janet D. 2010. *From the Mansion to the University: A History of Armstrong Atlantic State University, 1935–2010.* Savannah, GA: Armstrong Atlantic State University.

Stroud, Cynthia. 1980. "Writing Center Workshops: A Way to Reach Out." *Writing Lab Newsletter* 5 (2): 1–3.

Stuart, Reginald. 1981. "New Trend in College Desegregation Emerges." *New York Times*, September 3, A1.

Stuart, Reginald. 1984. "Black Colleges Survive, but Students Are Fewer." *New York Times*, February 1, A18.

"A Study of Patterns of Institutional Response to Blacks in Higher Education." n.d. Department of Higher Ed, School of Education, Indiana University, Bloomington. Box 41, Folder 3. Lane Library Special Collections at Georgia Southern University, Savannah.

Sum, Paul E., Steven Andrew Light, and Ronald F. King. 2004. "Race, Reform, and Desegregation in Mississippi Higher Education: Historically Black Institutions after *United States v. Fordice.*" *Law and Social Inquiry* 29 (2): 403–435.

"A Survey of Faculty Views on Student Writing." 1981. Box 23B, Folder 2. Lane Library Special Collections at Georgia Southern University, Savannah.

Swann v. Charlotte-Mecklenburg Board of Education. 403 US 912 (S. Ct. 1971).

Tacorda, Ryan. 2003. "Acknowledging Those Stubborn Facts of History: The Vestiges of Segregation." *UCLA Law Review* 50: 1547–1583.

Tate, William F., Gloria Ladson-Billings, and Carl A. Grant. 1993. "The *Brown* Decision Revisited: Mathematizing Social Problems." *Educational Policy* 7 (3): 255–275.

Testing Center. 2017. Email to Annie Mendenhall. Savannah State University, July 25.

Thelin, John R. 2004. *A History of American Higher Education.* Baltimore: Johns Hopkins University Press.

Thornton, Toni Clark. 1972. "An Alternative Freshman English Program for Minority Students." *College Composition and Communication* 23 (5): 365–370.

Tinto, Vincent. 1975. "Dropout from Higher Education: A Theoretical Synthesis of Recent Research." *Review of Educational Research* 45 (1): 89–125.

Tinto, Vincent, and John Cullen. 1973. "Dropout in Higher Education: A Review and Theoretical Synthesis of Recent Research." Washington, DC: US Office of Education.

Toth, Christie, and Laura Aull. 2014. "Directed Self-Placement Questionnaire Design: Practices, Problems, Possibilities." *Assessing Writing* 20: 1–18.

Tovatt, A. 1965. "Oral-Aural-Visual Stimuli for Teaching Composition." *English Journal* 54 (3): 191–195.

Turner, Caroline Sotello Viernes, Juan Carlos González, and J. Luke Wood. 2008. "Faculty of Color in Academe: What 20 Years of Literature Tells Us." *Journal of Diversity in Higher Education* 1 (3): 139–168.

Twomey, Steve. 1990. "Singleton's Disputed Record." *Washington Post*, October 25. https://www.washingtonpost.com/archive/politics/1990/10/25/singletons-disputed-record/cf2edd71-a733-4f25-9572-1571176606b0/.

United States v. Fordice. 505 US 717 (S. Ct. 1992).

United States v. Louisiana. 9 F.3d. 1159 (5th Cir. 1993).

United States v. Louisiana. 718 F.499 (E.D. La. 1989).

University System of Georgia. 1978. "1968–1978: Ten Year Enrollment Reports." https:// www.usg.edu/research/enrollment_reports.

University System of Georgia. 1981. "1971–1981: Ten Year Enrollment Reports." https:// www.usg.edu/research/enrollment_reports.

University System of Georgia. 1990. "1981–1990: Ten Year Enrollment Reports." https:// www.usg.edu/research/enrollment_reports.

University System of Georgia. 1996. "Regents Testing Program." https://www.usg.edu/re search/digest/1997/regents_prog.html.

University System of Georgia. 2003. "Policy Changes Adopted on Regents' Test." April 16. https://www.usg.edu/news/release/policy_changes_adopted_on_regents_test.

University System of Georgia. 2007. "Board Approves Recommendations on Regents Testing Policy." June 12. https://www.usg.edu/news/release/board_approves_recom mendations_on_regents_testing_policy.

University System of Georgia. 2010a. "Board Approves Recommendations on Regents Testing Policy." January 12. https://www.usg.edu/news/release/board_approves_recom mendations_on_regents_testing_policy1.

University System of Georgia. 2010b. "2.8 Board of Regents' Testing Program." Academic and Student Affairs Handbook, January 20. https://www.usg.edu/academic_affairs _handbook/section2/C757.

University System of Georgia. 2019. *Learning Support Manual.* https://www.usg.edu/assets /academic_affairs_and_policy/documents/transforming_remediation/LearningSup portManual.pdf.

Valles, Sarah Banschbach, Rebecca Day Babcok, and Karen Keaton Jackson. 2017. "Writing Center Administrators and Diversity: A Survey." *Peer Review* 1 (1). https://thepeerreview -iwca.org/issues/issue-1/writing-center-administrators-and-diversity-a-survey/.

Vasquez, James A., and Nancy Wainstein. 1990. "Instructional Responsibilities of College Faculty to Minority Students." *Journal of Negro Education* 59 (4): 599–610.

Victorelli, Laura. 2019. "The Right to Be Heard (and Understood): Impartiality and the Effect of Sociolinguistic Bias in the Courtroom." *University of Pittsburgh Law Review* 80 (3): 709–728.

Villanueva, Victor. 2006. "Blind: Talking about the New Racism." *Writing Center Journal* 26 (1): 3–19.

Vobejda, Barbara. 1987. "5 States Said to Default on College Desegregation; Racial Gap Wider than in '70s, Group Charges." *Washington Post*, August 7, A6.

Walker, Barbara A. 1977. Letter to Albert T. Hamlin, April 29. Box 41, Folder 16. Lane Library Special Collections at Georgia Southern University, Savannah.

Wallenstein, Peter. 2008. "Black Southerners and Nonblack Universities: The Process of Desegregating Southern Higher Education, 1935–1965." In *Higher Education and the Civil Rights Movement: White Supremacy, Black Southerners, and College Campuses,* edited by Peter Wallenstein. Gainesville: University Press of Florida, 17–59.

Wallenstein, Peter. 2015. "*Brown v. Board of Education* and Segregated Universities: From Kluger to Klarman—Toward Creating a Literature on Federal Courts and Undergraduate Admissions." *Virginia Social Science Journal* 50: 11–23.

Warnick, Marta. 1984. "Historically Black College Struggling to Desegregate." *Associated Press*, September 9.

Warnock, Caroline. 2017. Personal Interview. December 7, Savannah, GA.

Watters, Pat. 1979. "Faith, Hope, and Parity." *Change* 11 (7): 10–13.

Wellborn, Stanley N. 1980. "Education Department: Born in a Tempest." *U.S. News and World Report*, May 12, 49.

White, Edward M. 1978. "Mass Testing of Individual Writing: The California Model." *Journal of Basic Writing* 1 (4): 18–38.

White, Edward M., and Thomas Leon. 1981. "Racial Minorities and Writing Skills Assessment in the California State University and Colleges." *College English* 43 (3): 276–283.

Wilder, Craig Steven. 2013. *Ebony and Ivy: Race, Slavery, and the Troubled History of America's Universities.* New York: Bloomsbury.

Williamson-Lott, Joy Ann. 2018. *Jim Crow Campus: Higher Education and the Struggle for a New Southern Social Order.* New York: Teachers College Press.

Wilson, Cory Todd. 1994. "Mississippi Learning: Curriculum for the Post-Brown of Higher Education Desegregation." *Yale Law Journal* 4 (1): 243–282.

Wilson, Kenneth M. 1974. "The Validity of a Measure of 'Academic Motivation' for Forecasting Freshman Achievement at Seven Liberal Arts Colleges." Educational Testing Service, Princeton, NJ: College Entrance Examination Board.

Winkler, Karen J. 1974. "After a Decade, College Desegregation Still an Issue." *Chronicle of Higher Education,* May 28, 1, 6.

Women's Equity Action League v. Cavazos. 906 F.2d 742 (Court of Appeals, District of Columbia Circuit 1990).

Wooten, Melissa E. 2015. *In the Face of Inequality: How Black Colleges Adapt.* Albany: State University of New York Press.

Wright, Marion A. 1955. "How to Implement the Supreme Court Decision." *New South,* March, 3–7. Box 10596. Georgia Archives, Morrow.

"Writing across the Curriculums Newsletter: Winter 1984." 1984. Box 17, Folder 29. Lane Library Special Collections at Georgia Southern University, Savannah.

Yancey, Kathleen Blake. 1999. "Looking Back as We Look Forward: Historicizing Writing Assessment as a Rhetorical Act." *College Composition and Communication* 50 (3): 483–503.

Young, Art, and Toby Fulwiler, editors. 1986. *Writing across the Disciplines: Research into Practice.* Upper Montclair, NJ: Boynton/Cook.

Young, Vershawn Ashanti. 2009. "'Nah, We Straight': An Argument against Code Switching." *JAC* 29 (1–2): 49–76.

Zaluda, Scott. 1998. "Lost Voices of the Harlem Renaissance: Writing Assigned at Howard University, 1919–31." *College Composition and Communication* 50 (2): 232–257.

INDEX

academic skills, 41, 56, 60, 63–64
Academic Skills Laboratory, 78, 106
Academic Skills pilot, 56; writing assignments in, 57–59
academic standards, 26, 50, 80, 84, 99, 101, 104; of HWCUs, 7–8; HEW on, 86–87; in student writing, 106, 107; at white colleges, 132–33; in writing programs, 116–17
accreditation agencies, segregated, 15
Accuplacer testing, 26
ACT scores, 16, 17, 88, 148, 149
Adams cases, 13, 48, 82, 154–55(nn15–17); Black colleges and, 40–41
Adams v. Califano, 82, 83, 93, 155(n16)
Adams v. Richardson, 13, 18, 40, 155(n16)
admissions, 14, 24, 49; nondiscriminatory, 17, 56; obstacles to, 75, 154(n11)
admissions standards/requirements, 19, 22, 41, 69, 74–75, 144; Armstrong State, 78, 105; HEW on, 87, 102–3; Mississippi, 26–27, 147, 148; race and, 76–77, 82; segregated schools and, 16, 17; USG system, 95, 96–97; white colleges, 124–25
affirmative action, 20, 41, 88, 113; at Armstrong State, 55–56
African Americans, 10, 12, 13, 36, 42, 82, 150, 152; and CCCC, 46–47; as faculty, 61–62; segregated colleges and, 14–18. *See also* Black students
Ahmed, Sara, 7, 28
Alabama, 16, 18, 21–22, 39, 114, 154(n12), 155(n19)
Alabama State College/University, 39, 114
Alabama State Teachers Association v. Alabama Public School and College Authority (*ASTA*), 39, 94
Albany Junior College, 96
Albany State College, 95, 96, 98, 99, 126
"Alternative Freshman English Program for Minority Students, An" (Thornton), 46
Alternative Plan for the Desegregation of the University System of Georgia, An, 96, 97
American Missionary Association, 14

Anderson, Kelsey Kylene, 101
anti-Black linguistic racism, 9–10, 23, 65, 67, 80, 104
antiracism, 4, 23, 28
Appalachian State University, Center for Developmental Studies, 135
Applebee, Arthur N., 115
archives, 30, 31; white-informed, 28–29
Armstrong State University, 3, 6, 16–17, 21, 91, 93, 96, 100, 133; Black American Movement at, 59–60; Black students at, 38, 69, 74; desegregation, 8, 30, 31, 76, 82, 83, 110; Regents' Test scores, 101–2, 126, 127; remediation at, 55–60; and Savannah State University, 29, 40; Special Studies program, 78–80; USG desegregation plans, 98–99; writing programs, 104–9, 131
Ashmore, Henry L., 55, 59, 61, 76–77
assessment, 4, 136, 147; in Regents' Test, 50–51; writing, 89–93, 121–22, 138, 140; writing program, 73, 145–46
assimilation, 27; of Black colleges, 40–41
Association of Black Psychologists, 88
ASTA. *See Alabama State Teachers Association v. Alabama Public School and College Authority*
attrition rates, 6, 24, 41, 136
Auburn University, 39, 114
Aull, Laura, 149
auto-tutorial methods, 137
Ayers v. Allain, 18
Ayers v. Fordice, 18, 19, 25, 26, 27, 148–49, 155(n21)

Bainbridge Junior College, 129
Baker, Scott, 100
Baker-Bell, April, 151
Ball, Arnetha, 122–23
BAM. *See* Black American Movement
Banks, Adam J., 25, 42
Basic Skills Examination (BSE), 94, 103
basic writing, as segregation, 117
Bazerman, Charles, 120
Bell, T. H., 113
bidialectism, 24, 36–37, 57, 58, 59, 155(n20)